THE

GENESIS

FACTOR

THE
GENESIS
FACTOR

Myths and Realities

RON J. BIGALKE JR.
COMPILATION EDITOR

First printing: January 2008

ISBN-13: 978-0-89051-480-1
ISBN-10: 0-89051-480-1
Library of Congress Number: 2007939091

Unless otherwise indicated, Scripture quotations in the introduction and chapters 8–9 are taken from the King James Version of the Holy Bible.

Unless otherwise indicated, Scripture quotations in chapters 3–4 are from the New American Standard Bible, © 1960, 1962, 1963, 1968, 1971, 1972, 1973, 1975, 1977, 1995 by The Lockman Foundation.

Unless otherwise indicated, Scripture quotations in chapter 7 are from the American Standard Version of the Holy Bible, 1901.

The views expressed in each chapter of this book are those of each individual author and may not necessarily reflect the views of every other author.

Cover design by Left Coast Design, Portland, Oregon

Printed in the United States of America

Please visit our website for other great titles:
www.masterbooks.com

For information regarding author interviews, please contact the publicity department at (870) 438-5288.

Master
Books

A Division of New Leaf Publishing Group

This book is dedicated to Dr. Thomas Ice, colleague, friend, and mentor, whose contagious desire to grow in the grace and knowledge of our Lord and Savior Jesus Christ and his continual example of applying a consistent literal hermeneutic to the pages of Scripture — so that God may be God — has meant so much throughout the years. I have been blessed to witness his godly example and I value his friendship.

Acknowledgments

Since there is ever growing confusion regarding the interpretation of the Genesis record of creation, it was obvious this volume needed to be written and published as quickly as possible. The nine contributors were equally concerned about the creationist compromises within the church and the need to present another defense for a young earth in addition to a refutation of such compromises. Each author finished his chapter in remarkable time, was diligent to comments, and was thorough to answer any questions or recommendations throughout the writing (or revision) of his chapter. Therefore, acknowledgment is given to the great dedication and sacrifice of each of these godly authors to the completion of this project.

An exceptional thanks is to Jim Fletcher, former editor-in-chief at Master Books, for his encouragement to complete the manuscript. Thank you also to the New Leaf Publishing Group team, especially: Amanda Price for her accuracy and detail to the final published project; Judy Lewis and Laura Welch for their tremendous communication throughout the editing and gracious professionalism with those edits; and Tim Dudley for his insights with key elements. Thank you to those brothers in Christ who were perceptive in providing critical commentary. A special thanks also goes to my church, family, and friends for their patience with me, and understanding of the time and effort to organize and oversee this project to completion.

Contents

INTRODUCTION

THE DAYS DO MATTER

Henry M. Morris

Most everyone has been taught all through their school years that the earth, life, animals, and man have all been developing from primordial beginnings over billions of years of natural evolution. Many have tried to "baptize" this process, so to speak, by calling it "theistic" evolution or "progressive" creation, saying that God may have used evolution as His process of creation.

It is because of this ubiquitous indoctrination that even many evangelical Christians have felt they must conform to this evolutionary world view, especially in relation to the so-called "deep time" that is so essential to evolutionism. One respected leader of the "Intelligent Design" movement, for example, recently wrote to this author that he would prefer to believe in a "young earth," but science had proved the earth was very old, so he had to go with science. Two other leaders of the Intelligent Design movement told this author personally (on two separate occasions) that they could not even afford to listen to my arguments for a young earth because they were afraid they would be convinced and that this would halt their opportunities to speak to college groups and others about Intelligent Design.

So this brief introduction is written to show once again that the Lord Jesus himself believed in recent creation and the young earth. Assuming that a Christian is a person who believes in the deity and inerrant authority of Christ, it would seem that this fact should be sufficient to convince him or her.

What will be done here, therefore, is to list three key reasons for concluding that our Lord Jesus Christ believed and taught literal recent creation of all things essentially instantaneously by the omnipotent command of God, who "spake, and it was done" (Ps. 33:9).

The Bible nowhere allows for long ages. One can search the Scriptures from beginning to end without finding even a hint of evolution or long ages. To Jesus, every jot and tittle of Scripture was divinely inspired (Matt. 5:18), and He warned severely against adding any other words to it (Rev. 22:18). The Bible, therefore, would certainly not leave the vital doctrine of creation open to human speculation.

The Bible explicitly states how and when creation occurred. Although many evangelicals have long equivocated as to the meaning of the *days* of creation, this type of *ad hoc* handling of Scripture is never justified in the context, and Christ himself would never have interpreted them as indefinite ages of some kind. Not only is *day* (*yôm*) defined in this context the first time it is used (Gen. 1:5), but the writer also conclusively restricted its interpretation to the literal meaning by numbering the days (*first day*, *second day*, etc.) and by indicating their boundaries (*evening and morning*), both of which restrictions elsewhere in the Old Testament limit the meaning to literal days. The question seems to have been even more firmly settled when God wrote with His own finger that "in six days the LORD made heaven and earth, the sea, and all that in them is, and rested the seventh day: wherefore the LORD blessed the [seventh] day, and hallowed it" (Exod. 20:11), thereby basing our calendar's seven-day week on this primeval creation week. Jesus referred to this divine example when He said, "The sabbath was made for man" (Mark 2:27) to meet our weekly need of rest from work.

The Lord Jesus recognized that men and women existed from the beginning. The current opinion is that the cosmos evolved about 16 billion years ago, the earth about 4.6 billion, primitive life perhaps 2 billion, and human life about 1 million years ago. The Lord Jesus, conversely (who was there, having himself created all things — see John 1:1–3) taught that men and women were made essentially at the same time as the cosmos itself, when He said, "From the beginning God . . . made them male and female" (Mark 10:6). *The beginning* obviously was a reference to Genesis 1:1, and Christ was specifically citing Genesis 1:26.

On another occasion, speaking especially of Adam's son Abel, He referred to "the blood of all the prophets, which was shed from the foundation of the world" (Luke 11:50–51), thereby acknowledging that Abel was the first prophet, martyred in the very first generation — not 4.6 billion years after the formation of the earth. Jesus also said that Satan, using Cain to slay Abel, "was a murderer from the beginning" (John 8:44).

Note also that the father of John the Baptist, prophesying when filled with the Holy Spirit, said that God's holy prophets had been predicting a coming Savior "since the world began" (Luke 1:70). Then the apostle Peter later preached that the second coming of Christ and the ultimate removal of the great Curse on the earth had even been events that "God hath spoken by the mouth of all His holy prophets since the world began" (Acts 3:21). The apostle Paul wrote that evidence of God as Creator should have been "clearly seen" (by men, of course) ever "since the creation of the world."

There can be no reasonable doubt that Jesus was what evolutionists today (both theistic and atheistic) would call a "young-earth creationist." It would seem that this should settle the question for all true Christians, who should certainly — on the authority of Christ himself — completely reject the notion of geologic ages. But they don't! For one thing, not all who consider themselves Christians really believe the Bible, especially its unpopular teachings. Unfortunately, many who think they are Bible-believing Christians have become adept at "wresting" the

Scriptures (see 2 Pet. 3:17), even the recorded words of Jesus and the Apostles, to make them conform to the scientism of evolutionary speculation. As previously stated, there is not the slightest suggestion of millions and billions of years anywhere in the Bible when it is taken simply to mean what it says. It is for this reason that "young-earth creationists" must continually reemphasize the pervasive Bible teaching of just thousands of years of earth and cosmic history.

Nevertheless, the battle rages against the reality of a young earth as revealed by God in Scripture. For example, in his latest book,[1] Dr. Hugh Ross mounted the most vigorous attack yet against literal biblical creationism and its defenders. The book is replete with references to creationist writings, to not only this author, but also those of John Morris, Ken Ham, Walter Brown, and many others. There are also many references to those of secular astronomers in connection with his spirited promotion of the big-bang theory.

Although Hugh Ross has a Ph.D. in astronomy from Toronto plus post-doctoral work at Cal-Tech, he has spent most of his career as a minister of evangelism and (since 1986) leading his "Reasons to Believe" organization. The purpose of the latter is that of winning people to Christ through scientific apologetics. Dr. Ross repeatedly (but unjustifiably) maintains that what he calls "young-earth creationism" is a hindrance in doing this. The purpose of his new book, therefore, is to promote the "day-age theory" of Genesis interpretation and to defend the standard evolutionary belief in long geological ages with their billions of fossils of dead animals entombed in the sediments of those alleged ages.

Dr. Ross does claim to believe the Bible to be the inspired Word of God and in salvation through Jesus Christ. Although he does not use the term himself, his position is apparently what most of its advocates call "progressive creation" — the idea that God's creative activity did not take place in six literal days, but rather at different times during the supposed 4.6 billion years

---

1. Hugh Ross, *A Matter of Days* (Colorado Springs, CO: NavPress, 2004).

of earth history demanded by evolutionary geologists. It differs slightly from "theistic evolution" in that the latter assumes God's overall guidance of the process of evolution but without any occasional interjections of special creation.

There is no scientific way, however, of distinguishing between progressive creation and theistic evolution. Both systems rely on the geologic ages as real history and interpret the "days" of creation in Genesis to correlate in some vague way with those ages. Both systems incorporate billions of years of suffering and dying among the animals before man appeared. However, this implies a God who is either sadistic or incompetent — certainly not the God of the Bible who cares when even a sparrow dies. Animal suffering in the present order, of course, is part of God's "curse" on man's dominion because of human sin.

Ross devoted many pages to arguing for a non-literal meaning of the "days" of creation and then also tried to justify the suffering of those billions of animals before Adam's sin brought death into the world. There are many compelling evidences against such notions, but space does not allow their repetition here. Exodus 20:8–16, for example, inscribed by God himself with the Ten Commandments, clearly stresses that the whole universe was made in six literal days. There are now thousands of fully credentialed scientists who have become "young-earth creationists." The change is not only because of the preponderance of biblical evidence, but also because they are satisfied that the real scientific evidence agrees with it. The only real reason for following the Ross approach is to avoid disagreement with evolutionary geology and astronomy.

Many of these scientists (including this author) were once evolutionists. They have found (as did this author) that there is not a hint anywhere in the Bible of the long ages of geology. The latter are based on their premise of uniformitarianism, which the Bible declares to be wrong (2 Pet. 3:3–6), and on their rejection of the global cataclysmic flood so plainly described in Genesis 6–9.

Dr. Ross only mentions the biblical flood in passing, but it can account for the geological deposits better than uniformitarian geology does and the modern revival of literal creationism is believed by many to be attributable largely to the recent revival of biblical geology. In other writings, Ross has indicated that he believes the Flood was only a local flood, despite the clear teachings of God's Word otherwise.

A good portion of the Ross book is devoted to defending the big bang, which Ross thinks may correspond with the primeval creation of Genesis 1. Although the section is the most impressive part of the book, he ignored the reality of many outstanding astronomers who reject the big-bang theory altogether and only a minority who think it might have something to do with Genesis 1:1.

In one strange tangent, he accused literal creationists of being "hyper-evolutionists" because they believe the biblical teaching that all present land animals are descendants of those preserved on Noah's ark (Gen. 7:21–22; 8:19). The different varieties that developed from the original "kinds" after the Flood did not "evolve," of course, by mutation or any other evolutionary process. They simply diversified by recombination of the genetic information already present in their parents in response to environmental factors in the barren world after the Flood, with all such diversification occurring within the originally created "kinds." The development was not evolution but simple variation.

In his personal references to this author, Dr. Ross made a number of errors. For example, after referring to the rapid growth of the Creation Research Society following publication of *The Genesis Flood*, he said that the Society soon "began to splinter because of differences in personalities and objectives."[2] His statement is not true: the Institute for Creation Research was formed in order to have a full-time creationist educational ministry, but membership in and support of the Society continues to this day.

Another example was in his discussion of the 1982 meeting of the International Council of Biblical Inerrancy (ICBI) that dealt primarily with biblical hermeneutics. He said that Walter Bradley, Gleason Archer, and this author each presented "full-length"

---

2. Ibid., p. 33.

papers on how to interpret the Genesis record of creation. Again, his statement is wrong. Dr. Bradley presented the only full-length paper. The presentations by Dr. Archer and this author were merely discussions of Bradley's paper. The "stacking" of the ICBI program was evident in that both Dr. Bradley and Dr. Archer were known to be opposed to the literal day record of Genesis. The statement finally adopted by the Council was so innocuous on the subject of origins that it would not even exclude evolution as an acceptable interpretation. It was this reason why the author could not sign their statement on biblical hermeneutics (a decision which Ross deplores).

The fact that Ross is wrong about these facts with which this author was personally familiar might raise questions about his reliability in other sections of the book. However, the book is copiously documented and impressively argued.

Ross tried to criticize a few of the scientific evidences for recent creation.[3] However, questioning a few of them in no way obviates the fact that there are still scores of others, all of them in-dicating an age far too small to be accommodated in the standard geological system. Furthermore, there are many more processes that yield young ages than the handful that yield old ages.

Ross twice quoted,[4] in apparent disagreement, this author's contention that if one truly wanted to know the age of the earth or the universe, God must tell him. This God has done in His written Word, but Ross refuses to believe what the Bible says.

Dr. Ross is evidently a sincere Christian who earnestly desires to win skeptics to Christ (of course, so do "young-earth creation-ists" and have indeed seen many come to real faith in Christ and His Word). However, he thinks this purpose can best be served by adopting the whole uniformitarian world view of origins, and then superimposing the gospel upon that world view.

The contributors to this volume disagree: each has found that more scientists and other intelligent men and women can be won by taking God at His Word, accepting the biblical world view,

---

3. Ibid., p. 185–206.
4. Ibid., p. 36, 211.

and trusting Christ on His own terms, without compromise. This may be a harder task, because it demands more study and rethinking, in addition to ridicule from naturalists (and compromising Christians), but it is a higher task and actually more productive. The vigor of the creationist revival of the past several decades bears witness.

Dr. Ross maintained in his book that his goal is to reconcile the two world views and bring peace, but this to him seems to mean that those who believe in a literal Genesis should abandon this belief and accept his belief that there were long ages of suffering and death long before sin entered the world. To the contributors of this volume, however, such a compromise dishonors the clear teaching of Scripture and even undermines the gospel. Furthermore, the day-age and progressive creation concepts are not accepted by the scientific establishment any more than is young-earth creationism.

When John Morris and this author met with the "Reasons to Believe" board several years ago, Hugh urged us to accept and treat their position as a valid biblical position in order to bring about the peace they discussed. We in turn suggested that they reciprocate by accepting and treating literal six-day biblical creationism as a valid scientific position. However, Hugh Ross still refuses to do this. The present author is afraid the progressive creationist view is widening the chasm, not helping to bridge it.

What are Christians supposed to do when the Bible disagrees with the majority of scientists regarding the Genesis record of creation? Christians are to believe the Bible — that is what! When the teachings of men conflict with the Word of God, it would be wise to submit to God's revelation.

There is also a rapidly growing body of scientific data that not only shows the impossibility of macroevolution but also much that repudiates the so-called evidences of "billions of years." Creationist geologists have been developing an abundance of evidence of global catastrophism instead of uniformitarianism in earth history — thus confirming the biblical record of the great Flood as the major explanation for the fossil-bearing rocks in the earth's crust, instead of having to invent imaginary long ages of evolution to account for them.

It is possible now even to amass a list of dozens of worldwide natural processes (e.g., accumulation of salt in the sea) which, even on uniformist assumptions, will yield ages much too brief for evolution. Therefore, even without referring to the Bible, it is possible to make an impressive case for recent creation. One cannot determine the exact age of the earth by science, of course, and these various processes may yield various values, but all prove too small for evolutionism to be possible — with the supposed exception of radiometric dating, that is. The decay of uranium into lead, rubidium into strontium, and a few other such processes can be made to show extremely long ages, so radioactive decay processes have been considered by evolutionists to be firm proof of the billions of years.

However, Christians need to remember that such calculations, like all the others, are based on the arbitrary assumption of uniformitarianism, which not only is unprovable but also contrary to the Bible. The apostle Peter called it *willing ignorance* (2 Pet. 3:3-6) when this assumption ignores the world-changing impact of special creation of all things in the beginning and the worldwide geologic impact of the global deluge in the days of Noah. Furthermore, as Dr. DeYoung has documented in the Appendix, the RATE Initiative demonstrated strong scientific evidence that even these radioactive decay processes really provide convincing arguments that the earth is thousands of years old — not billions!

Therefore, the contributors to this volume plead once again with our Christian theistic evolutionists, progressive creationists, gap creationists, and intelligent design minimalists to come back to the Bible for their view of the world and its history. It is for this reason the present volume is written in defense of the Genesis record of creation. We should most certainly believe the words of our Lord Jesus Christ on this vital subject. *"And why call ye me, Lord, Lord,"* He might well say, *"and* [believe] *not the things which I say?"* (Luke 6:46).

Henry M. Morris, M.S., Ph.D., LL.D., Litt.D., (1918–2006) was founder and president emeritus of the Institute for Creation Research, and was professor of hydrogeology at the Graduate School of the Institute for Creation Research, Santee, California.

It is widely recognized today that the modern creation movement had its genesis in the early 1960s through the release of Dr. Morris's groundbreaking book *The Genesis Flood* (coauthored with Dr. John Whitcomb). Soon after the book's publication, invitations for Dr. Morris to speak nationally, combined with a growing network of Bible-believing scientists and engineers he assembled, led him (along with now-famous Christian novelist Tim LaHaye) to start the Institute for Creation Research in 1970.

Dr. Morris and his wife of 66 years, Mary Louise, were the parents of five children (including Dr. John Morris, president of ICR), in addition to 17 grandchildren and 9 great-grandchildren.

Chapter 1

The History of Biblical/ Scientific Creationism in the Church

Christopher Cone

I
t was not until Darwin's generation that the idea of biblical creationism became a minority view. Moreover, while some critics of biblical creationism purport that the six-day creation view is a recent development, history tells us otherwise. It must be admitted that the terms *creationism* and *creationist* are fairly recent terms — dating back to Darwin's day, and initially referring to "the doctrine that God creates a new soul whenever a human being begins to live. . ."[1] (in contrast to the traducian view), but Darwin himself used the term to describe opponents of his evolutionary theory.[2] As the theological and scientific significance of this issue has become more and more evident, the terms find a more prominent place at the center of the debate. Nevertheless, while the terms may be recent, the historically evidenced view of biblical creationism certainly is not; rather, there has been

---

1. *The Practical Standard Dictionary of the English Language* (New York: Funk & Wagnalls Company, 1943), 1:282.

2. F. Darwin, *The Life and Letters of Charles Darwin* (New York: D. Appleton, 1889), 2:28.

held historically a diversity of views with prominent early representation for the literal six-day creation account.

Although not the first proponent (in the human sense) of biblical creationism (there are numerous Old Testament acknowledgments of the literal Genesis account, i.e., Gen. 1–2; Deut. 4:32; Ps. 148:5; Isa. 40:26; 41:20; 42:5; 45:12, 18; 54:16; Mal. 2:10; etc.), Jesus Christ was very clear regarding His hermeneutically literal approach to the Genesis record (Mark 13:19; Luke 24:27; John 5:46–47). Note His confirmation in Matthew 19:4–6 and Mark 10:6, of both creation accounts (Gen. 1 and 2). He was both Creator (John 1:3; Col. 1:16) and witness to His own creative work. It is on His authority (in Old and New Testament revelation) that the church found its basis for the literal understanding of the Genesis account of creation.

Apostolic Era (A.D. 40–95)

James, the half brother of Jesus[3] and apostle (Gal. 1:19), in A.D. 48 confirmed creation *ex nihilo* by the Word of God (James 1:17–18) and acknowledged man as originating directly from God and in His image (James 3:9).

Paul the apostle, throughout his ministry (roughly A.D. 32 to A.D. 68), demonstrated a literal understanding of the creation account. He testified to the men of Athens that God was the lifegiver, and that all mankind originated from Adam (Acts 17:22–31). He presented to the Roman church that man existed from creation (Rom. 1:18–25), that Adam's sin was the cause of human death (Rom. 5:12–19), and that creation (all that is created) groans from sin and yet God is sovereign over it (Rom. 8:19–23). He identified to the Corinthian church the order of the creation of man and woman, based on the Genesis account (1 Cor. 11:8–12), traced death to Adam (1 Cor. 15:20–21), differentiated types of flesh, again based on Genesis (1 Cor. 15:37–41), and identified God as the Creator of light (2 Cor. 4:3–6). He affirmed to the Colossian church Christ as Creator and Sovereign (Col. 1:15–20) and Lifegiver (Col. 3:9–10).

---

3. C. Cone, *The Promises of God, A Bible Survey* (Arlington, TX: Exegetica Publishing, 2005), p. 231.

The **author of Hebrews** (possibly Apollos[4]), around A.D. 64–67, made reference to creation as a divine act through Jesus Christ (Col. 1:2–3), to God as Creator of all things (Col. 3:4), and to the creative work being completed in six literal days (Col. 4:3–4, 10–11).

The **apostle Peter** (A.D. 66–67) was very detailed in his recounting of creation, identifying uniformitarianism as the message of mockers (2 Pet. 3:3–4), affirming the methodology of creation as *by the word of God* (2 Pet. 3:5), and reiterating specific elements contained in the Genesis account (2 Pet. 3:5–6).

The beloved disciple (John 21:7, 20) **John**, in his Gospel (A.D. 65–69) presented Jesus as the Creator of all (John 1:1–3), and later in his Apocalypse (A.D. 85–95) he recorded the testimony of the 24 elders who affirmed the same fact (Rev. 4:11).

It is upon this framework that the church historically built its understanding of the creation doctrine. Inherent in this framework were two major issues necessary for the biblical creationism/young-earth conclusion: (1) the idea that God created all things *ex nihilo* (out of nothing) — which would make the creation of Genesis 1:1 the beginning of all matter and time — and, (2) the literal understanding of the days of creation, which would therefore submit the earth to the dating of the Old Testament chronologies, beginning with Adam, and thus provide biblical evidence for a young earth. While it must be admitted that there was some diversity on these views even among the church fathers in the post-Apostolic church, it is evident that the majority did indeed hold to biblical creationism and the young-earth conclusion.

Ante-Nicene Era (A.D. 95–325)

Hermas (90–150) held to creation *ex nihilo*. He stated, "First of all, believe that there is one God who created and finished all things, and made all things out of nothing."[5]

---

4. Ibid., p. 262–266.

5. "The Shepherd of Hermas (Book II, Commandment 1)" [online] (New Advent, 2004, accessed September 19, 2005) available from http://www. newadvent.org/fathers/0201201.htm.

Clement of Alexandria (150–215), in his chronology defending the antiquity of Moses over the Greek philosophies, traced 6,148 years from Adam to the death of the Roman Emperor Commodus in A.D. 192, thus dating creation as being newer than 6,000 years. In yet another strand of his chronology, he quoted Eupolemus (seemingly as authoritative) who dated Adam as late as 5438.[6] His conclusions support a literal understanding of the days of creation and a young-age earth.

Theophilus of Antioch (115–188), in his letter to Autolycus (2:11–12), recognized the magnificence of creation and its six-day scope: "Of this six days' work no man can give a worthy explanation and description of all its parts. Not though he had ten thousand tongues and ten thousand mouths; nay, though he were to live ten thousand years, sojourning in this life, not even so could he utter anything worthy of these things, on account of the exceeding greatness and riches of the wisdom of God which were in the six days' work above narrated."[7] Theophilus's emphasis on the amazing work accomplished in such a short time illustrates the profundity of the doctrine (of six-day creationism) and his respect for the One who orchestrated it.

Iranaeus (115–202) understood creation to be *ex nihilo*: "For, to attribute the substance of created things to the power and will of Him who is God of all, is worthy both of credit and acceptance. . . . He Himself called into being the substance of His creation, when previously it had no existence."[8] Additionally, he believed the creation days to be literal, developing his eschatology, as was commonly done, on the day-age principle:

> For in as many days as this world was made, in so many thousand years shall it be concluded. And for this reason the Scripture says: "Thus the heaven and the earth

---

6. A. Roberts and J. Donaldson, eds., *The Ante-Nicene Fathers* (1886; reprint, Grand Rapids, MI, Eerdmans, 1989), 2:332.

7. Ibid., 2:99.

8. St. Irenaeus of Lyons, "Adversus Haereses (Book II, Chapter 10)" [online] (New Advent, 2004, accessed September 19, 2005) available from http://www.newadvent.org/fathers/0103210.htm.

were finished, and all their adornment. And God brought to a conclusion upon the sixth day the works that He had made; and God rested upon the seventh day from all His works." This is an account of the things formerly created, as also it is a prophecy of what is to come. For the day of the Lord is as a thousand years; and in six days created things were completed: it is evident, therefore, that they will come to an end at the sixth thousand year.[9]

Tertullian (160–225) reasoned for *ex nihilo* throughout his argument *Against Hermogones*.

Hippolytus of Rome (170–236), in his commentary on Daniel (2:4) — written in context of the coming of Messiah — acknowledged a creation date of 5,500 years before the appearance of Christ[10] and seemed to understand the creation days to be literal, although he did reference the day-age idea of 6,000 years as typified by the creation days,[11] but this does not seem to impact his literal interpretation of the creation days themselves.

Julius Africanus (160–240) — like Hippolytus — specifically reckoned the creation date as 5,500 years before the incarnation of Christ. He regarded the chronology seriously, saying, "For the Jews . . . together with the truth by the spirit of Moses, have handed down to us, by their extant Hebrew histories, the number of 5,500 years as the period up to the advent of the Word of salvation, that was announced to the world in the time of the sway of the Caesars."[12] His statement indicates an inarguably literal approach.

Theophilus of Antioch (180) remarked: "But the power of God is manifested in this, that out of things that are not He makes whatever He pleases; just as the bestowal of life and motion is the prerogative of no other than God alone. For even man makes indeed an image, but reason and breath, or feeling, he

---

9. *Against Heresies* 5:28:3 — http://www.newadvent.org/fathers/0103528.htm.

10. Roberts and Donaldson, *Ante-Nicene Fathers*, 5:179.

11. Ibid.

12. Ibid., 6:131.

cannot give to what he has made. But God has this property in excess of what man can do, in that He makes a work, endowed with reason, life, sensation. As, therefore, in all these respects God is more powerful than man, so also in this; that out of things that are not He creates and has created things that are, and whatever He pleases, as He pleases."[13]

Origen (185–253) stated, "The Mosaic account of the creation . . . teaches that the world is not yet ten thousand years old, but very much under that."[14] Moreover, while disagreeing with Celsus's sources, he agreed with Celsus' conclusion that the earth is less than 10,000 years old (*Against Celsus* 1.20).[15] Although he was a notorious allegorist, Origen's acknowledgment here requires a literal interpretation of the creation account. Origen did alter the discussion slightly; however, as he (as did Philo and others) understood that creation took place in a moment, and tried to reconcile momentary creation with the six-day work. Nonetheless, he recognized a young earth.

Lactantius (240–320), in his *Divine Institutes* (1.3), identified God as authority over all by virtue of His creative work *ex nihilo*, stating that He "created all things and governs them with the same energy by which He created them."[16]

Eusebius of Caesarea (263–339), in his *Chronicle*, reckoned the year of creation to be 5228 B.C., stating, "And from Adam to the flood, is 2,242 years. So the overall total, from Adam until the second year of Dareius and the second building of [the temple in] Jerusalem, is 4,680 years. And from the second year of Dareius which was the first year of the 65th Olympiad [520 B.C.] [until the ministry of Christ], is 137 Olympiads and 548 years."[17]

---

13. Theophilus of Antioch, "To Autolycus (Book 2)" [online] (New Advent, 2004. accessed September 20, 2005) available from http://www.newadvent.org/fathers/02042.htm.

14. Roberts and Donaldson, *Ante-Nicene Fathers*, 4:404.

15. Ibid.

16. Ibid., 7:11.

17. "Eusebius: Chronicle" [online] (Attalus, February 3, 2005, accessed September 20, 2005) available from http://www.attalus.org/translate/eusebius1.html.

Methodius (311), in his *Banquet of the Ten Virgins* (or *Concerning Chastity*), identified man as being created at once by the Almighty, who "alone breathes into man the undying and undecaying part, as also it is He alone who is Creator of the invisible and indestructible."[18] His statement reflects a clear supposition of creation *ex nihilo* in addition to an acknowledgment of the divine origin certainly of human life. Methodias acknowledged man's formation from clay,[19] evidencing his literal view of the substance of the creation account — that God created man from the dirt. He also held to a literal meaning of day in the creation account.[20]

Victorinus of Pettau (304) presented a literal understanding of the creation days: "In the beginning God made the light, and divided it in the exact measure of twelve hours by day and by night, for this reason, doubtless, that day might bring over the night as an occasion of rest for men's labours; that, again, day might overcome, and thus that labour might be refreshed with this alternate change of rest, and that repose again might be tempered by the exercise of day. 'On the fourth day He made two lights in the heaven, the greater and the lesser, that the one might rule over the day, the other over the night,' — the lights of the sun and moon and He placed the rest of the stars in heaven, that they might shine upon the earth, and by their positions distinguish the seasons, and years, and months, and days, and hours."[21]

Even the **Creed of Nicea** (325) reads, "We believe in one God, the Father, the Almighty, maker of heaven and earth, of all things visible and invisible." Creation *ex nihilo* is expressly communicated here as the majority view of the young church.

Post-Nicene Era (A.D. 325–590)

Ephrem the Syrian (306–373), in his *Commentary on Genesis* (1.1), held that the earth was created in six 24-hour days, saying

---

18. Roberts and Donaldson, *Ante-Nicene Fathers*, 6:316.

19. Ibid., 6:317.

20. Ibid., 6:333.

21. Victorinus, "On the Creation of the World" [online] (New Advent, 2004, accessed September 21, 2005) available from http://www.newadvent.org/fathers/0711.htm.

adamantly, "So let no one think that there is anything allegorical in the works of the six days. No one can rightly say that the things that pertain to these days were symbolic . . ."[22], and again he said, "Because everything that was created was created in those six days. . . ."[23] He was emphatic about both *ex nihilo* and the literalness of the days, going even to the lengths of reducing the days in terms of hours: "The light remained a length of twelve hours so that each day might also obtain its own hours just as the darkness had obtained a measured length of time . . . the day and the night of the first day were each completed in twelve hours."[24]

Basil (329–379) argued that creation was "not spontaneous, as some have imagined, but drew its origin from God."[25] He supposed further that *In the beginning God created* was "to teach us that at the will of God the world arose in less than an instant, and it is to convey this meaning more clearly that other interpreters have said: 'God made summarily' that is to say all at once and in a moment."[26] He also held to a literal understanding of the creation day, saying in that regard, "Scripture means the space of a day and a night."[27] He clarified his position with further detail, as he explained why Genesis 1:5 refers to *one day* rather than *the first day*: ". . . it is from a wish to determine the measure of day and night, and to combine the time that they contain. Now twenty-four hours fill up the space of one day — we mean of a day and a night."[28] Basil's work in the Hexaemeron (the six-day work) stands as a significant and lasting defense of the historicity of the young church's prominently literal understanding of the creation account.

---

22. T. Halton, ed., *The Fathers of the Church: St. Ephrem the Syrian*, trans. E.G. Matthews and J.P. Amar (Washington DC: Catholic University of America Press, 1994), p. 74.

23. Ibid., p. 77.

24. Ibid., p. 80.

25. P. Schaff and H. Wace, *The Nicene and Post-Nicene Fathers* (1886-1889; reprint, Grand Rapids, MI: Eerdmans, 1989), 8:52.

26. Ibid., 8:55.

27. Ibid., 8:64.

28. Ibid.

Jerome (340–420), the earliest church father with fluency in all the biblical languages, broke with the tradition of utilizing only the Latin text and relied on the Hebrew Old Testament, with Augustine (*City of God* 15.13) agreeing that on conflicting passages, Hebrew is final authority. It is because of his attention to the Hebrew grammar of the creation account, he came to the *ex nihilo* conclusion. He called a truism the statement, "God has been, is, and will be the maker of men, and that there is nothing either in heaven or on earth which does not owe its existence wholly to Him."[29]

Cyril of Jerusalem (387) recognized creation as a six-day process,[30] and understood the breadth of its scope: ". . . if of the wild beasts we know not even the mere names, how shall we comprehend the Maker of them? God's command was but one, which said, Let the earth bring forth wild beasts, and cattle, and creeping things, after their kinds: and from one earth, by one command, have sprung diverse natures. . . ."[31]

Ambrose of Milan (339–397) recognized creation *ex nihilo*, stating that God "commanded the world to come into being out of no matter and no substance,"[32] and upon this truth built his argument for the sensibility of the doctrine of resurrection, saying, "But if God made all these things out of nothing (for 'He spake and they were made, He commanded and they were created'), why should we wonder that that which has been should be brought to life again, since we see produced that which had not been?"[33]

Augustine of Hippo (354–430), demonstrating his agreement with Eusebius's chronology, and referring to those who believed in an old earth, said, "They are deceived, too, by those highly mendacious documents which profess to give the history of many thousand years, though reckoning by the sacred writings we find that

---

29. Ibid., 6:284.
30. Ibid., 7:73.
31. Ibid., 7:54.
32. Ibid., 10:184.
33. Ibid.

not 6,000 years have yet passed."[34] It is notable that the Egyptian and Greek chronologies also dated the world in terms of thousands of years (not millions), yet Augustine saw indisputable biblical evidence for their correction.

Augustine went further than simply suggesting a young earth, as he argued that "in the beginning" referenced not only the beginning of God's creative work, but also the beginning of time.

> I do not see how He can be said to have created the world after spaces of time had elapsed, unless it be said that prior to the world there was some creature by whose movement time could pass. And if the sacred and infallible Scriptures say that in the beginning God created the heavens and the earth, in order that it may be understood that He had made nothing previously . . . then assuredly the world was made, not in time, but simultaneously with time.[35]

Augustine left no consideration, in these two statements, for anything other than a literal six-day creation resulting in a young earth. Furthermore, in his *Against the Manichees* (Book 1), although he admitted a generally allegorical approach to Genesis,[36] he dealt literally with the creation days.[37] He also had a clear understanding of *ex nihilo*, stating, "Holy, Holy, Holy, Lord God — Almighty, didst in the beginning, which is of Thee, in Thy Wisdom, which was born of Thy Substance, create something, and that out of nothing."[38]

---

34. Ibid., 2:232.

35. Ibid., 2:208.

36. T. Halton, ed., *The Fathers of the Church: St. Augustine On Genesis*, trans. R. Teske (Washington DC: Catholic University of America Press, 1991), p. 42.

37. Ibid., p. 63–64.

38. St. Augustine of Hippo, "Confessions (Book XII)" [online] (New Advent, 2004, accessed September 20, 2005) available from http://www.newadvent.org/fathers/110112.htm.

John Chrysostom (347–419) supported *ex nihilo* in his *Homily on Genesis*. He regarded as literal the order of creation,[39] and spoke of literal days from darkness and light: "Then, when he had assigned to each its own name, he linked the two together in the words 'Evening came, and morning came: one day.' He made a point of speaking of the end of the day and the end of the night as one, so as to grasp a certain order and sequence. . . ."[40] He later referred to the teaching of the Holy Spirit as "narrating to us detail by detail all the items of creation and going through the works of the six days. . . ."[41]

Medieval Era and the Middle Ages (A.D. 590–1517)

Isidore of Seville (560–636) identified a literal view of the creation day: "Wherefore, beginning with the day, whose creation appears first in the order of visible things. . . ."[42] He also showed a fascination with number symbolism that betrayed his views of God's creative work as numbering 22,[43] which he paralleled with the number of generations between Adam and Jacob. Nevertheless, this shows his agreement with the traditionally held Hebrew chronology. He held to creation *ex nihilo*, saying that God "created all things out of nothing."[44] The literal six-day creation was the prevalent view of his day.[45]

The **Venerable Bede** (672–735) developed a history of the world from biblical chronology, relying on six literal days of creation; he estimated 3952 B.C. as the creation year.[46]

---

39. T. Halton, ed., *The Fathers of the Church: St. John Chrysostom Homilies on Genesis*, trans. R. Hill (Washington DC: Catholic University of America Press, 1985), p. 35.

40. Ibid., p. 44.

41. Ibid., p. 157–158.

42. E. Brehaut, *An Encyclopedist of the Dark Ages: Isidor of Seville* (New York: Columbia University, 1912), p. 15.

43. Ibid., p. 37.

44. Ibid., p. 39.

45. Ibid., p. 46.

46. B. Ward, *The Venerable Bede* (Kalamazoo, MI: Cistercian Publications, 1998), p. 33.

John of Damascus (676–749) recognized creation *ex nihilo*, saying, "He brings all things from nothing into being and creates them, both visible and invisible. . . . By thinking He creates."[47] Although he did not deal with the creation days of Genesis, he went to great lengths to explain the anatomy of a day as being quite literal,[48] and he regarded the elements of the creation account literally.[49]

Thomas Aquinas (1225–1274) adopted the geocentric cosmology of Aristotle and Ptolemy apart from a literal interpretation of Scripture, yet he held to creation *ex nihilo*, stating "creation — our name for the issuing of all existence — must proceed from what is not existent at all, from nothing."[50] He also acknowledged the six-day work of creation in a literal sense, recognizing the distinguishing between night and day of the creation days,[51] and the order of creation as stated in Genesis: "Just as days one, two, and three saw the distinction and forming of the heavens, the waters and the earth, so days four, five, and six saw the adornment of the heavens with the lamps of sun, moon, and stars, of the waters and air with fish and birds, and of the earth with animals and men."[52] He also understood, "Adam's body was formed by God immediately, there being no preceding human body that could generate a body of like species to itself."[53]

The **Fourth Lateran Council** (1215) proclaimed *de nehil condidit*: "God created all that is from nothing."

Bishop Ettiene Tempier of Paris (1277) issued a list of heresies that included the belief that the world is eternal, reemphasizing the fact that the world is finite and created from nothing.

Copernicus (1473–1543) developed the great heliocentric postulation that the earth and other planets revolved around the

47. R. J. Deferrari, ed., *The Fathers of the Church: Saint John of Damascus*, trans. F. H. Chase Jr. (New York: Fathers of the Church, Inc., 1958), p. 205.

48. Ibid., p. 212.

49. Ibid., p. 213.

50. T. Aquinas, *Summa Theologiae*, ed. T. McDermott (Allen, TX: Christian Classics, 1991), p. 85.

51. Ibid., p. 103.

52. Ibid., p. 103–104.

53. Ibid., p. 142.

sun, and set the tone for correcting the church's hermeneutical error of submitting the scriptural text to the science of the day, despite criticisms from Luther (based on Luther's own hermeneutical mistake in approaching Joshua 10:12 — a mistake that Kepler later corrected).

Reformation (A.D. 1517–1605)

Martin Luther (1483–1546) was particularly critical of Augustine's soft approach (sometimes allegorical, sometimes literal . . .). He held firmly to the literal interpretation of the creation account and the six creation days, leaving no consideration for anything other than biblical/scientific creationism. His literal understanding extended throughout the first 11 chapters of Genesis.[54] He championed the young-earth view, saying, "We know from Moses that the world was not in existence before 6,000 years ago."[55]

Philip Melancthon (1497–1560) understood creation to have taken place both instantaneously and in six days. He calculated the creation of man at 3963 B.C.

John Calvin (1509–1564), in his commentary on Genesis, saw the antithesis of literal six-day creation not as the day age or forms of gap theory, but rather as the idea that God created all things in a moment (an idea perpetuated by Philo, Origen, and others):

> Here the error of those is manifestly refuted, who maintain that the world was made in a moment. For it is too violent a cavil to contend that Moses distributes the work which God perfected at once into six days, for the mere purpose of conveying instruction. Let us rather conclude that God himself took the space of six days, for the purpose of accommodating his works to the capacity of men.[56]

---

54. M. Luther, *Luther's Works*, ed. J. Pelikan (St. Louis, MO: Concordia, 1958), 1:122-123.

55. Ibid, 1:3.

56. J. Calvin, *Genesis* (1554; reprint, Edinburgh: Banner of Truth, 1984), p. 78.

Consequently (despite Warfield's assessment[57]), Calvin communicated a literal understanding of the creation time frame, as he also characterized the *days* of Genesis 1 with two descriptives: artificial (referring to the time of day in which there is daylight) and natural (which would include the night).[58]

Pope Gregory XIII (1502–1585) declared that the creation of man occurred 5,199 years before Christ.

Modern Era (A.D. 1606–present)

Joseph Justus Scaliger (1540–1609), in emphasizing Jewish (Old Testament) chronologies, estimated 3949 B.C. as the creation year.

Francis Bacon (1561–1626) believed "the book of nature" answered things temporal and the Scriptures answered the eternal. He believed the student of both should proceed with caution in an attempt to intermingle the two; yet, he did understand a complementary relationship between the two, and his conclusions led him to maintain a literal understanding of the six-day creation.

> It is so then, that in the work of the creation we see a double emanation of virtue from God; the one referring more properly to power, the other to wisdom; the one expressed in making the subsistence of the matter, and the other in disposing the beauty of the form. This being supposed, it is to be observed that for anything which appeareth in the history of the creation, the confused mass and matter of heaven and earth was made in a moment; and the order and disposition of that chaos or mass was the work of six days. . . . So in the distribution of days we see the day wherein God did rest and contemplated his own works, was blessed above all the days wherein he did effect and accomplish them [*Advancement of Learning* 1.6.16].[59]

---

57. Warfield was criticized by some for his seemingly baseless interpretation of Calvin as a sort of theistic evolutionist.

58. Calvin, *Genesis*, 83.

59. F. Bacon, *Advancement of Learning* (Oxford: Oxford University Press, 1906), p. 40–41.

Johannes Kepler (1571–1630) was a devoted Christian who approached biblical chronology with the same scientific approach as he did his astronomy. He dated creation at 3993 B.C.

Galileo (1564–1642) supported Copernicus's heliocentric theory with some scientific evidence, and suggested that his view was consistent with Scripture, not opposed to it — contradicting the generally held Ptolemaic cosmology, which was geocentric. The "Galileo Affair" further provided a warning to the church against the scientific hermeneutic of submitting Scripture to the so-called scientific opinions of the day. This development would bolster the plain-sense hermeneutic in the church and give further credence to the literal six-day approach to the creation account. He believed science could be a useful tool in the exposition of Scripture: "nothing physical which sense-experience sets before our eyes, or which necessary demonstrations prove to us, ought to be called in question (much less condemned) upon the testimony of biblical passages which may have some different meaning beneath their words. . . . On the contrary, having arrived at any certainties in physics, we ought to utilize these as the most appropriate aids in the true exposition of the Bible."[60] He adhered generally to the literal interpretation of Scripture, saying that only in the instance of a demonstrated scientific truth opposing the literal interpretation should there be consideration for any other approach.[61]

James Ussher (1581–1656), a professor of theology at Trinity College, Dublin, and archbishop of Armagh, in 1650 published *Annals of the Ancient and New Testaments*, in which he concluded through his study of Scripture alone that the biblical chronology suggested a specific creation date of 4004 B.C. Ussher's chronology was readily accepted, and unity of thought regarding the

---

60. G. Galilei, *Letter to the Grand Duchess Christina* (1615), translated and reprinted in S. Drake, *Discoveries and Opinions of Galileo* (New York: Doubleday, 1957), p. 182–183, reprinted in D. C. Goodman, ed., *Science and Religious Belief 1600–1900: A Selection of Primary Sources* (Berkshire: The Open University Press, 1973), p. 32–33.

61. C. Hummel, *The Galileo Connection* (Downers Grove, IL: InterVarsity Press, 1986), p. 107.

young earth was evident. In spite of this, opposition to Ussher's approach to Hebrew chronology began to arise, and with it, new challenges to the young-earth conclusion. These challenges were somewhat quelled by men such as Dr. John Lightfoot, vice chancellor of Cambridge and noted rabbinical scholar, who, by way of his expertise in Hebrew language and culture declared, "Heaven and earth, center and circumference, were created all together, in the same instant, and clouds full of water," and again he said, "this work took place and man was created by the Trinity on October 23, 4004 B.C., at nine o'clock in the morning."

The **Westminster Confession of Faith** (1646) evidenced the majority view holding to Ussher's conclusions, as the Confession proclaimed, "It pleased God the Father, Son, and Holy Ghost, for the manifestation of the glory of his eternal power, wisdom, and goodness, in the beginning, to create or make of nothing the world, and all things therein, whether visible or invisible, in the space of six days, and all very good."

John Lightfoot (1602–1675), Vice-Chancellor of Cambridge, in 1642–1644 published a chronology based on Ussher's work, and therefore, like Ussher, arrived at a young-earth conclusion, dating creation at 3923 B.C.

John Ray (1627–1705), known as the father of English natural history, wrote the *Wisdom of God Manifested in the Works of the Creation*, in which he strongly opposed theistic evolution. He held to *ex nihilo*, saying that God's creative works were "the works created by God at first, and by Him conserved to this day in the same state and condition in which they were first made."[62]

Isaac Newton (1642–1727), seeing a strong unity between God and nature, by virtue of His sovereignty over nature, refused to speculate on origins (to the chagrin of some of his followers[63]). His comments on origin are limited, as in his *Principia*, he only mentioned God once, saying, "Thus God

---

62. H. Morris, *Men of Science, Men of God* (Green Forest, AR: Master Books, 1984), p. 40.

63. W. Kaiser, *Creation and the History of Science* (Grand Rapids, MI: Eerdmans, 1991), p. 190.

arranged the planets at different distances from the sun."[64] Newton, a few years earlier, "offered by way of conjecture a view on how the planets might have been arranged by God in an initial act of creation and their motion steadily accelerated until the desired tempo for their coordinated movements had been reached. . . ."[65] He seemed to give approval, as patron, of William Whiston's postulation, "The Mosaick creation is not a nice and philosophical account of the origin of all things, but an historical and true representation of the formation of our single earth out of a confused chaos, and of the successive and visible changes thereof each day, till it became the habitation of mankind."[66] Note the acknowledgment both of God as the origin of that which is created (*ex nihilo*) and the seemingly literal understanding of the creation day.

Thomas Burnet (1635–1715), a clergyman and geologist in England, took a literal approach to the creation account, and utilizing the Genesis account of the flood, developed a basic approach toward interpreting the earth's history.[67]

William Whiston (1667–1752), a protégé and successor to Newton at Cambridge, took a literal approach to the Genesis account (see quote under Isaac Newton), and believed there to be a very tangible harmony between the creation and flood accounts of Genesis and scientific data.

To this point, it had been most commonly held in the church that "God created the world in six twenty-four hour days,"[68] yet the century of Darwin was nearly devoid of adherents to biblical creationism, as many theologians deferred to Darwin's thought, either seeking a compromise with evolution or ignoring it altogether: "To find a creationist who insisted on the recent appearance of all living things in six literal days, who doubted the evidence of progression in the fossil record, and who attributed

64. F. Manuel, *The Religion of Isaac Newton* (Oxford: Clarendon Press, 1974), p. 31.

65. Ibid., p. 37.

66. Ibid.

67. Morris, *Men of Science, Men of God*, p. 47.

68. Hummel, *Galileo Connection*, p. 212.

geological significance to the biblical deluge, one has to look far beyond the mainstream of scientific thought."[69]

Due in large part to the supposition of theology as an empirical science (and therefore the submission of theology *to* empirical science), generations of theologians and thinkers (i.e., B.B. Warfield, C.I. Scofield, etc.), began to accept the concept of theistic evolution and other non-literal approaches to the creation account, as their presuppositions and approach to world view could not negate the seemingly overpowering arguments of Darwinian (so-called) science. This tendency signaled a humanism-influenced departure from the long-held authority of Scripture, and thus weakened both the position of and the perceived need for biblical creationism. With a proper epistemological and hermeneutical approach to both theology and science, the young-age creationist approach could have otherwise been more widely esteemed, but this tragic departure would later result in even greater theological abandonments.

While there was much criticism of Darwin's evolutionary theory during this time among theologians,[70] it primarily came against the idea that man was not a special creation of God. However, there was a grave failure to hold to the literal interpretation of the creation account, which resulted in growing popularity of day age and gap theory positions.

Charles Hodge (1797–1878) recognized the importance of rightly understanding Scripture separate from a scientific hermeneutic; yet regarding the six days of creation, he seemingly abandoned the literal hermeneutic in favor of the interval theory (the French view that the six days are not literal days, but rather symbolic of creative eras of indefinite time),[71] and thereby, regarding the Bible and science, undermined the very thing he sought to defend — the authority of the biblical record over science. Hodge

---

69. R.L. Numbers, *The Creationists* (Berkeley, CA: University of California Press, 1992), p. 11.

70. For example, Guyot, Dawson, Burr, Armstrong, Hodge, Hitchcock, Morris, Hastings, Townsend, Patterson, Dabney, et al.

71. J. Wells, *Charles Hodge's Critique of Darwinism* (New York: Edwin Mellen Press, 1988), p. 53.

was not alone in his error, as even men such as Moody and Spurgeon seemed to ignore the issue entirely.[72]

Dr. Adam Clarke (1760–1832) avoided the allegorical problem, and played an important role in the debate as he steadfastly maintained the divine inspiration of the Old Testament record, saying, "To preclude the possibility of a mistake, the unerring Spirit of God directed Moses in the selection of his facts and the ascertaining of his dates."[73]

Eleazar Lord (1788–1871), in his *Epoch of Creation* (1851), written eight years previous to the publishing of Darwin's *Origin of Species*, and his brother David Lord (1792–1880), in *Geognasy* (1855) seem to be the last and loudest voices of their generation to defend biblical creationism and the six-day creation of all things.

Under "creation" in his analytical concordance, Robert Young quoted Dr. William Hales regarding a young earth: "Dr Hales, in his work entitled, 'A New Analysis of Chronology and Geography, History and Prophecy,' (Vol. 1, p. 210 [published in 1830]), remarks: 'In every system of chronology, sacred and profane, the two grand eras — of the *Creation of the World*, and of the *Nativity of Christ* — have been usually adopted as standards, by reference to which all subordinate epochs, eras and periods have been adjusted.' He gives a list of 120 dates, commencing BC 6984, and terminating BC 3616, to which this event has been assigned by different authorities, and he admits that it might be swelled to 300. He places it at BC 5411. The date commonly adopted is BC 4004; being that of Ussher, Spanheim, Calmet, Blair, etc., and the one used in the English Bible [KJV]."[74]

Philip Henry Gosse (1810–1888) proposed the *Ompholos* (from the Greek word for *navel*, as the theory addressed Adam's need for a bellybutton) theory, suggesting that the earth was

---

72. H. Morris, *The Long War Against God* (Grand Rapids, MI: Baker, 1989), p. 97.

73. A. Clarke, *Clarke's Commentary on the Old Testament* [CD-ROM] (Albany: Sage Software, 1996), 1:7.

74. R. Young, *Analytical Concordance to the Bible* (Peabody, MA: Henrickson Publishers, n.d.), p. 210.

young, in agreement with Ussher's chronology, yet created with the appearance of age.

During the 19th century, a plurality of **scriptural geologists** began to bring biblical creationist considerations to the forefront, recognizing that the scientific data was indeed compatible with a literal rendering of the Genesis account of creation and the flood. Such men as George Young, George Fairholme, John Murray, and William Rhind (addressed by Dr. Terry Mortenson in the subsequent chapter) gave biblical in addition to geological evidence opposing the recently formulated old-earth conclusions.

During the early 20th century, the strongest defenders of biblical creationism were Seventh Day Adventists, such as **George McCready Price** (1870–1963), who emphasized the young earth, and appealed to scientific data: "Unlike virtually all other non-Adventist creationists at the time, who accepted the antiquity of the earth and attached little or no geological significance to Noah's flood, Price insisted on the recent appearance of life on earth and assigned most of the fossil-bearing rocks to the work of the deluge."[75]

Biblical creationism began its modern return to prominence through the published work *The Genesis Flood* by Drs. John C. Whitcomb and Henry M. Morris in 1961. The work of these men helped influence the spawning of think tanks such as the Creation Research Society (1963) and the Institute for Creation Research (1972), of which Henry Morris served as president, and provided great momentum for the return to the literal interpretation of the creation account.

Today, countless scientists are realizing that God's truth is all truth, and that true science will indeed be compatible with the Word of God. Furthermore, as they hunger to know the Creator more intimately, they continue to search the wonders of creation, returning to the church's roots of biblical, scientific creationism, to the church's edification and gratitude.

---

75. R.L. Numbers, ed., *Selected Works of George McCready Price* (New York: Garland Publishing, Inc, 1995), p. ix–x.

Christopher B. Cone, M.A.B.S., M.Ed., Th.D., is president and professor of Bible and theology at Tyndale Theological Seminary and Biblical Institute, Ft. Worth, Texas, and Shreveport, Louisiana.

He is the author of *Prolegomena: Introductory Notes on Bible Study & Theological Method* and of *The Promises of God: A Bible Survey*. He has also taught at Southern Bible Institute and at the University of North Texas.

CHAPTER 2

BOUNDARIES ON CREATION AND NOAH'S FLOOD

EARLY 19TH CENTURY BRITISH SCRIPTURAL GEOLOGISTS

Terry Mortenson

The purpose of this chapter[1] is to present a little-known controversy in the early 19th century that focused on the age of the earth. The participants were, on the one hand, the leading geologists of the day and on the other hand, a group of scientists and non-scientists, primarily in Britain, who collectively became known as the "scriptural geologists."[2] Like

---

1. The chapter is a revision of an earlier edition published as follows: T. Mortenson, "The Early 19th Century British 'Scriptural Geologists': Opponents of the Emerging Old-Earth Theories of Geology," *Proceedings of the Fifth International Conference on Creationism* (Pittsburgh, PA: Creation Science Foundation, 2003), p. 539–550. It is used here with kind permission.

2. The title was given to them by their opponents. To this author's knowledge, it was never used by these men to describe themselves, though two of their books bore the title *Scriptural Geology*. Indeed, none of them claimed to be geologists. However, at the time most of them wrote, there were hardly any geologists in the modern sense of the word. Most "geologists" in the early 19th century, until approximately 1840, were geologists by avocation, not vocation. It was a hobby (largely self-learned) of wealthy men. Nevertheless, they, like a few of the "scriptural geologists" developed an impressive knowledge of the rocks and fossils.

contemporary young-earth creationists, the scriptural geologists held to the dominant Christian view within church history[3] and at the beginning of their own time, namely, that Genesis 1–11 is inspired, inerrant Scripture which should be interpreted literally as a reliable, fully historical account. Their conviction led them to believe that Noah's flood was a unique global catastrophe, which produced most of the geological record, and that the earth was roughly 6,000 years old, having been created and furnished with all kinds of life in six literal days. From this young-earth creationist position, they opposed with equal vigor both the "uniformitarian" and "catastrophist" old-earth geological theories. They also opposed all the old-earth reinterpretations of Genesis, such as the gap and day-age theories, the tranquil and local flood theories, and the "Genesis is myth" theory, all of which were developed and popularized in the church at this time.

The early 19th century debate is an interesting and important one for students of the history of science, especially the history of the relationship of science to Christianity. The scriptural geologists have been greatly misrepresented, both by their contemporary old earth opponents and by nearly all later historians, whether secular or evangelical. However, the battle the scriptural geologists fought in the 19th century is also very relevant for understanding the current growing debate about evolution and creation and especially the debate among Christians about the age of the earth.[4] To understand both the 19th century debate and the current one, the reader needs first to consider briefly the historical context.

---

3. See D. Hall's thorough historical research on this matter in chapters 3–5 of his book, *Holding Fast to Creation* [online] (Covenant Presbyterian Church, accessed April 25, 2005) available from http://capo.org/holdfast0.html.

4. A fully documented analysis of the scriptural geologists and their opposition to old-earth geology may be found in the author's dissertation: T.J. Mortenson, "British Scriptural Geologists in the First Half of the Nineteenth Century" (unpublished Ph.D. thesis, Coventry University, 1996). It is available from the British Library Thesis Service by visiting http://www.bl.uk/services/document/brittheses.html.

The Relation of Scripture and Science

Two important people in the 16th century greatly influenced the Genesis-geology debate of the early 19th century. The two men were Galileo and Francis Bacon. As is well known, **Galileo** (1564–1642) was a proponent of Copernicus's theory that the earth revolves around the sun, not vice versa. Initially, the Roman Catholic Church leadership had no problem with this idea, but for various academic, political, and ecclesiastical reasons, in 1633 the pope changed his mind and forced Galileo to recant his belief in heliocentricity on threat of excommunication. However, eventually heliocentricity became generally accepted and with that many Christians absorbed two lessons from the so-called "Galileo affair." One was from a statement of Galileo himself. He said that the Bible tells man how to go to heaven, but it does not tell us how the heavens go. In other words, it was reasoned, the Bible teaches man theology and morality, but not astronomy or science. The other closely related lesson was that the Church will make big mistakes if it tries to tell scientists what to believe about the world.[5]

Galileo's contemporary in England, Francis **Bacon** (1561–1626), was a politician and philosopher who significantly influenced the development of modern science. He emphasized observation and experimentation as the best method of gaining true knowledge about the world. He also insisted that theory should only be built upon the foundation of a wealth of carefully collected data. However, although Bacon wrote explicitly of his belief in a recent, literal, six-day creation,[6] he, like Galileo, insisted on not mixing the study of what he called the two books of God: creation and the Scriptures.[7]

---

5. Much has been written about this complex Galileo affair. Helpful analysis can be found in T. Schirrmacher, "The Galileo Affair: History or Heroic Hagiography?" *CEN Technical Journal* 14 (April 2000): p. 91–100; W.R. Shea, "Galileo and the Church," in *God and Nature*, eds. D.C. Lindberg and R.L. Numbers (Berkeley, CA: University of California Press, 1986), p. 114–135; P. Redondi, *Galileo Heretic* (London: Penguin, 1989).

6. F. Bacon, *The Works of Francis Bacon* (London, 1819), 2:480–488.

7. F. Bacon, *Advancement of Learning* 1.6.16 (1605; reprint, Oxford: Oxford University Press, 1906), p. 46.

Therefore, because of the powerful influence of Galileo and Bacon, a strong bifurcation developed between the interpretation of creation (which became the task of scientists) and the interpretation of Scripture (which is the work of theologians and pastors). When one reaches the 19th century, one finds that often the old-earth geologists, whether Christian or not, referred to Bacon and Galileo's dictums to silence the objections of the scriptural geologists. The warning was obvious and powerful on the minds of the public, namely that defenders of a literal interpretation of Genesis regarding creation and Noah's flood were repeating the same mistake the Roman Catholic Church made three centuries earlier in relation to the nature of the solar system, which retarded the progress of science.

New Theories about the History of Creation

In contrast to the long-standing young-earth creationist view, different histories of the earth began to be developed in the late 18th century, which were evolutionary in character. Three non-Christian French scientists were prominent and all were either atheists or very skeptical theists. In 1778, **Buffon** (1708–1788), a nominal Catholic, but probably a secret skeptic, postulated that the earth was the result of a collision between a comet and the sun and had gradually cooled from a molten lava state over at least 78,000 years.[8] **Laplace** (1749–1827), an open atheist, published his nebular hypothesis in 1796.[9] He imagined that the solar system had naturally and gradually condensed from a gas cloud during a very long period of time. In his *Zoological Philosophy* of 1809, **Lamarck** (1744–1829), who vacillated between deism and atheism, proposed a theory of biological evolution over long ages, known as the inheritance of acquired characteristics.

New theories in geology were also being advocated at the turn of the 19th century as geology began to develop into a disciplined field of scientific study. Abraham **Werner** (1749–1817) was a German mineralogist and probably a deist. Although he published very little, his impact on geology was enormous

---

8. Buffon, *Epochs of Nature* (1778).

9. Laplace, *Exposition of the System of the Universe* (1796).

because many of the 19th century's greatest geologists had been his students. He theorized that the strata of the earth had been precipitated chemically and mechanically from a slowly receding universal ocean. In his mind, the earth was at least one million years old. His oceanic theory was quickly rejected, but the idea of an old earth remained with his students.

The Scotsman James **Hutton** (1726–1797) was trained in medicine but turned to farming for many years before eventually becoming interested in geology. In his *Theory of the Earth*, published in 1795, he proposed that the continents were gradually and continually being eroded into the ocean basins. These sediments were then gradually hardened and raised by the internal heat of the earth to form new continents, which would be eroded into the ocean again. With this slow cyclical process in mind, Hutton could see no evidence of a beginning to the earth, a view that precipitated the charge of atheism by many of his contemporaries, though he too may have been a deist.

Neither Werner nor Hutton paid attention to the fossils in rocks. Nevertheless, another key person in the development of old-earth geological theories who did was the Englishman William **Smith** (1769–1839). He was a drainage engineer and surveyor and helped build canals all over England and Wales, which gave him much exposure to the strata and fossils. He is called the "Father of English Stratigraphy" because he produced the first geological maps of England and Wales and he developed the method of using fossils to assign relative dates to the strata.[10] As a vague sort of theist who embraced a catastrophist theory like Cuvier's, he too imagined that the earth was much older than the Bible taught.

The Frenchman Georges **Cuvier** (1768–1832) was a comparative anatomist and a Lutheran who popularized the catastrophist theory of earth history. By studying fossils found largely in the Paris Basin, he believed that over the course of untold ages there had been at least four regional or nearly global catastrophic

10. W. Smith, *Strata Identified by Organized Fossils* (London, 1816) and *Stratigraphical System of Organized Fossils* (London, 1817).

floods, the last of which probably was about 5,000 years ago.[11] Obviously, his views coincided with the date of Noah's flood, but Cuvier never explicitly made this identification in his published theory.[12]

Finally, Charles **Lyell** (1797–1875), a trained lawyer turned geologist and probably a deist or Unitarian, began publishing his three-volume *Principles of Geology* beginning in 1830. Building on Hutton's uniformitarian ideas, Lyell insisted that the geological features of the earth can, and indeed must, be explained by slow gradual processes of erosion, sedimentation, earthquakes, and volcanism operating at essentially the same rate and power observed today. By the 1840s, his view became the ruling paradigm in geology. Therefore, at the time of the scriptural geologists there were three views of earth history (see Appendix 1).

It should be noted that two very influential geologists in England (and in the world) at this time were William **Buckland** (1784–1856) and Adam **Sedgwick** (1785–1873). Buckland became the head professor of geology at Oxford University in 1813, and Sedgwick gained the same position at Cambridge in 1818. Both were ordained Anglican clergy and both initially promoted old-earth catastrophism. However, under the influence of Lyell, they both converted to uniformitarianism with public recantations in the early 1830s. Buckland is often viewed as a defender of Noah's flood because of his 1823 book, *Reliquiae Diluvianae*. However, this apparent defense of the Flood was actually a subtle attack on it, as scriptural geologists accurately perceived. It is because of their powerful positions in academia and in the Church that Sedgwick and Buckland led many Christians in the 1820s to

---

11. G. Cuvier, *Theory of the Earth* (Edinburgh, 1813). The Edinburgh volume was the first English translation of the French original, "Discours Préliminaire," in *Recherches sur les ossemens fossils de quadrupèdes* (Paris, 1812).

12. The identification was made by the editor and publisher of Cuvier's English editions, Robert Jameson, who made the clear connection between Cuvier's last catastrophe and Noah's flood, no doubt to make it more compatible with British thinking at the time. The Oxford geologist William Buckland made this idea even more popular. See M. Rudwick, *The Meaning of Fossils* (Chicago, IL: University of Chicago Press, 1985), p. 133–135.

abandon their faith in the literal interpretation of Genesis and in the unique and geologically significant Noachian flood.

One more thing needs to be mentioned about geology at this time. The world's first scientific society devoted exclusively to geology was the London Geological Society, founded in 1807. From its inception, which was at a time when very little was known about the geological formations and fossils in them, the London Geological Society was controlled by the assumption that earth history is much older and different from that presented in Genesis. Moreover, a few of its most powerful members were Anglican clergy.

Christian Compromises with Old-Earth Geological Theories

During the early 19th century, many Christians attempted to harmonize these old-earth geological theories with the Bible. In 1804, the gap theory began to be propounded by the young pastor Thomas **Chalmers** (1780–1847), who soon became one of the leading Scottish evangelicals.[13] The gap theory became the most popular reinterpretation of Genesis among Christians for about the next half-century. The respected Anglican clergyman George Stanley Faber (1773–1854) began advocating the day-age theory in 1823.[14] The theory was not widely accepted by Christians until Hugh **Miller** (1802–1856), the prominent Scottish geologist and evangelical friend of Chalmers, revived it in the 1850s.[15]

Furthermore, in the 1820s, the evangelical Scottish zoologist Reverend John Fleming (1785–1857) began arguing for a tranquil Noachian deluge,[16] and in the late 1830s, the prominent

---

13. W. Hanna, *Memoirs of the Life and Writings of Thomas Chalmers* (Edinburgh, 1849–1852), 1:80–81; T. Chalmers, "Remarks on Curvier's *Theory of the Earth*," *The Christian Instructor* (1814), reprinted in *The Works of Thomas Chalmers* (1836–1842), 12:347–372.

14. See volume 1, chapter 3 of G.S. Faber, *Treatise on the Genius and Object of the Patriarchal, the Levitical, and the Christian Dispensations* (1823).

15. H. Miller, *The Two Records: Mosaic and the Geological* (1854) and *Testimony of the Rocks* (1856), p. 107–174.

16. J. Fleming, "The Geological Deluge as Interpreted by Baron Cuvier and Buckland Inconsistent with Moses and Nature," *Edinburgh Philosophical Journal* 14 (1826): p. 205–239.

evangelical Congregationalist theologian John **Pye Smith** (1774–1851) advocated a local creation and a local flood, both of which supposedly occurred in Mesopotamia.[17] Subsequently, as German liberal theology was beginning to spread in Britain in the 1830s, the view that Genesis is a myth, which conveys only theological and moral truths, started to become popular.

Consequently, it should be clear at this point, that by 1830, when Lyell published his uniformitarian theory, most geologists and much of the Church already believed the earth was much older than 6,000 years and that the Noachian flood was not the cause of most of the geological record. Lyell is often given too much credit (or blame) for the Church's loss of faith in Genesis. Actually, most of the damage was done before Lyell, often by Christians who were otherwise quite biblical, and this compromise was made at a time when geologists knew very little about the rocks and fossils of the earth.

Nevertheless, many evangelicals and high churchmen still affirmed the literal view of Genesis. Indeed, until about 1845, the majority of Bible commentaries on Genesis taught a recent six-day creation and a global catastrophic flood.[18] In the early 19th century, there were competing old-earth geological theories of the earth and competing interpretations of the early chapters of Genesis. Moreover, the scriptural geologists fought against all these ideas.

Philosophical Developments

As a prelude to this Genesis-geology controversy, the 18th century also witnessed the spread of two competing world views: deism and atheism. The two world views naturally developed from the Enlightenment, in which human reason was elevated to the place of supreme authority for determining truth. Apart from the deists' belief in a Creator God and a supernatural beginning to the creation, they were indistinguishable from atheists in their

---

17. John Pye Smith, *Mosaic Account of Creation and the Deluge illustrated by Science* (1837) and *Relation between the Holy Scriptures and Some Parts of Geological Science* (1839).

18. See the detailed analysis of commentaries before and during this period in Mortenson, "British Scriptural Geologists," p. 53–67.

views of Scripture and the physical reality. In deism, the Bible is merely a human book, containing errors, and not the inspired Word of God, and the history and function of the creation can be totally explained by the properties of matter and the "inviolable laws of nature." Deists and atheists often disguised their true views, especially in England where they were not culturally acceptable. Many of them gained influential positions in the scientific establishment of Europe where they subtly promoted what is today called "philosophical naturalism." However, the effects of deistic and atheistic philosophy on biblical studies and Christian theology also became widespread on the continent in the late 18th century and in Britain and America by the middle of the 19th century. Reventlow concluded in his thorough study:

> We cannot overestimate the influence exercised by Deistic thought, and by the principles of the Humanist worldview which the Deists made the criterion of their biblical criticism, on the historical-critical exegesis of the 19th century; the consequences extend right down to the present. At that time a series of almost unshakeable presuppositions were decisively shifted in a different direction.[19]

The biblical world view, which had dominated the Western nations for centuries, was rapidly being replaced by a naturalistic world view.

The Scriptural Geologists

It was in the midst of these revolutions in world view and the reinterpretation of the phenomena of nature and the Bible that the scriptural geologists expressed their opposition to old-earth geology. Who were these men? The scriptural geologists were a very diverse group of individuals. The author discovered over 30 authors writing between about 1815 and 1855, but there were probably more. Although some of them knew of each other and appreciated each other's writings, they never formally organized themselves into a group. Most of them were from Great Britain,

---

19. H.G. Reventlow, *The Authority of the Bible and the Rise of the Modern World*, translator, John Bowden (London: SCM Press, 1984), p. 412.

although this author found a few in America also and maybe there were some in continental Europe.[20]

Some of the scriptural geologists were clergy and some were not. Some were highly trained scientists, and others had no such training. A few were very competent in geology, both because of extensive reading and field study of geological formations and fossils in Britain and on the European continent. Their writings ranged from short pamphlets to massive, well-documented books, and they raised biblical, philosophical, and geological objections against old-earth theories.

What was most interesting for this author, as a historian, was the fact that the old earth opponents of the scriptural geologists, including fellow Christians, generally misrepresented them as being opposed to science and being ignorant of geological facts. None of the old-earth geologists responded to the arguments of the geologically most competent scriptural geologists, even though it was clear, in a couple of cases at least, that old-earth geologists personally knew one or more of these scriptural geologists.

In the author's book (based on his Ph.D. thesis), *The Great Turning Point: The Church's Catastrophic Mistake on Geology — Before Darwin*,[21] he wrote individual chapters on each of seven scriptural geologists, giving a biographical sketch and a detailed summary of their arguments against the old-earth theories.[22] In

---

20. B. Nelson, in his *The Deluge Story in Stone* (Minneapolis, MN: Bethany Fellowship, 1968), briefly referred to several American and European scriptural geologists at that time. See also R.L. Stiling, "Scriptural Geology in America," in *Evangelicals and Science in Historical Perspective*, eds. D.N. Livingstone, D.G. Hart, and M.A. Noll (New York: Oxford University Press, 1999), p. 177–192. With regard to Germany, help may also be found in S. Holthaus, *Fundamentalismus in Deutschland: Der Kampf um die Bibel im Protestantismus des 19. und 20. Jahrhunderts*, Biblia et Symbiotica 1 (Bonn: Verlag für Kultur und Wissenschaft, 1993); it is a Ph.D. dissertation from ETF-Leuven.

21. T. Mortenson, *The Great Turning Point: The Church's Catastrophic Mistake on Geology—Before Darwin* (Green Forest, AR: Master Books, 2004).

22. The Ph.D. thesis had chapters on 6 other men. Many of those have been published in the *CEN Technical Journal* and can be found within the archive list at http://www.answersingenesis.org/tj/archive/archive.asp.

this chapter, he is limited to briefly introducing the reader to four of the most geologically competent scriptural geologists. To set the context, it is helpful to see what Charles Lyell, the leading uniformitarian geologist in the 19th century, had to say about the opponents of old-earth-geological theories. Lyell described them as "wholly destitute of geological knowledge" and unacquainted "with the elements of any one branch of natural history which bears on the science." He said they were "incapable of appreciating the force of objections, or of discerning the weight of inductions from numerous physical facts." Instead, he complained, "they endeavour to point out the accordance of the Mosaic history with phenomena which they have never studied" and "every page of their writings proves their consummate incompetence."[23] As will be clear, these men were far from being the anti-geology, scientific ignoramuses that Lyell, most of their other contemporary critics, and nearly all historians have portrayed them.[24]

---

23. C. Lyell, Review of *Memoir on the Geology of Central France* by G.P. Scrope, *Quarterly Review* 36 (1827): p. 482. Lyell likely had in mind, among others, G. Penn, G. Bugg, and G. Young, who all wrote substantial works on the subject before 1827 and who feature in the author's thesis.

24. Even D. Young, the professing evangelical old-earth geologist at Calvin College, who has influenced so many other evangelical scholars in the last few decades, has misled his readers on this subject. In his *Christianity and the Age of the Earth* (Grand Rapids, MI: Zondervan, 1982, p. 54), he implied that these scriptural geologists had no real geological knowledge: "A torrent of books and pamphlets were published on 'Scriptural' geology and Flood geology, all designed to uphold the traditional point of view on the age and history of the world. The 'heretical' and 'infidel' tendencies of geology were roundly condemned by some churchmen, few of whom had any real knowledge of geology. Those who had geological knowledge were now largely convinced that the Earth was very old." In his more recent work, *The Biblical Flood* (Grand Rapids, MI: Eerdmans, 1995), p. 124–128, he was a little more generous, when he stated, "a few were competent field observers who had described regional geology." He named G. Young, but briefly discussed only the views of G. Penn, G. Fairholme, and W. Kirby. He did not mention J. Murray or W. Rhind, who, along with Young and Fairholme, were the most geologically competent scriptural geologists. All these men except Kirby are discussed thoroughly in the author's thesis.

George Young

George Young (1777–1848) was born into a poor but godly farming family in Scotland. He earned his first degree from the University of Edinburgh, where he focused on mathematics and natural philosophy and was a favorite student of professor John Playfair, who at this time was in the process of becoming the articulate interpreter of James Hutton's uniformitarian theory. Young then studied theology for five years under a leading Scottish theologian. In 1805, he moved to the little port of Whitby in Yorkshire and became the pastor of a Presbyterian congregation, called Whitby Chapel, where he served faithfully until his death in 1848. After beginning his pastoral ministry, he also received an M.A. and an honorary Doctor of Divinity.

As a godly pastor, Young was respected for his concern for the poor and his generous, self-denying Christian spirit, because of which he delighted to unite with Christians of other Protestant denominations in joint efforts of witness and service. His congregation fixed a monument over the pulpit of the church after his death, which honored Young for having "preached the Word of God within these walls with unabated zeal for 42 years, actuated and sustained throughout solely by a sense of duty, and an anxious desire for the salvation of souls."[25]

Additionally, his scholarly attainments were also considerable. He had a more than common knowledge of Hebrew, Greek, Latin, French, and Italian, in addition to an acquaintance with Arabic, Chaldee, and Syriac, and was considered quite an authority on the Anglo-Saxon language.

In 1823, he became a founding member and the first secretary of the Whitby Literary and Philosophical Society, a position he held until his death and which also included the establishment of the Whitby Museum. He was also a corresponding member of the Wernerian Natural History Society and an honorary member of several regional "philosophical societies" (which were very scientific in orientation since in those days science was often called "natural philosophy"). He served as an advisor to the Yorkshire

---

25. F.K. Robinson, *Whitby* (1860), p. 145.

Philosophical Society and as its coastal representative obtaining fossil and mineral collections.

Young published 21 books, which included books of sermons, theology, history, a biography, and scientific treatises. He was the most geologically competent of the scriptural geologists. Three of his books and six scientific journal articles dealt with geology and were based on wide reading and very thorough investigations of the strata of his home area of Yorkshire, where a great percentage of the so-called "geological column" was exposed in the mines and on the sea coast. He gave the most thorough analysis of the geological record done by any scriptural geologist. One of Young's journal articles was about a fossil crocodile found near Whitby.[26] He also sought to answer in a gracious and respectful yet challenging manner the specific geological and theological arguments of the leading old-earth geologists. He contended that the rocks and fossils gave abundant evidence that most of the geological record was the result of Noah's flood. His *Geological Survey of the Yorkshire Coast*, published in 1822 and revised and expanded in 1828, was praised by leading geologists of his day for its accurate observations, although they ignored his lengthy theoretical interpretations at the end of the book. Ten years later, in 1838, he published *Scriptural Geology* to defend Genesis against old-earth geology. The work was followed two years later by *Appendix to Scriptural Geology* (1840), in which he responded to John Pye Smith's theory that Genesis merely described a local creation and local Noachian flood.

George Fairholme

George Fairholme (1789–1846) was born into a wealthy Scottish family. His early education probably resulted from home tutoring and self-education. There is no record of him attending any of the major universities of the United Kingdom, but he became well educated nonetheless. His wealth enabled him and his family to travel extensively in England, Scotland, and Ireland,

---

26. G. Young, *Geological Survey* (1828), 299–300; "Account of a Fossil Crocodile Recently Discovered in the Alum Shale Near Whitby," *Edinburgh Philosophical Journal* 13 (1825): p. 76–81.

in addition to the European continent, especially in Belgium, France, and Germany. His devout Christian faith was expressed in his writings on geology and in his will.

Besides being well read in the leading British and foreign geological and scientific literature of his day, Fairholme also did considerable geological fieldwork and studied other aspects of nature during his extensive travels. He personally visited or corresponded with other naturalists, developed his own collection of rocks and fossils, did investigations at leading museums and zoos, performed scientific experiments, and attended some of the meetings of both the German and British associations of science. On this basis, he published seven scientific journal articles on such diverse topics as coal, Niagara Falls, human fossils, spiders, elephants, woodcocks, and microscopic animals. His most significant writings, however, were his two 400-page books on geology: *The Geology of Scripture* in 1833 and *Physical Demonstrations of the Mosaic Deluge* in 1837. In these works, he sought to correlate the geological record with the order of events described in the biblical accounts of creation and the Flood. In his second book on the Flood, he carefully argued from the present state of the valley systems of the continents and the erosion rates of the seacoasts and several prominent waterfalls in Germany and America, concluding that the Flood must have occurred about 5,000 years ago.

John Murray

John Murray (ca. 1786–1851) was born in Stranraer, Scotland, and from an early age he demonstrated a great interest in science. Eventually he attained M.A. and Ph.D. degrees in science. He became well known throughout Great Britain as a traveling lecturer on the philosophy of physics and chemistry for much of his life and was described by a prominent contemporary as one of the best lecturers in the world. Although he was a loyal member of the Church of Scotland and a strong Calvinist all his life, the local paper said of him at his death, "His benevolent heart was a stranger to bigotry and sectarianism. He loved all who loved the Lord Jesus Christ. In the hours of sickness and of death he manifested the same meek, patient, and amiable spirit which had characterized his deportment through life."[27]

With great industry, he developed an impressive breadth of knowledge in many subject areas of both science and literature. He did not gain great eminence in any single field, though he contributed much to chemistry and to mining. Between 1816 and 1835, he wrote several scientific papers, conducted many experiments and lectured often on the subject of the safety lamps used by miners. The miner's lamp was one of Murray's many inventions. Due to his expertise, he was invited in 1835 to testify on safety lamps and mine ventilation before a committee of Parliament.

His knowledge and experience qualified him to become a Fellow of the Linnaean Society in 1819, the Society of Antiquities in 1822, the London Geological Society in 1823, and the London Horticultural Society in 1824. He was almost appointed in 1831 to the chemistry chair of King's College, London. His membership in the Geological Society continued throughout his career. Additionally, he was a member of the Meteorological Society of London, the Wernerian Natural History Society of Edinburgh, and many other regional scientific or medical societies in addition to the mechanics institutes[28] in several cities.

Besides lecturing and doing experimental research, he also traveled extensively to do his own firsthand archaeological and geological fieldwork, some of which was done at great physical risk (e.g., exploring the top of an active volcano). Additionally, he was a prolific writer, publishing 28 books and at least 60 articles in scientific journals, plus frequent correspondence over many years to the *Mechanics' Magazine* and the *Mining Journal*. He had

---

27. "Death of Dr. Murray, Ph.D., &c.," *Galloway Advertiser and Wigtownshire Free Press* (July 3, 1851).

28. In the 1820s, mechanics institutes began to form in a number of provincial cities. The Institutes were intended to teach artisans and mechanics the scientific information that would be practically useful in their trades. For a number of reasons, they failed in this objective, though they did help to encourage young people to pursue scientific studies, and some of the institutes became polytechnics or universities.

nearly 20 inventions that came into practical use. His journal articles addressed subjects in chemistry, physics, medicine, geology, natural history, and manufacturing. His books, some of which went through two or more editions, covered such diverse topics as the cultivation of the silkworm, modern paper, atmospheric electricity, ventilation, disinfection and other sanitation measures, poisons, diamonds, a method for forming an instantaneous contact with shore during a shipwreck, and plant physiology. He also wrote a passionate pamphlet calling for the end of slavery in the colonies, a book of minor poems, and a scientific/historical travel memoir of his three-month journey through Switzerland in 1825.

Murray wrote two books that directly related to geology and the Bible. *The Truth of Revelation* was published in 1831, with an expanded second edition appearing in 1840. In this book, he endeavored to demonstrate the truth and inspiration of the Bible by an appeal to the existing monuments, sculptures, gems, coins, and medals from ancient peoples of the Near East and elsewhere. His 1838 *Portrait of Geology* was written primarily to give proofs from geology of divine design in creation, and secondarily to add verification of the truth of Scripture by presenting his geological and biblical reasons for rejecting old-earth theories.

William Rhind

Finally, William Rhind (1797–1874) was yet another Scotsman who was a geologically competent scriptural geologist. His university studies at Marischal College, Aberdeen, were devoted to medicine and he became a Licentiate of the Royal College of Surgeons of Edinburgh in 1818. Shortly thereafter, he began his medical practice in London but soon reestablished it in Scotland. Although he became quite successful as a doctor, his real love was literature and scientific research; consequently, in the mid-1820s, he moved to Edinburgh where he spent nearly 40 years of his life writing and lecturing on various subjects of natural science, primarily botany, zoology, and geology. In 1854, he became a lecturer in botany for a few years in the medical faculty at Marischal College and then spent the last decade of his life in poor health living with his older brother near New-port, Fife.

Rhind was likely a member of the Church of Scotland and his writings reflect a strong commitment to the Scriptures. Accord-ing to one biographer, "He was universally loved for his character and bearing, and a most amiable man. He was unassuming and retiring in his manner, but a most agreeable and interesting mem-ber of society."[29] In addition to his early membership in the Royal College of Surgeons of Edinburgh, by 1830 he also had become a member of the Royal Medical Society and Royal Physical Society of Edinburgh, and sometime before 1858 he became an honorary member of the Natural History Society of Manchester.

Rhind was also a voluminous writer on many subjects. His non-scientific books included a historical work on his home county and three tourist guides of Scotland. Of his scientific writings, a number reflected his strong commitment to see good textbooks available for the education of children, aged 10–18 years. Many of these books went through several editions and included class books on the natural history of the earth, botany, geology, zoology, meteorology, physical geography, and elemen-tary geography. In 1829, he published the first thorough work on the nature and cure of intestinal worms in the human body. His magnum opus discussing living and fossil plants was his 700-page *History of the Vegetable Kingdom*, which first appeared about 1841 and went through eight editions until 1877. In addition to his books, Rhind published several scientific journal articles on various topics: a species of worm in sheep (1830), the errone-ous idea of spontaneous generation of living creatures (1830), the geological arrangement of the strata (1844), the hydrology of the British Isles (1855), and coal found in Seil Island, Argyleshire (1858).

He wrote three books at an adult level dealing directly with geology. In 1833, he produced a book of excursions around Ed-inburgh, which illustrated the geology and natural history of the area and received high scientific reviews, especially for its accurate

---

29. R. Douglas, *Sons of Moray* (1930), p. 6.

geological information. In 1842, he published *The Geology of Scotland and Its Islands* — a purely descriptive work — which he hoped would stimulate further geological research by local geologists. However, the work in which Rhind discussed geological theory was *The Age of the Earth*, published in 1838. In it he presented his biblical and geological reasons for rejecting the old-earth theories.

The Scriptural Geologists' Biblical Arguments against Old-Earth Geology

As would be expected, the scriptural geologists did not write identical works. However, there were a number of biblical and geological objections shared by many, and sometimes all, of the scriptural geologists. With regard to biblical objections, some of them gave quite detailed refutations of the various old-earth re-interpretations of Genesis. Nevertheless, two important general criticisms commonly appeared. First, they contended that these old-earth compromise views were only possible if Christians *superficially read Genesis 1–11* and ignored other relevant Scriptures. Nearly all old-earth proponents *ignored* two critically important passages, even though they insisted that their views did not contradict Scripture. The passages ignored were the account of Noah's flood in Genesis 6–9 and the fourth commandment in Exodus 20:11. Nonetheless, the scriptural geologists referred to nearly all of these passages, since they understood them as fatal to the old-earth theories. Therefore, the scriptural geologists insisted that one could not legitimately speak of the harmony between the Bible and old-earth geological theory if one gave scant attention to what the Bible actually says.

Another major biblical objection of the scriptural geologists was related to the *biblical teaching about death*. The old-earth theories postulated long ages of violence, death, and destruction in the creation before the creation and fall of man. However, the scriptural geologists argued that the Bible teaches that God brought death into the world when He judged man and the whole creation because of man's sin. Therefore, the vast geological ages proposed by the old-earth geologists could not possibly have occurred. Rather, the geological evidence of death, violence, and extinction pointed primarily, though not exclusively, to Noah's flood. Modern young-earth creationists are still using this argument today.[30]

The Scriptural Geologists' Geological Arguments against Old-Earth Geology

With respect to geological evidence, the scriptural geologists raised five important objections, though the geologically competent scriptural geologists also gave many different detailed objections to old-earth theories. The scriptural geologists believed that the old-earth geologists were closing their minds to evidence that was contrary to their theories and that there were logical errors in their old-earth interpretations of their otherwise accurately described geological evidence.

One important geological objection related to the *gradual transitions* between different mineralogical formations. Several scriptural geologists[31] and many old-earth geologists[32] observed that it was quite common in the geological record to find one

---

30. For a popular treatment, see J. Stambaugh, "Death Before Sin?" *Impact* 191; and, K. Ham, "The God of an Old Earth," *Creation* 21 (September 1999): p. 42–45. For scholarly discussions, see J. Stambaugh, "Creation and the Problem of Evil," paper presented at the national meeting of the Evangelical Theological Society, November 17, 1995, and "Creation and the Curse," paper given at the Far West regional meeting of the Evangelical Theological Society, April 26, 1996. See also T.H. Ury, "The Evolving Face of God as Creator: Early Nineteenth-Century Traditionalist and Accommodationist Theodical Responses in British Religious Thought to Paleonatural Evil in the Fossil Record" (unpublished Ph.D. dissertation, Andrews University, 2001).

31. For example, G. Young, *Scriptural Geology* (1838), p. 22–23; and G. Fairholme, *Physical Demonstrations of the Mosaic Deluge* (1837), p. 12, 80, 285, 395–398.

32. For example, W. Smith, *Strata Identified by Organized Fossils* (1816), p. 1, 9-11, 13, 15, 21, 27, 32; T. Weaver, "Geological Observations on Part of Gloucestershire and Somersetshire," *Transactions of the Geological Society*, 2nd Ser. Vol. 1, Pt. 1 (1822), p. 323–324, 339, 343, 349, 360; A. Sedgwick and R.I. Murchison, "On the Structure and Relation of the Deposits Contained Between the Primary Rocks and the Oolitic Series in the North of Scotland," *Transactions of the Geological Society*, 2nd Ser. Vol. 3 (1835), p. 130, 132, 141, 147, 150.

kind of mineral deposit gradually changed into another kind (e.g., sandstone blending into limestone). Furthermore, the scriptural geologists noted, at this transition boundary, there was no evidence of soil erosion, as would be expected if the lower layer had been exposed to water or air for a long period of time. The theoretical implications of this observation were almost universally ignored by old-earth geologists when they accurately described this phenomenon, but it indicated to the scriptural geologists that the strata were deposited in rapid succession (as expected during a yearlong global flood), while the subjacent stratum were still rather soft and moist.

A second important geological objection related to certain *polystrate fossils*, which were often found in an upright position and cutting through two or more strata of rock.[33] One of the most famous polystrate fossils of the early 19th century was a tree found in a quarry in Scotland in 1830, which can be seen to be passing through many strata of rock. Two theories to explain such fossils were proposed and debated by leading geologists well into the 1840s, namely, either: 1) the trees had been gradually buried where they grew; or, 2) the trees had been uprooted, transported, and deposited by flood waters, which buried them rapidly in sediments. Since a dead tree would rot and disintegrate over hundreds or thousands of years, the scriptural geologists, along with some old-earth geologists,[34] believed that these trees had been transported and buried catastrophically. Moreover, since the formations where

---

33. For example, Fairholme, *Physical Demonstrations*, p. 392–394; Young, *Scriptural Geology*, p. 12-14; Rhind, *The Age of the Earth* (1838), p. 36–37.

34. S.P. Hildreth, "Notice of Fossil Trees, near Gallipolis, Ohio," *Philosophical Magazine*, N.S., 2 (October 1827): p. 311–313; H.L. Pattinson, "On the Fossil Trees Found in Jefferies Rake Vein at Derwent Lead Mine in the County of Durham," *Philosophical Magazine*, N.S., 7 (March 1830): p. 185–189; J. Phillips, *Illustrations of the Geology of Yorkshire* (1829–1836), 1:95; J. Phillips, *Treatise on Geology* (1837–1839), 1:160; J. Lindley and W. Hutton, *The Fossil Flora of Great Britain* (1831–1837), 2:xx–xxi; H. Witham, "A Description of a Fossil Tree Discovered in the Quarry of Craigleith," *Transactions of the Royal Society of Edinburgh*, Vol. 12, Pt. 1 (1834), p. 147–152.

these trees were found were analogous in their mineralogical characteristics to other formations where no trees were found, the scriptural geologists saw them as an important piece of evidence that most of the strata were deposited rapidly by Noah's flood. Polystrate fossils are still being used (by both young-earth creationists and old-earth, evolutionary "neo-catastrophists") to argue for the rapid, catastrophic deposition of the strata in which they are found.[35]

A third important geological objection related to *shell creatures*. Since these were the majority of fossils, they had a great, if not singular, importance for old-earth geologists in developing their history of the earth. William Smith, the "Father of English Stratigraphy," based his depiction and relative dating of the geological record primarily on shell creatures.[36] In 1828, Lyell formulated his interpretation of the Tertiary formation (or Cenozoic, as it is called today) solely on the basis of shells.[37] Buckland stated that fossil shells were "of vast importance in investigating the records of the changes that have occurred upon the surface of our globe" and "in fact without these [organic remains], the proofs of the lapse of such long periods as Geology shows to have been occupied in the formation of the strata of the earth, would have been comparatively few and indecisive."[38] In 1838, geologist James Smith said judging the age of a deposit purely on the basis of shells was a sound rule of geological reasoning.[39] Even in 1888, shells were still the primary tools used to date the strata. The highly touted, but

35. For example, J. Morris, *The Young Earth* (Green Forest, AR: Master Books, 1994), p. 100–102; and D. Ager, *The New Catastrophism* (Cambridge: Cambridge University Press, 1993), p. 47–50.

36. W. Smith, *Stratigraphical System of Organized Fossils* (London: 1817), p. vi [also see, "Geological Table," following page xi]. Most of the fossils he discussed were shell creatures.

37. C. Lyell, *The Antiquity of Man* (London, 1863), p. 3–5.

38. W. Buckland, *Bridgewater Treatise* (London: John Murray, 1836), 1:110, 112.

39. J. Smith, "On the Last Changes in the Relative Levels of the Land and Sea in the British Islands," *Memoirs of the Wernerian Natural History Society* 8 (1838), p. 84–85.

now demonstrably unreliable, radiometric dating methods were not developed until the early 20th century.[40] Fossil shells remain the dominant index fossils (OHT) used for dating geological formations.[41]

---

40. For information exposing the fatal problems with the radiometric dating methods, see the following arguments written for non-specialists but with full documentation: M. Lubenow, *Bones of Contention* (Grand Rapids, MI: Baker, 1992), p. 247–266; S. Austin, *Grand Canyon: Monument to Catastrophe* (El Cajon, CA: Institute for Creation Research, 1994), p. 111–132; Morris, *Young Earth*, p. 45–68. For a thorough technical analysis see J. Woodmorappe, *The Mythology of Modern Dating Methods: Why Million/Billion-Year Results Are Not Credible* (El Cajon, CA: Institute for Creation Research, 1999); and, L. Vardiman, A.A. Snelling, and E.F. Chaffin, eds., *Radioisotopes and the Age of the Earth: A Young-Earth Creationist Research Initiative* (El Cajon, CA: Institute for Creation Research, 2000). The latter scholarly book set the stage for a five-year scientific research project involving many Ph.D. young-earth scientists working to solve the riddle of radiometric dating (for they are convinced by the existing scientific research that this method is not giving the true age of the rocks).

41. J. Thackray, *The Age of the Earth* (London: Institute of Geological Sciences, 1980), p. 8–9, 10, 13. Referring to his Figure 21 on page 10 (showing predominantly shell creatures), Thackray wrote, "Two ideas form the basis of [time] correlation [of the strata] using fossils today: first that all members of a species evolve together over their whole geographical range, so that evolutionary changes can be regarded as taking place at the same time wherever they occur, and second that evolution is a process which does not repeat itself, so that once a species or fauna has gone, it will never reappear. For a fossil to be useful in time-correlation it must be widely distributed in a variety of rock types, reasonably common and easy to recognize, and a member of a well-defined, rapidly evolving lineage. No fossil satisfies all these requirements and all have their particular problems. The most useful are those like graptolites and ammonites which moved freely in the surface waters and are therefore found over wide areas in many different rock types. Less adequate are those like corals, gastropods, and bivalves, which evolved slowly and which were confined to a narrow range of environments. Widely used fossils, including some of the unfamiliar microscopic forms which are very important in borehole correlation, are shown in figure 21" (8–9).

Nevertheless, a number of scriptural geologists,[42] along with several respected conchologists (experts on shell creatures) and even a few old-earth geologists, objected that these shells were an unreliable means of dating the rock formations for several reasons.[43] First, the taxonomic classification of shell creatures was very controversial and confusing at this time. Often different species or even genus names were given to what in reality was a single species. Secondly, there was experimental and observational evidence that the same creature could produce different shells depending on slight changes in such variables as the salinity or temperature of the water, or the surface to which the creature frequently attached itself. Thirdly, it was known that marine shell creatures could adapt to fresh water and that freshwater shell creatures could adjust to life in the sea. The conclusions meant that the distinction of freshwater and saltwater deposits solely on the basis of shells was questionable (to say the least).

A fourth major geological objection related to *human fossils*. An intriguing specimen was found in Guadaloupe and reported in a scientific journal in 1814. A primary reason that the majority of geologists at that time believed that most of the geological record was deposited long before the creation of man was apparently that no fossil human bones had been found with extinct animals in lower formations but only in recently formed deposits close to the earth's surface. However, several scriptural

---

42. For example, T. Gisborne, *Considerations on the Modern Theory of Geology* (1837), p. 19, 51; G. Bugg, *Scriptural Geology* (1826–1827), 1:210–211; and G. Young and J. Bird, *Geological Survey of the Yorkshire Coast* (1828), p. 329–332.

43. For example, G. Cuvier, *Theory of the Earth* (1813), p. 58–60; F.S. Beudant, "Extract From a Memoir Read To The Institute on the 13th of May 1816 on the Possibility of Making the Molluscae of Fresh Water Live in Salt Water, and Vice Versa," *Philosophical Magazine* 48 (1816), p. 223–227; J.E. Gray, "Remarks on the Difficulty of Distinguishing Certain Genera of Testaceous Mullusca By Their Shells Alone, and on the Anomalies in Regard to Habitation Observed in Certain Species," *Philosophical Transactions*, Pt. 2 (1835), p. 301–310.

geologists[44] argued that there were several fossil discoveries that refuted this widespread opinion, but that this evidence had been misinterpreted due to superficial investigations or that the correctly interpreted evidence had been ignored or suppressed by old-earth geologists.

Finally, another important objection of the scriptural geologists to the old-earth theories was since *geology was in its infancy* as a science in the early 19th century, geological knowledge was far too limited to justify a theory of the whole earth based solely on the geological data.[45] Again, however, the scriptural geologists were not the only ones raising this objection.[46] It is important to note that Werner based his theory only on his knowledge of the sedimentary rocks around his home in Saxony, Germany.[47] Hutton first sketched his theory of the earth in a journal article *before* he had done hardly any fieldwork, and he traveled very little inside or outside Scotland to look for confirmation of his theory.[48] Cuvier built his catastrophist theory exclusively on the fossils and formations of the Paris Basin, most of which he did not

44. See, for example, Fairholme, *Physical Demonstrations*, p. 41–52; J. Murray, *A Portrait of Geology* (1838), p. 82–96; G. Penn, *Comparative Estimate of the Mineral and Mosaic Geologies* (1825), 2:124–134, 394–412.

45. See for example, Rhind, *Age of the Earth*, p. 111–114; Young and Bird, *Geological Survey*, p. 2–3, 8–9; Gisborne, *Modern Theory of Geology*, 6; J. Murray, *The Truth of Revelation* (1840), p. 137–138, 142; Bugg, *Scriptural Geology*, 1:10–14, 2:289, 343.

46. For example, T., anonymous review of Bakewell's *Introduction to Geology* (3rd ed.), *Magazine of Natural History* 1 (1829): p. 250–251; W. Conybeare, "Report on the Progress, Actual State, and Ulterior Prospects of Geological Science," *Report of the BAAS: 1831–32* (1833), p. 410–13; W. Whewell, *The History of the Inductive Sciences* (1837), 3:621–622.

47. M. Millhauser, *Just Before Darwin* (Middleton: Wesleyan University Press, 1959), p. 42–43. Millhauser, a respected historian of science, bluntly stated that Werner "drew the broadest generalizations from the scantiest and most haphazard supply of facts; untraveled, indifferent to contemporary studies abroad, he evolved out of local formations and his own consciousness an intricate, largely hypothetical, immensely influential, and almost completely wrong theory of the world."

48. "Hutton," in *Dictionary of National Biography* (United Kingdom), p. 354; C. Lyell, *Principles of Geology* (1830), 1:62.

personally investigate in the field. Furthermore, in a candid and revealing admission, he stated that almost all of the fossils upon which he based his theory were found by people who did not carefully observe or record the precise geological location where the bones were found.[49] Charles Lyell developed the essential points of his whole uniformitarian theory after only a few years of geological observations in England and before his first major geological tour on the European continent.[50] These theories were indeed based on a very limited knowledge of the geology of Britain and Europe (to say nothing of the rest of the earth). The scriptural geologists rightly concluded that this theorizing on skimpy data was contrary to the method taught by Bacon.

Accordingly, because of these major geological objections and other minor ones, along with biblical objections, the scriptural geologists argued that the old-earth theories were false and that the acceptance of them would not only undermine the Christian faith and morality, but would also slow the progress of geology in the acquisition of true knowledge.

The Actual Concern of the Debate

In spite of these significant objections against the theories of both the catastrophists and the uniformitarians, the writings of the most geologically competent scriptural geologists were ignored or misrepresented, but never refuted. Why? Well, the historical evidence clearly shows that they were not rejected because their objections had no basis in the science of their day. They were not naïve Bible students nor "wholly destitute of geological knowledge," as their opponents and historical critics said.[51] Rather, this author believes the reason they were ignored is that they were in a conflict of philosophical or religious world views.

---

49. Cuvier made his revealing admission of ignorance in his *Theory of the Earth* (1822), p. 111–113.

50. M.J.S. Rudwick, "Lyell on Etna, and the Antiquity of the Earth," in *Toward a History of Geology*, ed. C.J. Schneer (Cambridge: MIT Press, 1969), p. 289.

51. The quoted words are from C. Lyell, Review of *Memoir on the Geology of Central France* by G.P. Scrope, *Quarterly Review* 36 (1827): p. 482.

The scriptural geologists were not opposed to geological facts but to the interpretation of those facts. Moreover, they argued that old-earth interpretations were based on anti-biblical philosophical assumptions. Although they did not label those assumptions with the modern term of "philosophical naturalism," they clearly perceived them as such. They also insisted that there was a difference between, on the one hand, the experimental scientific studies which use observations of presently occurring processes and repeatable experiments to determine how the present creation operates and, on the other hand, the historical scientific studies which use circumstantial evidence and written records to try to reconstruct the origin of the creation and its historical development to its present state. The scriptural geologists insisted that in constructing a history of the earth, geologists should not limit themselves to the circumstantial evidence of rocks and fossils, but should also carefully consult the more important eyewitness testimony of God's Word.

Therefore, the Genesis-geology debate was really a conflict of world views — that is, deism, or vague forms of theism and atheism joined against biblical Christianity. Sadly, many Christians, including clergy, absorbed many of the anti-biblical philosophical assumptions hidden in scientific writings in those days (and the current day), and so they unconsciously became semi-deists, as society was enjoying the lush and seemingly boundless fruits of human reason at work in the Industrial Revolution. The author believes this is the ultimate reason that the writings of the geologically competent scriptural geologists were rejected without refutation by the leading geologists of their day. By the publication of Darwin's theory in 1859, the scriptural geologists as a "species" of thinkers had almost passed into extinction. Their thinking about both Scripture and the geological evidence surprisingly resurfaced in the last half of the 20th century with the modern young-earth creationist movement that is now worldwide.

The battle the scriptural geologists fought is very relevant for today, for at least two reasons. First, their existence helps to expose the fallacy of the recent charge by evangelical church historian

Mark Noll, who followed the former Seventh Day Adventist and now agnostic historian of science Ronald Numbers. Both men have discredited modern young-earth creationism by attempting to base it in the teachings of Seventh Day Adventism and stated that young-earth geology began in the early 20th century with Adventist George McCready Price.[52] Certainly, Price's geological writings influenced men such as Henry Morris. However, Price and the earlier scriptural geologists made many of the same observations and interpretations of the geological phenomena that modern creationists have also observed. Moreover, the scriptural geologists, the early Adventists, and the modern creationists all obtained their young-earth ideas from a literal interpretation of Genesis, which freed their minds from anti-biblical philosophical assumptions in geology (which is the way Genesis was almost universally interpreted in the church prior to the 19th century). Therefore, Mark Noll is badly misinformed as a historian and greatly misleads his readers when he states in his influential book *The Scandal of the Evangelical Mind* that young-earth creationists use "a fatally flawed interpretive scheme of the sort that no responsible Christian teacher in the history of the church ever endorsed before this century."[53]

A second lesson from the scriptural geologists' battle with old-earth Christians of their day is that the increasingly popular old-earth Intelligent Design movement (ID), led by Phillip Johnson, is fatally flawed. This writer appreciates the efforts of the ID writers to expose the inadequacy of theories of biological evolution to explain the incredible design witnessed in living creatures and to challenge the philosophical naturalism that controls science. Nevertheless, many Christians are led astray regarding

---

52. M. Noll, "The Scandal of the Evangelical Mind," *Christianity Today* (October 25, 1993): p. 29–32, and *The Scandal of the Evangelical Mind* (Grand Rapids, MI: Eerdmans, 1994), esp. p. 12–14; and R. Numbers, *The Creationists* (New York: Knopf, 1992).

53. Noll, *Evangelical Mind*, p. 14. For an incisive review of the preceding book by a leading creationist, see C. Weiland, "Book Review: *The Scandal of the Evangelical Mind*," *CEN Technical Journal* 10 (April 1996): p. 18–20.

geological and astronomical (or cosmic) evolution, which most ID people uncritically accept as proven fact. Like the early 19th-century old-earth advocates, Phillip Johnson and the ID movement are only focusing on design in creation and overlooking the obvious witness in creation to God's wrath outpoured at the Fall and at the Flood. Additionally, they apparently fail to see (or at least explain to others, if they do see), that philosophical naturalism controls geology and astronomy as much as, if not more than, it controls biology, and that naturalism did not take control of science through Darwin but through old-earth geology and astronomy half a century earlier. Ultimately, the age of the earth controversy is not just a philosophical argument; rather old-earth geology and old-universe astronomy, like evolutionary biology, are massive assaults on the authority and clarity of the Word of God. Furthermore, as in the 19th century, ID proponents insist on keeping the Bible, or at least Genesis, out of the discussion, or when they do allow the Bible in the discussion, they give only a superficial attention to the text. In his recent book, Johnson encouraged Christian readers, "The place to begin is with the biblical passage that is most relevant to the evolution controversy. It is not in Genesis; rather, it is the opening of the Gospel of John."[54] He then quoted and discussed John 1:1–3.

The same kind of old-earth, intelligent design approach by Christians almost 200 years ago failed to halt the rising tide of skepticism and unbiblical religion. All the early 19th century Christian old-earth proponents used or supported intelligent

---

54. P. Johnson, *The Wedge of Truth* (Downers Grove, IL: InterVarsity Press, 2000), p. 151. He has said similar things many times to Christian audiences. In a recent interview in Australia [P. Hastie, "Designer Genes: Phillip E. Johnson Talks to Peter Hastie," *Australian Presbyterian* 531 (October 2001): p. 4–8], he stated, "I think that one of the secondary issues [in the creation-evolution debate] concerns the details of the chronology in Genesis. . . . So I say, in terms of biblical importance, that we should move from the Genesis chronology to the most important fact about creation, which is John 1:1. . . . It's important not to be sidetracked into questions of biblical detail, where you just wind up in a morass of shifting issues."

design arguments against pre-Darwinian evolutionary theories.[55] Furthermore, all of them gave very superficial attention to the text of Genesis. However, the old-earth geology they supported actually paved the way for Darwin's victory. The author sees no reason to think that the present strategy of the ID movement will lead the culture or individuals back to the God of the Bible and to His inspired, inerrant, and authoritative Word.

One final point can be made here. Several of the scriptural geologists expressed their concerns that if the early chapters of Genesis were rejected as literal accurate history, it would only be a matter of time before other parts of the Bible would also be rejected, leading inevitably to the spiritual decline of the Church and its evangelistic mission, and the moral decay of society. In 1834, one of the scriptural geologists, Reverend Henry Cole, explained:

> Many reverend Geologists, however, would evince their reverence for the divine Revelation by making a distinction between its *historical* and its *moral* portions; and maintaining, that the latter only is inspired and absolute Truth; but that the former is not so; and therefore is open to any latitude of philosophic and scientific interpretation, modification or denial! . . . According to these impious and infidel modifiers and separators, there is not one third of the Word of God that *is* inspired; for not more, nor perhaps so much, of that Word, is occupied in abstract moral revelation, instruction, and precept. The other two thirds, therefore, are open to any scientific modification and interpretation; or (if scientifically required), to a total denial! It may however be safely asserted, that whoever professedly, before men, disbelieves the inspiration of any part of Revelation, disbelieves, in the sight of God, its inspiration altogether. If such principles were permitted of the most High to proceed to

55. Next to William Paley's *Natural Theology* (1802), probably the most famous examples of design arguments against naturalistic explanations for the origin of living things were the series of eight *Bridgewater Treatises*. The *Treatises* were written from 1833–1836 by eight different prominent authors, only one of whom (William Kirby, an entomologist) was a young-earth proponent.

their ultimate drifts and tendencies, how long would they be sweeping all faith in revealed and inspired Veracity from off the face of the earth? ...

What the consequences of such things must be to a revelation-possessing land, time will rapidly and awfully unfold in its opening pages of national scepticism, infidelity, and apostacy [*sic*], and of God's righteous vengeance on the same![56]

The last 170 years in the western world has confirmed the scriptural geologists' worst fears. The denial seems particularly obvious in Britain and America, where the gospel has previously had such great cultural influence.

Therefore, in light of all that has been stated, this author will stand with his scriptural geologist forefathers and insist that the age of the earth and its history matter enormously. It is not a secondary side issue, but it strikes at the very heart of philosophical naturalism's stranglehold of science, culture, and much of the Church, a stranglehold that began in the early 19th-century Genesis-geology debate. Christians need to realize that biological evolution (in whatever form) is only one strand of naturalistic interpretations of the physical creation. Ecclesiastes 4:12 states, "A cord of three strands is not easily torn." Removing one strand may weaken the rope. However, the Church will not be liberated from the bondage to philosophical naturalism if only biological evolution is rejected. Old-earth geological evolution and old-universe astronomical evolution must also be rejected. Both the Bible and the demonstrated scientific facts require it. The scriptural geologists of the early 19th century were convinced of this and wrote to persuade other Christians. Today, Christians likewise need to become informed and convinced of the plain and literal truth of Genesis and contend for that truth, when the scientific evidence

---

56. H. Cole, *Popular Geology Subversive of Divine Revelation* (London: Hatchard and Son, 1834), p. ix–x, 44–45 (fn.), emphasis in original. In this book, Cole, an Anglican minister, was responding to the writings of old-earth Cambridge University geologist and fellow ordained Anglican, Adam Sedgwick.

is more clearly on the side of Genesis than it was even in the early decades of the 19th century.

Appendix 1
Early 19th Century Views of Earth History

Biblical View (Scriptural Geologists)
SB---F-----------------P------------SE
(Time to Present: ca. 6000 years)

God supernaturally created the world and all the basic "kinds" of life in six literal days (SB) and then judged the world with a global flood (F) at the time of Noah, which produced most of the geological/fossil record, and all present day (P) processes have continued essentially since the Flood. Earth history will continue until God supernaturally brings the world to an end (SE).

Catastrophist view (e.g., Cuvier, Smith)
SB----C----C----C----C--------------------P-----C?---NE?
(Time to Present: "untold ages")

During the earth's long history (at least millions of years) there have been at least four natural regional or global catastrophic floods, since God created the world (SB), which produced most of the geological/fossil record and current geography of the earth. After each catastrophe (C), God supernaturally created some new forms of life. Since the past catastrophes were natural events, there may be another in the future, which may also have a natural (or supernatural) end (NE).

Uniformitarian View (e.g., Hutton, Lyell)
SB?---P---------NE?
(Time to Present: "untold ages")

All geological processes on the earth (maybe) began (SB) millions of years ago. These processes (e.g., erosion, sedimentation, volcanoes, earthquakes) continued into the present and will continue into the future at the same rate and intensity as observed today (P). No one knows if there will be an end to the current natural processes (NE?).

Terry Mortenson, M.Div., Ph.D., is lecturer and researcher at Answers in Genesis, Petersburg, Kentucky. Like most people, Dr. Mortenson grew up in an education system that taught evolution as fact. He started to see the fallacy of billions of years of evolution shortly after becoming a Christian during his first year in the university and has been studying and speaking on the creation-evolution issue since the late 1970s.

Much of his M.Div. studies focused on various (biblical, historical, and philosophical) aspects of this subject. His Ph.D. thesis analyzed the origins of old-earth geology in the early 19th century and particularly the writings of the "scriptural geologists," a group of scientists and non-scientists who wrote biblical, geological, and philosophical arguments against old-earth theories. He has spoken on the subject to various kinds of audiences in various settings and in many countries.

CHAPTER 3

GENESIS I–II AS LITERAL HISTORY

Eugene H. Merrill

The question of whether Genesis 1–11 should be viewed as literal history has long been an issue in biblical scholarship.[1] In more recent times it has become a matter of interest at the level of the Church as well. The Church is generally 25 years behind scholarship, so topics that engage the academy do not reach the popular level immediately, though they inevitably do in time.

The consensus of critical scholarship is that the first 11 chapters of Genesis are not to be construed as genuine history.[2] This chapter attempts to present arguments to counteract such skepticism and to give the Church reasons for renewed confidence in the historicity of the early Genesis accounts. This first section of the book recounts what is sometimes called the primeval or

1. The author read an earlier draft of this article at the first annual regional meeting of the Conservative Theological Society on August 8, 2003, at Living Word Church, New Port Richey, Florida.

2. See especially H. Gunkel, *Genesis*, trans. M.E. Biddle (Macon, GA: Mercer University Press, 1997), p. vii–xix. Gunkel's original work in German appeared in 1901. That the consensus still holds may be seen, for example, in N.P. Lemche, *Prelude to Israel's Past*, trans. E.F. Maniscaleo (Peabody, MA: Hendrickson Publishers, 1988), p. 12–26.

pre-patriarchal period because Genesis 12 begins the story of Abraham, followed by those of Isaac, Jacob, and Joseph, which comprise the remainder of the Genesis narrative. It should be acknowledged in passing that mainstream Old Testament scholarship denies the historicity of Genesis 12–50 in addition to the first 11 chapters, relegating Abraham to the realm of legend or saga.[3] Particularly disturbing, however, is the fact that at least moderate use of source critical methods has also made inroads into evangelicalism.[4]

Usually Genesis 1–11 is thought to be problematic in terms of the so-called Bible-science debate, specifically the matter of creationism versus evolutionism. The intent of this chapter is not to address that particular aspect of the topic except to note that the historicity of Genesis is rejected by nearly all evolution-oriented scientists. The author will argue here that since a sound biblical theology must be based on actual events, Genesis 1–11, as well as the rest of the biblical testimony, must be understood as literal history.[5] Otherwise, the theology of this part of the Bible — and of the whole — cannot be regarded as authentic and authoritative.

The Qualification of Genesis 1–11 as History

What is there about Genesis 1–11 that would lead one to think it is history? Is there literature there and elsewhere in the Bible other than historical literature? Clearly there is. For example, there is poetry, wisdom, and prophetic literature, very little of which can be regarded as history writing. Whenever it does speak in historical terms, it should, of course, be understood as such. This said, is there anything in Genesis 1–11 that would lead one to conclude that these chapters are anything but an attempt

---

3. J.M. Miller and J.H. Hayes, *A History of Ancient Israel and Judah* (Philadelphia, PA: Westminster, 1986), p. 58–63.

4. See, for example, the equivocations of G.J. Wenham, *Genesis 1-15*, in the Word Biblical Commentary series (Waco, TX: Word, 1987), p. xxi–liii.

5. E.H. Merrill, "Old Testament History: A Theological Perspective," in *A Guide to Old Testament Theology and Exegesis*, ed. W.A. VanGemeren (Grand Rapids, MI: Zondervan, 1999), 66-68.

to convey a message founded on actual historical events? The evidence points decidedly away from such a supposition. Genesis 1–11 presents what may be called primeval or pre-patriarchal history, which, despite its antiquity, conforms to standard and acknowledged criteria of genuine historiography.

The Hallmarks of History Writing

At least seven hallmarks characterize authentic historiography and thus qualify Genesis 1–11 as literal history.[6]

1. History is usually composed in narrative form (at least good history is). The reason many people have no interest in history is that often it is not written in good narrative. However, good history tells a story. Genesis 1–11 does so, since it is narrative in the same tradition as standard historical writing.

2. History is person and event centered. Without persons and events, there is no history. It is that simple. As one looks at Genesis 1–11, one observes that persons and events constitute the narrative.

3. History writing is purposeful, with a clearly definable objective and movement in a certain direction. Students of history seldom, if ever, understand the purpose of historical events unless it be theological history, which, as such, contains its own interpretation. One may study American history, for example, and fail to discern any kind of a pattern, any movement toward which that history is driven (perhaps, indeed, there is none from a human perspective). The Christian may resort to the theological idea that even the history of America is part of a divine plan, and that God is accomplishing some kind of a mysterious purpose but it is highly presumptuous for anyone to claim to understand exactly what that plan might be from a historical narrative standpoint. However, one can discern — by retrospection — patterns and

---

6. For these and others, see B. Halpern, *The First Historians* (San Francisco, CA: Harper & Row, 1988), p. 6–15.

plans in biblical history, that is, a way of viewing it as is sometimes called "sacred" or "redemptive" history. It is possible, for example, to recognize that God placed everything in Genesis 1–11 in some kind of a purposeful arrangement moving forward toward a climax.

4. History writing is coherent. It makes sense. The narrative holds together, which means there are no irrelevant details and that every part contributes to the whole. This is true not only of biblical history, but also of history in general. If written well, it ought to have a storyline that integrates the whole account and provides it a central core.

5. It is self-consistent and non-contradictory. History, understood properly, may indeed relate inconsistencies in human behavior, but the narrative must be internally consistent as a narrative and free of illogical or self-negating elements. For example, there cannot be two sets of dates for a given event since one of those has to be wrong. It may be reasonable to have doubts about dates or even the events of which they speak and to suggest solutions to these problems. However, the events must be presented as having occurred in a certain manner at a certain time and in a certain sequence.

6. It must be focused. It is impossible to write an exhaustive history of anything. Recently, the author finished reading a very technical and detailed history of the Jewish people in Europe from 1789 until 1939 (a book of a thousand pages in small print). It was of special interest because the author had previously visited Central Europe, specifically Budapest, Prague, Vienna, and Bratislava. Among many other reasons for the travel was to visit some of the old Jewish communities (many of which, sad to say, no longer exist) and to view synagogues, cemeteries, and other places of interest referenced in the book. Even that lengthy book is focused. The author had a plan, pattern, agenda, and objective.

It is obvious that Genesis 1–11 adheres to this sixth criterion and therefore should be construed as history writing on these grounds alone. One recalls John's observation in chapter 20 of his Gospel that if all the things that Jesus said and did had been recorded, the world itself, he supposed, could not contain the books. Certainly, that is true as well of the first 11 chapters of Genesis. Had God determined to record everything that had occurred from creation until the time of Abraham, the world could hardly contain that information. In just the brief compass of 11 chapters, one reads of the history of the world from the beginning until approximately 2100 B.C. The fact that it can all be contained in 11 chapters demonstrates that it is highly focused history (i.e., with a very narrowly conceived pattern and plan).

7. A hallmark of history is that it must be interpretive by its very nature. There are no such things as brute facts in history.[7] Facts come to the reader already interpreted with some kind of meaning. This is true of biblical history also since events it recounts must be viewed through the prism of interpretation. A bare event has scarcely any kind of meaning; it must be accompanied by a clarifying word in order for it to be intelligible and profitable.

These seven criteria should be applied to any kind of history writing, including Genesis 1–11. The author intends to argue that when this is done, Genesis 1–11 will be shown to be literal history because it satisfies all seven criteria of ordinary history writing. Before proceeding, however, it will be well to raise further methodological questions. First, what are some common objections that ought not in fact disqualify Genesis 1–11 from being history writing? Second, what appears to disqualify it as such from the standpoint of modern rationalistic, enlightenment, and humanistic skepticism?

---

7. R.G. Collingwood, *The Idea of History* (Oxford: Clarendon, 1946), p. 231–233.

What Cannot Disqualify

1. The supernatural. Beginning with the very first words of Genesis, "In the beginning, God . . ." the first 11 chapters of Genesis are filled with the supernatural. The moment one has said "God" is to testify to the supernatural, in particular to creation. When one speaks of creation, one is speaking of the transcendent, that is, something beyond normal human experience. However, can the supernatural by itself disqualify these chapters from being historical? Who is to say simply because an event is supernatural it cannot be considered historical? If one follows such thinking to its logical conclusion, then, of course, the Resurrection (a prime example) cannot be considered a historical event because it is clearly supernatural. There is no precedent for disqualifying an event of the past as history simply because it cannot be explained in rationalistic, experiential terms.

2. The miraculous. Should a text containing the story of a miracle disqualify itself as a historical text simply because it recounts a miracle? If so, great portions of the New Testament and the Old Testament (not just Genesis 1–11) must be regarded as fable, fiction, legend, or myth because so much of them contain miracle stories. The presence of the miraculous cannot by itself disqualify a text as history writing.

3. Uniqueness. Merely because an event occurred only once cannot mean it did not happen. How many resurrections have there been in the history of the world? The answer is, only one! There have been resuscitations, as in the case of Lazarus and others, but only one triumphant glorious resurrection — that of our Savior. Therefore, if uniqueness is a disqualification for historicity, one again must disqualify the Resurrection as an historical event. Applying such thinking to Genesis 1–11, since there has been only one creation, the record of its occurrence must be fiction. To extend the idea further, if it be accepted that

an event that has allegedly occurred only once cannot be historical, then one must, to be consistent, hold the so-called big-bang hypothesis to be pure fiction inasmuch as it surely must have occurred only once.

4. Antiquity. The notion is rampant that one can believe something that occurred last week but cannot believe something that took place thousands of years ago. The implication is that the ancients were incapable of recording actual historical events, and only with the arrival of the Enlightenment has man finally become intelligent enough to engage in historical research and get his facts straight. Thus, some argue that the first 11 chapters of Genesis cannot be historical because they refer to such an ancient time.

5. Religious or theological content. Texts that embrace such concepts are automatically disqualified as being historical. If God is ever mentioned in a narrative, it cannot be historical since the presence of deity in the text renders it religious and therefore non-historical. Accordingly, God is either erased from the narrative, the narrative itself is rejected because it refers to God, or there is some act or movement attributed to a superhuman power that disqualifies the account from being historical. Who is to say that God cannot have a part to play in history or that religion and theology have no place in historical narrative?

6. Selectivity of content. This refers to authorial intent in what is to be included or excluded in a given narrative. Such selectivity is not as apparent in the first 11 chapters of Genesis as it is in later Old Testament history. For example, many events well documented from the ancient Near Eastern world by means of Sumerian, Babylonian, Egyptian, Assyrian, and other inscriptions are never referred to in the Old Testament. Consequently, the critic alleges that since these events are mentioned in secular history but not in the Old Testament, the Old Testament

cannot qualify as serious history writing. The assumption is that the Old Testament ought to recount every event recorded in every extra-biblical inscription. Alternatively, many events mentioned in the Old Testament find no attestation elsewhere, the exodus being a classic case.

Since there is no allusion to the climactic and decisive deliverance of Israel from Egypt in extra-biblical literature, does this mean the exodus did not occur simply because it is mentioned only in the Bible? By what standard of history writing must any event be mentioned in a host of texts for its historicity to be validated? The Old Testament as a whole, and the first 11 chapters in particular, are written not to recount the history of the world in detail, but to reveal specific incidents or events that are important to redemptive history (i.e., God's plan and program of bringing the world back into fellowship with himself).

7. Non-narrative. Significant sections of the first 11 chapters of Genesis are not narrative. These include genealogies, especially in Genesis 5 and 11, and the so-called Table of Nations in Genesis 10. While it is true that most historiography consists of narrative, other genres are commonly interspersed. Such things as lists, statistical tables, addresses, geographic descriptions, and the like are regular features and as non-narrative texts cannot be precluded from having historical value on that account.

The preceding principles are introductory to examining the historical character of Genesis 1–11, but are at the same time essential in supporting its integrity as a credible historical account.

The Structures of Genesis 1–11

The Tôl°dôt

The author and reader now turn to an examination of the literary structures of Genesis 1—11, beginning with a consideration of the Hebrew word *tôl°dôt*, generally translated "generations" or "account." The term first occurs in Genesis 2:4: "This is the account of the heavens and the earth when they were created, in the day that the LORD God made earth and heaven." To understand the Book of Genesis as a literary piece, one must view the term *tôl·dôt* as a key in identifying the various sections of the book, since the book as a whole appears to be arranged around it.[8]

The word is derived from the Hebrew verb *yālad*, "to give birth," "to bear," and thus *tôl·dôt* usually means "generation" (i.e., "that which is brought forth," "that which is born"). It also has a secondary meaning of "narrative" or "account." One may therefore read Genesis 2:4 as "this is the account" or "this is the record of the heavens and the earth when they were created" (referring in this case to the previous creation narrative of Gen. 1:1–2:3). The first *tôl·dôt* is the creation story of Genesis 1 (a separate, independent narrative) and the second *tôl·dôt* the account of the heavens and the earth (Gen. 2:4–26).

The term occurs elsewhere in Genesis 5:1–6:8 (the *tôl·dôt* of Adam); 6:9–9:29 (the *tôl·dôt* of Noah); 10:1–11:9 (the *tôl·dôt* of the sons of Noah); 11:10–26 (the *tôl·dôt* of Shem); 11:27–25:11 (the *tôl·dôt* of Terah); 25:12–18 (the *tôl·dôt* of Ishmael); 25:19–35:29 (the *tôl·dôt* of Isaac); 36:1–8; 36:9–37 (used twice for the *tôl·dôt* of Esau); and, 37:2–50:26 (the *tôl·dôt* of Jacob). As for the creation narratives, it is clear that *tôl·dôt* has the dual function of summarizing the cosmocentric account of Genesis 1:1–2:3 and forming a heading for the anthropocentric account in 2:4–25. The dual function is clear from the pivot pattern of 2:4 which reads, "The heavens and the earth when they were created ... made the earth and the heavens." Therefore, the text employs a common Hebrew literary device to specify "heavens and earth" balanced by "earth and heavens," and "created" balanced by "made."

The Placement of Genealogies

Genealogies are also structurally significant in Genesis 1–11, always occurring at certain crisis points.[9] The genealogy of Cain

8. A.P. Ross, *Creation and Blessing* (Grand Rapids, MI: Baker, 1988), p. 69–74.

9. K.A. Mathews, *Genesis 1–11:26*, in the New American Commentary series (Nashville, TN: Broadman & Holman, 1996), p. 34–35.

appears immediately after Genesis 4:15 ("So the LORD said to him, 'Therefore whoever kills Cain, vengeance will be taken on him sevenfold.' And the LORD appointed a sign for Cain, lest anyone finding him should slay him"). The next is Genesis 4:25 ("And Adam had relations with his wife again; and she gave birth to a son; and named him Seth; for, she said, 'God has appointed me another offspring in place of Abel; for Cain killed him'"). In Genesis 4:15 ("lest anyone finding him should slay him") and 4:25 ("for Cain killed him") there is clearly common wording, and the genealogy of Seth occurs immediately after 4:25. It is worth noting that the genealogy of Cain comes immediately after a threat on his life, and that of Seth follows a repetition of the account of the death of Abel at the hands of Cain.

Likewise, Genesis 10:1 reads, "Now these are the records of the generations of Shem, Ham, and Japheth, the sons of Noah; and sons were born to them after the flood." The great crisis event of the Flood is followed by not just one genealogy, but three, those of the sons of Noah. It culminates in the genealogy of Shem, who is the founder of the line of which Messiah would come, the Shemites (or Semites). Indeed, Genesis 10:25 draws attention to Eber in a special way because Eber is the father of the Hebrew people, a matter hinted at previously in 10:21. The narrator clearly wanted his readers to understand the significance of Shem, the ancestor of Eber. Eber does not in chronological fact occur immediately after Shem. The reason his name appears twice immediately after the name Shem is to point forward to the fact that Eber would be an important personality, one listed precisely in the middle of the genealogy that follows.[10]

Genesis 11:9 ("Therefore its name was called Babel, because there the LORD confused the language of the whole earth; and from there the LORD scattered them abroad over the face of the whole earth") recounts the next great crisis events, the building and destruction of the Tower of Babel and the dispersion of the human race. These are immediately followed by another genealogy, this a

---

10. The name Eber (*'ēber*) occurs in the gentilic form *'ibrî*, "Hebrew."

second genealogy of Shem (one ending this time with Abraham) which brings the reader to the end of the first 11 chapters. Therefore, it is possible to arrange the narrative around the *tôl*dôt* as well around the genealogies, which appear to interrupt the narrative but are in fact very important to it.

The Creation Accounts

The most common, almost intuitive, reaction of readers of the first two chapters of Genesis concerns the nature of the creation account. Did God create all things in six literal, 24-hour days, or are the days to be understood as epochs of indeterminable length? Indeed, some would ask whether the Bible is to be regarded as a scientific-historical account of beginnings in any way at all, or if it is merely a mythological explanation? Such discussion, though interesting and important, is likely to overshadow the more important question, namely, what is the theological meaning of the creation narratives? Rather than concentrating on the "how" of creation, it is more appropriate theologically to address the "why."

Bible students have long noted the two records of creation, one in Genesis 1:1–2:3 and the other in 2:4–25. Historical-critical analysis has typically viewed these as coming from two originally independent sources, one preferring the divine name *Elohim* (the "P" document) and the other the name *Yahweh* (the "J" document). Chapter 1 is thought to have come from one set of traditions, and chapter 2 from quite another one. Such thinking shows abysmal insensitivity to the theological differences of the names Elohim and Yahweh, and the cosmological (or cosmocentric) nature of the first chapter as opposed to the anthropocentric nature of the second chapter. Furthermore, it is being seriously challenged by recent literary-rhetorical approaches that make a case for unity of composition by a common author. The two creation texts are thus to be seen not as competing, but as complementary — viewing the event from two different angles.[11]

---

11. See the helpful critiques of U. Cassuto, *The Documentary Hypothesis*, trans. I. Abrahams (Jerusalem: The Magnes Press, 1961); D.A. Garrett, *Rethinking Genesis* (Grand Rapids, MI: Baker, 1991), p. 13–33.

The Literary Structure of the Creation Accounts

Beyond doubt, two creation accounts exist. The first, as noted above, is cosmological, having to do with the heavens and the earth in general. *Elohim*, the name used exclusively in 1:1–2:3, conveys the meaning "power." It is appropriate that it occurs in a creation story that describes the limitless expanse of the universe and, at the same time, almost casually mentions creation by the mere speaking of words. The focus in 1:1–2:3 is on the universe as a whole, with special attention to the earth and all its creatures.

In 2:4–25, the creation of man is the central theme of the narrative. It is important to note that there is no contradiction with Genesis 1, but only a different way of describing the event. Consequently, it is appropriate that the name Yahweh be employed since it is the name by which God relates to human beings, especially to His own people. Yahweh is the title that occurs throughout the Old Testament to speak of God as the immanent one, that is, He who deigns to have fellowship with humanity. When Israel was in need of deliverance from Egyptian bondage, Moses learned that it was by the name Yahweh that God would accomplish that mighty redemption (Exod. 3:13–16). In the act of creating all things, God demonstrated His special concern for humankind by employing that same name, which means, "He is." Yahweh is God's covenant name; it is the term used when He undertakes some purpose in partnership with those whom He calls to himself. Such a purpose is evident in the creation narrative of 2:4–25.[12]

The title *Yahweh Elohim* occurs no fewer than 11 times in 22 verses. The combination declares that the powerful God of the cosmos who created by only a word is also the condescending God who created the human race tenderly and carefully as a potter might shape a vessel from a lump of clay. Indeed, the verb used in the narrative to describe man's creation (*yāṣar*) is related to the noun meaning "potter" (*yēṣer*). God as Elohim elicits awe and wonder; God as Yahweh instills a sense of comfort and joy. Both facets were later celebrated by the poet-king David (Ps. 8, 19, 139).

---

12. C. Barth, *God with Us* (Grand Rapids, MI: Eerdmans, 1991), p. 66–73.

The emphasis in 2:4–25 is on humankind and its role in the design of God. The very names of God used to differentiate the alleged sources are theological keys that unlock the mystery of the existence of two narratives and how they combine to provide a full panorama of the divine design. There is a perfectly good theological reason why Genesis should contain two creation accounts and why the first account has one divine name and the second has the other.

The Theological Structure of the Creation Accounts

A central theme of the creation narratives is the sovereignty of God as exercised through His image bearer, the human race. The pivotal text, Genesis 1:26–28, climaxes the stages of creation leading to it, and from it flows the fundamental expression of what it means to be the servant of God at work in accomplishing His will. The first narrative (1:1–2:3) describes the arena of divine sovereignty and the second (2:4–25) testifies of its agent. In the former case, the place of its exercise is presented in universal terms — the heavens and the earth (1:1). However, the focus narrows quickly to the earth, and by a series of separations, the structures of divine sovereignty are delineated. On day 1, light is separated from darkness (1:2–5); on day 2, the waters are separated from each other (1:6–8); on day 3, the land is separated from the waters (1:9–13); on day 4, night is separated from day (1:14–19); on day 5, marine creatures are separated from those in the air (1:20–23); and on day 6, man is separated from all other creatures (1:24–31). Finally, the Sabbath day is separated from all other days (2:1–3). The series of separations reaches its culmination with man firmly in place and with the stage fully set for his role in implementing the dominion task for which he was created.

The second narrative recapitulates the creation story from an entirely different viewpoint. The circumstances that prevailed before his creation (2:4–6) not only clarify why man must come into being, but they also elucidate his qualifications. He must be a creature unlike all others, a truth underscored by the fact that only he would be the recipient of divine inbreathing (2:7).[13] His

---

13. H.W. Wolff, *Anthropology of the Old Testament* (Philadelphia, PA: Fortress, 1974), p. 59–60.

uniqueness qualified him to undertake the awesome responsibilities of servanthood. He was placed in a garden, a microcosm of the entire earth (2:8–14), and there he received instruction as to what it means to be God's image bearer — to work and supervise the garden (2:15). There were limits to his dominion (2:16–17), and it was the violation of those limits that resulted in the downfall of the entire human race (3:1–21). However, there was also partnership in the person of the woman, the only creature that complemented and corresponded to him (2:18–25). Therefore, the divine plan was in place. Its failure because of human sin was grievous indeed, but what God proposes He also brings to pass. Through the "second Adam" (1 Cor. 15:45, 47), He has provided a way for all His creation purposes to be fulfilled, a way seen now darkly but someday in the full light of God's perfect redemption (Rom. 8:18–23).

The Fall

Genesis 3 consists of the narrative of the Fall, and chapters 4 and 5 the consequences of it. The account of the Fall is well known, so there is no need to elaborate on it in detail. At the same time, it may be helpful to explain how Genesis 4 and 5 relate to the account of the Fall in chapter 3. First, as already suggested, Genesis 4 provides the genealogy of Cain, which proceeds in a downward spiral to the seventh generation. The seventh name that appears in the list of the Cainite genealogy is Lamech (a name first introduced in 4:18–19). There is a brief narrative attached to the name Lamech, the seventh descendant from Cain, one that anticipates the deterioration of human civilization reflected and epitomized in the life of ungodly Lamech within the genealogy of Cain.

In the genealogy of Seth (Gen. 5), there is an upward spiral that ends in Enoch, who was also of the seventh generation. Enoch, of course, was a man so godly that he did not die and was translated into heaven. Therefore, the seventh generation of the Cain dynasty is interrupted by a narrative about Lamech; the seventh generation of the Seth dynasty is brought to an end by a brief narrative about Enoch, who is translated into heaven.

A study of the genealogy of Seth may reveal an interesting message based on the following names: Adam ("mankind"), Seth ("to appoint," "to place, "to set"), Enosh ("to be weak," "to be sick," "to be mortal," "to be frail"), Kenan ("a lament"), Mahalalel (from two verbs meaning "praise" and "God"), Jared ("to descend," "to go down"), Enoch ("to train," "to dedicate"), Methuselah (from two verbs meaning "man" and "send"), Lamech ("to vanquish"), and Noah ("to rest"). With a little creativity, this seems to yield the following message: Mankind was substituted by weak humanity with a lamentable result; praise God, He will descend, dedicating a man sent forth to vanquish, and to bring rest. Is there a message of redemption already in the genealogy? Possibly, and this may show that even in the genealogical sections, which are not often regarded as very interesting reading, there might indeed be some kind of a redemptive message.

The Flood

The largest narrative of the beginning chapters of Genesis is the narrative of the Flood (6:1–9:29). Although this treatment will not enter the debate as to whether the Flood was universal or not, one cannot but wonder how a reading of the story is possible that does not view it as teaching that the Flood covered the entire world. Some have advanced arguments in favor of a local flood, but when the text speaks in such extravagant terms as "the water covered the whole earth and the highest mountains in the earth were covered with the water," it seems that the author is trying to convey the notion of a universal flood by every type of adjective, verb, and noun possible in any kind of a language to communicate it.

The Table of Nations

Following the Flood account is a quasi-genealogy (Gen. 10:1–32, the Table of Nations) that speaks of the distribution of the human race. To understand chronologically the flow of history here, one must recognize that the Table of Nations presupposes the story of the Tower of Babel in Genesis 11 because it explains how the nations came to be distributed, whereas Genesis 10 describes where they were distributed. That is, chronologically Genesis 10 ought to follow Genesis 11. However, for the purpose of linking the dispersion of the nations to their later redemption and regathering, the narrator chose to place the result of the dispersion ahead of the event that precipitated it.[14]

The Tower of Babel

As a result of the chronological rearrangement just proposed, the Tower of Babel incident (Gen. 11:1–9) is followed by the genealogy of Shem in 11:10–32. God responded to the flagrant disobedience to the covenant conditions by scattering mankind across the earth, a scattering that seems to follow naturally the confusion of human speech. Since people would not spread throughout the earth voluntarily, God confused their language so they were unable to conduct the most ordinary affairs of life; consequently, they lost a sense of fellowship with every other person.

The Genealogy of Shem

According to Noah's prophecy, the Shemites (or Semites) were selected to bear the covenant promises. Therefore, the interest of the narrator from this point centers on them. The Semitic genealogy is traced from Shem to Abram, the man who was to become the father of a chosen people through whom God would manifest himself in saving grace to the remainder of the world. The genealogy of Shem is interesting in many respects. It is noteworthy that the ages of the individuals listed are much shorter than those of the pre-Flood patriarchs. The shortened ages may suggest a change in the environment in which people lived, one detrimental to their health. Alternatively, it may simply reflect the increasingly deadly toll of humanity's cursed existence. Additionally, by calculating the years of the various generations, it is possible to arrive at approximate dates for the period between Abraham and the Flood, though the probability of gaps in the genealogy and careful interpretation of the data contained therein may well extend the period considerably longer than that reached by a simple addition of the figures.[15]

14. E.H. Merrill, "The Peoples of the Old Testament According to Genesis 10," *Bibliotheca Sacra* 154 (January 1997): p. 6–7.

15. E.H. Merrill, "Chronology," in *Dictionary of the Old Testament: Pentateuch*, ed. T.D. Alexander and D.W. Baker (Downers Grove, IL: InterVarsity, 2003), p. 113–122.

The way the genealogy of Genesis 11 proceeds leaves no doubt that the family of Terah of Ur, especially as traced through his son Abram, was to occupy a special place in redemptive history. The whole course of the Genesis historical account oscillates from national and international considerations to the biographical account of Abram (Abraham) and his family, particularly those of his descendants who were chosen by God to mediate the covenant blessings. To these individuals, known initially as the patriarchs, the story turns in chapters 12–50.

The Story of Genesis 1–11

What is the story of Genesis 1–11? What is the stance of the narrator, or the historian? Who wrote the text? Adam surely did not, nor did Abraham, for the sacred record attests that Moses wrote the account thousands of years after the events that are recorded. When Genesis was written, Moses and the nation of Israel were in the plains of Moab at about 1400 B.C. on the eve of conquest, the setting of the writing of the narrative. Perhaps there had been pre-existent narratives that Moses incorporated into his writing of the Book of Genesis. That there was a Flood story, a creation story, and so forth that Moses, under divine inspiration, gathered, edited, incorporated, and collected into the present Book of Genesis is not problematic to a high view of Scripture. As long as the final result of the process is the inerrant, infallible Word of God, the process matters little. Nevertheless, Moses, by every ancient Christian and Jewish tradition, is the ascribed author of the Pentateuch, and as such would have written Genesis 1–11 considerably later than the time of the events themselves.

The next question to be asked is regarding the immediate purpose of Genesis 1–11. Why did Moses write this narrative? It clearly addresses certain general matters such as the nature and purpose of mankind, and more specifically those questions on the lips of the Israelite people. Who are we, after all? What is our origin? What are our roots? Why are we here? Where do we go from here? The questions posed are the kinds of questions addressed by the Book of Genesis and certainly in Genesis 1–11. They are the kinds of things the people of Israel would have to know about themselves and the purpose that God had for them.

A new reading strategy might be brought to bear here. We suggest that the text should be read backward, as it were, commencing the reading of Genesis from the standpoint of 1400 B.C., understanding what is going on there in order to grasp the meaning of the Book of Genesis more accurately and with greater theological precision. Abraham, in a sense, is a focal point, moving forward toward Moses and backward toward creation, so that Abraham becomes the center of the Genesis narrative, theologically speaking. He is the climactic figure as clearly seen in Genesis 11:26–32. He descended from Eber, and hence, is called the Hebrew in Genesis 14. He originated in Shem, whose God was to be a blessing in 9:26.

What is the ultimate message? We suggest five principal themes. (1) God created all things to be perfect (Gen. 1:31). (2) God gave mankind stewardship over all things (Gen. 1:26–28). (3) Mankind forfeited his stewardship (Gen. 3). (4) History bears evidence of that forfeiture with all the narrated incidents of human sin and depravity that one finds in the first 11 chapters. (5) God has initiated a plan of redemption (3:15, 21; 6:8; 9:16; 12:1). Accordingly, there is narrative here, a story, and according to every reasonable criterion of authentic history writing, these 11 chapters reflect actual historical events. This admittedly becomes ultimately a matter of faith, but this is true of any part of the Bible whether Old or New Testament. After all, Jesus said to doubting Thomas, "Because you have seen Me, have you believed? Blessed are they who did not see, and yet believed" (John 20:29).

Eugene H. Merrill, M.A., M.Phil., Ph.D., is distinguished professor of Old Testament studies at Dallas Theological Seminary, Dallas, Texas; and distinguished professor of Old Testament interpretation at the Southern Baptist Theological Seminary, Louisville, Kentucky.

Dr. Merrill has been heavily involved in international Christian ministry in Europe, Asia, and the Near East. As a scholar, Dr. Merrill regularly contributes to leading journals, periodicals, dictionaries, encyclopedias, and commentaries. Academia runs in his family as his wife, Janet, holds a doctorate in counselor education from Columbia University and his daughter, Sonya, earned a Ph.D. in medical ethics from the University of London and an M.D. from Harvard University.

CHAPTER 4

THE PREEMINENCE OF BIBLICAL CREATIONISM

Ron J. Bigalke Jr.

There are only two viewpoints in regard to the origin of the universe and the earth: creation and evolution. Christians who believe the Genesis record of creation should be interpreted literally and that Scripture actually means what it says (namely, God created the universe and everything in it) are called "young-earth creationists." Darwinian evolution demands an old-earth cosmology. Just as there are only two viewpoints regarding the origin of the universe and the earth, there are only two views regarding the age of the earth, either the earth is young (about 6,000–15,000 years old) or the earth is old (about 4.6 billion years old).[1] The issues involved in the age of the earth have to do with answering the question of cosmology and geological evolution. How is it, then, that Christianity can address this issue? Is this not a question for the scientists to answer? The secularist would say yes, but Christians *should* know better. For instance, Scripture has specific statements concerning

---

1. It must be acknowledged that the age of the earth is a different issue than the age of the universe.

the creation of the present earth that has been given to men by the inspiration of God.

Each person has a responsibility to understand the particular truth of any given issue. In practical terms, everyone who has a love for the truth must uncover sources and in that sense function as a historian. Mommsen said, "There is no other way to understand the events that take place before your eyes. Every businessman who handles a complicated transaction, every lawyer who studies a case, is a searcher for sources and a practicing historian."[2] Christians, apart from scientific training, have always sought to correlate science and Scripture. John W. Klotz likewise commented:

> There must be a basic unity between facts as we determine them by observation and truth as it is given us by revelation. . . . Truth is *one* whether it is scientific truth or spiritual truth. For that reason the Christian should never oppose scientific research and investigation. He should not oppose the studies of honest scientists in their search for truth. Indeed he must encourage scientific study and research even in areas where there appears to be disagreement with Scripture, for he must be convinced that ultimately Scripture will be vindicated.[3]

The conclusion, then, is obvious. To answer the question of the age of the earth, Scripture must be studied diligently. Numerous Christians claim to believe the Bible but interpret the creation record quite non-literally. For instance, the Genesis record states that God created the universe and everything in it in just six days, and then rested on the seventh day (see also Exod. 20:8–11). In contrast, the Darwinian world view states that the universe has been evolving for approximately 15–17 billion years, and that the earth has been evolving for about 4.6 billion years. One has a choice at this point either to interpret the scientific data in light

---

2 J. Barzun and H.F. Graff, *The Modern Researcher* (New York: Harcourt, Brace, and World, 1970), p. v.

3. J.W. Klotz, *Modern Science in the Christian Life* (St. Louis, MO: Concordia Publishing House, 1961), p. 79.

of Scripture, which is God's revelation, or to interpret the Genesis record of creation in light of evolutionary research, which is man's wisdom.

Scripture and Science

Scripture teaches that God has given two revelations of truth: general revelation (nature) and special revelation (Scripture). In Romans 1, the apostle Paul stated that all mankind possesses general revelation of God's existence, apart from God's special revelation (2 Tim. 3:16–17; 2 Pet. 1:20–21). "For since the creation of the world His invisible attributes, His eternal power and divine nature, have been clearly seen, being understood through what has been made, so that they are without excuse" (Rom. 1:20). Bernard Ramm proposed the theory that God's general revelation and special revelation differ from one another, but there is no contradiction between the two because the same self-consistent God is the author of both.[4] The theologian interprets Scripture and the scientist interprets nature. In this view, if the theologian is in conflict with the findings of science, then he must reinterpret Scripture so that it is in harmony with current scientific discoveries. God's Word is not a textbook on science, but it does refer to things that can be ascertained by scientific study. The interpreter is posed with the problem of whether he will interpret science in light of God's revelation or interpret science to fit the current evolutionary theories. Dillow provided a cogent assessment of this issue.

> It is obvious that the Bible is not a scientific textbook in the sense of giving detailed technical descriptions and mathematical formulations of natural phenomena. But this is not an adequate reason for questioning the objective accuracy of the numerous portions of Scripture which do deal with natural phenomena and historical events. The Bible is not a mathematics text either, but we expect that Daniel understands sixty-nine weeks by the

---

4. B. Ramm, *The Christian View of Science and Scripture* (Grand Rapids, MI: Eerdmans, 1955), p. 17–64.

phrase, "seven weeks and sixty-two weeks" (Dan. 9:25). The Bible is not, strictly speaking, a historical textbook either, but we expect that when it alludes to things which can be historically verified, it should be accurate. Likewise, the Bible is not technically a textbook of modern science, but when it refers to things which can be measured and checked by modern science, it should be accurate.[5]

Though man's knowledge of science is incomplete, the Bible is inspired and inerrant. Many alleged errors of Scripture have been based on the incomplete and incorrect knowledge of the scientific theories of man. The studies of this particular author have drawn the conclusion that 95 percent of the Bible has been verified by archaeology, history, and science, and the trend is toward verification, not contradiction. Such a trend should encourage skeptics to give the Bible the "benefit of the doubt," so to speak, when verification is not immediate. Therefore, when one seeks to determine the age of the earth, the Word of God must be the basis. Dillow commented again as follows:

> So, for the Bible-believer, science as an investigative technique is used. However, science is rejected as an interpretive tool to reconstruct a world view. So the determining criteria for understanding the major outlines of ancient history are interpretative principles which govern the interpretation of the Bible. What the Bible teaches is what ancient history was really like.[6]

The main issue regarding the Genesis record of creation is the alleged conflict between the assertions of Scripture and the current scientific theories of the day. All Christians should affirm that the Genesis record is a factual description of creation that should be understood at face value. Furthermore, as Dr. Merrill has presented in the previous chapter, modern science should understand the Genesis record as an historical record.

5. J.C. Dillow, *The Waters Above* (Chicago, IL: Moody Press, 1981), p. 2.

6. Ibid., p. 4.

Those who disagree with this statement would say that the Genesis record is a mere mythical attempt to explain the origin of the universe and this attempt must be dismissed because of the evidence proposed by modern science. Another view of the Genesis record views the text as a poetic description of creation and maintains that God is the Creator and He used known physical causes and effect mechanisms to create the world as man knows it.[7]

The Genesis record certainly does not appear to be presented as a mythical account, and neither does it appear that Moses intended his material to be regarded as such. All serious study would lead to the conclusion that the Genesis record is intended to be interpreted as an historical narrative. The noted liberal scholar Gerhard von Rad even noted this in his comments on Genesis 1:1–2:4 as follows:

> What is said here is intended to hold entirely and exactly as it stands. There is no trace of the hymnic element in the language, nor is anything said that needs to be understood symbolically or whose deeper meaning has to be deciphered.[8]

The above statements do not mean to imply that Moses *could not* have included various figures of speech. Moses could certainly have used figures of speech such as metaphors, similes, and symbols and this would not mean that the text should be interpreted non-literally. The key is to recognize figures of speech and then seek to determine the authorial intent.[9] It is critical to interpret Genesis 1–2 accurately, since one's interpretation will ultimately lead to one's view of earth's history. Kaiser made the following comments:

---

7. Dr. M. Harbin, "Genesis" (unpublished class notes in BIB 217, Taylor University, 2001), p. 13.

8. G. von Rad, *Genesis: A Commentary* (Philadelphia, PA: Westminster Press, 1972), p. 47–48, as quoted in ibid., p. 14.

9. Ibid., p. 13–14.

As an example, let us compare the organization of Genesis 1–11 with that of Genesis 12–50. The writer used the rubric "These are the generations (i.e., histories) of . . ." (KJV) ten times throughout the book, six times in the first 11 chapters and four times in the remainder of the book. Since the historical nature of the patriarchal narratives of Genesis 12–50 is usually conceded to be "substantially accurate" even by many non-evangelical scholars, we believe it is fair to argue that the writer wanted to indicate that the prepatriarchal material is of similar nature.[10]

Science has contributed greatly to the progress of man. Through use of the empirical method, and by being exhaustive about every area of knowledge, scientists have made great discoveries that have been implemented. The scientific method has also removed numerous superstitions and false information concerning the earth and universe that were prevalent in the Church for hundreds of years until the modern era. However, one must recognize the limitations of science. The atheistic scientist's methodology is that everything must be tested by the scientific method. What happens, for example, when scientists make pronouncements contrary to what the Bible states concerning scientific matters? It has already been noted that the Bible is not a textbook on science, yet when the Bible refers to areas of science, then the believer cannot surrender those statements and surrender his interpretation to that of a scientist. The evolutionist must maintain the theory of an old earth since he needs millions of years for his theory to function. Obviously, there will be an antitheistic bias here. The Christian, conversely, *could* believe in either a young earth or an old earth. The conclusion of the matter must rest upon the interpretation of Scripture alone, but an examination of the scientific data will also prove beneficial and should not be ignored.

---

10. W.C. Kaiser Jr., "Legitimate Hermeneutics," in *Inerrancy*, ed. Norman L. Geisler (Grand Rapids, MI: Zondervan, 1979), p. 145.

The Interpretation of Scripture

To determine the age of the earth, the scientific data must be evaluated in light of God's revelation. Any theory that determines the age of the earth by reinterpreting the Genesis record to fit the current evolutionary theories will be unsatisfactory. One of the biggest problems in determining the age of the earth is to identify the key term "day." Many assumptions occur at this point. For instance, those who begin with naturalistic evolution as their basic presupposition are constrained to understand the word "day" as a long period of time to provide enough time for the evolutionary process to occur. Some creationists argue that God created a universe that was fully operational from the beginning and others argue that God used the evolutionary process as a tool. For this simple reason, a number of scholars regard the issue of the age of the universe as an independent issue from the concern of creation.[11] However, since the function of this evolutionary tool is a "naturalistic process" that God allegedly used, then the evolutionary process must be able to be demonstrated scientifically.[12]

One's understanding of the word "day" is the key distinction between the young-earth creationist and the old-earth creationist. It is true that the Hebrew word *yôm*, similar to the English equivalent "day," can indicate a long period of time. However, this does not appear to be the indication when it is designated as a specific day, as in *one day* (Gen. 1:5) and following. By itself, the word *yôm* or "day" can refer to a long period of time, that is, more than 24 hours. For example, phrases such as the "day of the Lord" or the "day of Jehovah" are actually seven years long. However, when the word *yôm* is used with a numeral, it can only refer to a 24-hour period. If the Genesis record of creation did not have a numeral following the word "day," then it could be reasonably argued that the reference was to a longer period of time than just 24 hours.[13]

---

11. H.M. Morris and G.E. Parker, *What Is Creation Science?* (Green Forest, AR: Master Books, 1987), p. 253.

12. Harbin, "Genesis," p. 14.

13. Dr. A. Fruchtenbaum, class notes of this author in GB 334 Survey of Genesis, Tyndale Theological Seminary, 2000).

Therefore, one would need to read (eisegete)[14] evolutionary theories into the Genesis record to interpret the reference to "day" as a longer period of time. Furthermore, the additional phrase "evening and morning" merely reemphasizes the fact that "day" is referring to 24 hours only. The Sabbath law was given to Israel centuries later and was based upon the six days of creation and seventh day of rest. It is not possible that it could be applied if not for a literal 24 hour time period. Additionally, the fourth day mentions "days," "years," "signs," and "seasons," demonstrating that this was the normal system of time as it operates to this very day. Of course, some Christians think such an interpretation is foolish. Bradley and Olsen, for example, wrote the following:

> The Hebrew word *yom* and its plural form *yamim* are used over 1,900 times in the Old Testament. . . . Outside of the Genesis 1 case in question, the two-hundred plus occurrences of *yom* preceded by ordinals all refer to a normal twenty-four hour day. Furthermore, the seven-hundred plus appearances of *yamim* always refer to a regular day. Thus, it can be argued that the Exodus 20:11 reference to the six *yamim* of creation must also refer to six regular days.

---

14. Exegesis is from *exēgeisthai* which means "to explain" or "to interpret" from the preposition *ex* ("out of") and *ēgeisthai* ("to lead"). Exegesis is opposed to eisegesis (from *eisēgeisthai*, "to introduce") which is to interpret the text of Scripture by introducing one's own ideas. Exegesis is a critical interpretation, or "drawing out," of a text or portion of Scripture (A.B. Mickelsen, *Interpreting the Bible* [1963; reprint, Grand Rapids: Eerdmans, 1984], p. 56–57; W.F. Bauer, W.F. Arndt, and F.W. Gingrich, *A Greek-English Lexicon of the New Testament and Other Early Christian Literature*, 2nd ed., revised, F.W. Gingrich and F.W. Danker [Chicago, IL: University of Chicago Press, 1979], p. 343). The interpreter is not to eisegete meaning into the text. Indeed, he is to abandon himself of presuppositions and biases in order to understand the intended meaning of the divine Author. Those who introduce a deeper sense and secondary meaning into the text, produce an element of obfuscation and confusion into biblical interpretation.

These arguments have a common fallacy, however. There is no other place in the Old Testament where the intent is to describe events that involve multiple and/or sequential indefinite periods of time. . . .[15]

The problem with the statement of Bradley and Olsen is the Genesis record was written as a straightforward account that does not seem to imply "events that involve multiple and/or sequential indefinite periods of time." A plain reading of the creation account in Genesis would indicate that God created the heaven and earth in six literal days. It would appear that God intended Scripture to be understood by a plain reading of the text. Certainly, if God intended to convey the idea of long geological eras, then He would have used language that would accomplish this. The ancient Hebrews were familiar with the concept, since the idea was prevalent in many of the nature religions. Therefore, the teaching of six days of creation would have been in contrast to the common understanding of that time. For this reason, God was clear to define the meaning of "day" in the creation record. "And God called the light day, and the darkness He called night. And there was evening and there was morning, one day" (Gen. 1:5).

In every instance that *yôm* is used in connection with numbers, it always refers to a 24-hour day. Numbers 11:19–20 ("not one day, nor two days, nor five days, nor ten days, nor twenty days, but a whole month"), 1 Kings 8:65 (*seven days and seven* more *days, even fourteen days*), and Daniel 1:12 ("Please test your servants for ten days") are a few clear examples. Most of the remaining uses of *yôm* should be regarded as 24-hour days based on the context, as in Hosea 2:3 ("as on the day when she was born").[16] The Genesis record even uses the words *evening* and *morning,* causing it to

---

15. W.L. Bradley and R. Olsen, "The Trustworthiness of Scripture in Areas Relating to Natural Science," in *Hermeneutics, Inerrancy, and the Bible,* eds. E.D. Radmacher and R.D. Preuss (Grand Rapids, MI: Zondervan, 1984), p. 299.

16. W.W. Fields, *Unformed and Unfilled* (Green Forest, AR: Master Books, 1976, 2005), p. 169–172.

become painstakingly obvious to the reader that *yôm* is referring to 24-hour days. *Evening* comes first because in Jewish reckoning, the day begins with the evening. The evening and morning phraseology does not allow for anything but a 24-hour period.

The first day of creation ends with the words "one day." In Hebrew, the number is represented by the cardinal form ("one") rather than the ordinal form ("first"). Moses did not use the ordinal form for the other days (e.g., second, third, fourth, fifth, sixth, and seventh). However, for the first day, the writer simply recorded *one day*. Weston Fields explained the principal problem with the day age theory, as old-earth creationists apply it:

> ... the biblical account of creation is wrested to fit the dictums of a certain brand of science. Those who believe in a young earth are branded as "medieval" and charged with incorrectly interpreting Genesis. Most importantly, the primary argument for the Day-Age Theory is shown to be based merely on the fact that the word "day" *can* (not *must!*) be used either literally or figuratively in the Bible, the argument most commonly used by those defending this position.[17]

It has been demonstrated that the basis of the old-earth position is a reinterpretation of the Hebrew word *yôm* to fit the claims of modern science. Old-earth creationists argue strongly that there are many scientific evidences that the universe is approximately 15 billion years old. The problem is that only one side of the evidence is commonly given. There are also a number of scientific evidences that the universe is much younger. The old-age theory of the universe is based on the assumption that the universe evolved gradually from nothing and rejects the idea that God could have created a fully functional universe. It also assumes that the findings of current dating methods are entirely without fault. It is pertinent now to address the scientific issues involving the age of the earth.

---

17. Ibid., p. 169.

The Literal Week of Creation

Is it possible that God could have created the entire universe in just seven literal days? All Christians should offer a resounding "yes." However, the chief problem among Christian intellectuals and evolutionists[18] with understanding the term "day" as a literal 24-hour period of time is that this does not seem to compare well with the scientific evidence regarding the age of the earth and universe. Numerous scientists assert there are many evidences that the universe is approximately 15–17 billion years old, while the earth is approximately 4–5 billion years old. Harbin noted, "The dating of the universe is much more inferential, while the dating of the earth is based on various observed processes. Standard dating procedures look at two or three." Morris and Parker[19] listed "68 additional different processes which are just as valid, *given the same assumptions*, but which provide dates ranging from an earth which is 100 years old to 500,000,000 years old."[20] Clearly, some of these are inaccurate, which is why one must begin and end with the objective Word of God.

The Big-Bang Theory

There are numerous scientific evidences cited as proof for an old earth. However, there are also numerous scientific evidences that can be cited as proof for a young earth. Dr. Hugh Ross is perhaps one of the most vocal advocates today for an old-earth cosmology. A major component of his argument is the belief that the big-bang theory fits the biblical account of creation perfectly.

Atheistic evolutionists will argue the big bang occurred independent of God, whereas theistic evolutionists will argue the big bang occurred because "God pulled the pin" and there was an explosion. The phenomenon of an explosion is characterized by both a degradation and expansion. Since the universe and earth are subject to the law of entropy and the universe gives

18. A distinction between evolution as a process that God used to create and evolutionism as a belief system that completely nullifies the existence of God must be maintained in the current argument.

19. Morris and Parker, *Creation Science*, p. 288–291.

20. Harbin, "Genesis," p. 15.

the appearance of an expansion, then scientists conclude that the big bang is responsible.[21] Ross stated, "And if the universe is 'exploding,' there must have been a start and a Starter to that explosion."[22]

The big-bang theory would seem to suggest a primordial particle that once exploded. There are two responses to that statement. Either the particle was eternal or it began abruptly resulting in an explosion. Most evolutionists believe the particle began abruptly. However, there is no scientific evidence offering an explanation of the particle's origin. Once the "big bang" occurred abruptly, it is then theorized that a gradual evolution from the space residue developed the different elements of the observable universe.[23]

The majority of the research for the big bang comes from the Hubble Space Telescope, which has been able to detect the red shift of light. This red shift is believed to demonstrate an expansion of the universe. The assumption by the evolutionist is that the red shift of light is a necessary corollary of a Doppler effect, hence rejecting any other possibilities. The problem is that it is quite possible God created a universe with apparent age, that is, a fully functional universe. Therefore, the light from the farthest stars in the galaxy would have been already present at the most distant extremes of the universe at the point of creation.

Most old-earth creationists think that it would have been deceitful on the part of God to create a universe with apparent age. This is a *petitio principii* (circular) fallacy of presumption since there are no present signs that would indicate the given age of the universe. Anyone that dates the age of the universe has to rely on inferential presuppositions, including the theory that everything had to evolve. There are scriptural evidences that suggest the notion of apparent age, such as when Adam was created as a mature

21. The popularity of this argument among apologists was evident at the 1997 National Apologetics Conference (Frank Turek, "Ten Ways to Refute Evolution," paper presented at Southern Evangelical Seminary).

22. H. Ross, "The Cosmic Holy Grail," *Christian Single* (May 1995): p. 27. See also H. Ross, *The Creator and the Cosmos*, rev. ed. (Colorado Springs, CO: NavPress, 1995), p. 52–55.

23. Harbin, "Genesis," p. 15.

man. Likewise, Jesus turned water into wine during the wedding reception at Cana of Galilee and the wine had all the characteristics of having been through the entire process of fermentation.[24]

The problem with the big-bang theory is that it is incapable of explaining why the expansion of gases in the universe created constellations and gases. For instance, the rate of expansion according to the big bang is too vast for the gravity of the particles in order to begin the formation of stars. Furthermore, if the expansion rate were to be less than it actually is at present, then the whole mass would disintegrate upon itself.[25]

The red shift of light that is so favorably referenced to indicate an expanding universe is incapable of explaining double stars that interact with one another. Additionally, W.R. Bird has demonstrated that inter-stellar dust and gravity are other explanations of a red shift that are contrary to the Hubble expansion.[26] Wieland mentioned the existence of other problems.

> It turns out that most of the galaxies at high red shifts are indeed dominated by blue stars (this is the color which present theory expects from stars which have been burning as long as red ones), and there is a "striking variety of shapes."... The "most perplexing" such galaxy to date has an apparent age (again according to evolutionary theories) of 3.5 billion years, which is far too "old" for a galaxy at such an allegedly early stage (red shift 1.5) of the universe's history. In addition, the distant universe is causing a headache by being far too "clumpy" for the popular "big bang" scenario.[27]

The law of entropy is the most observable law of science that demonstrates that all energy is the result of a higher, more stable

24. Ibid., p. 15.

25. Ibid., p. 22; M.D. Lemonick and J.M. Nash, "Unraveling Universe," *Time* (March 6, 1995): p. 77–84.

26. W.R. Bird, *The Origin of Species Revisited*, 2 vols. (Nashville: Regency, 1991), 1:449–452.

27. C. Wieland, "Hubble, Hubble, 'Big Bang' in Trouble?" *Creation* 18 (September 1996): p. 26–27.

form of energy. Physics teaches that energy becomes less and less in a closed system, even though the total energy remains constant.[28] Consequently, the universe and earth "should degenerate rather than evolve to higher states."[29] Therefore, it needs to be admitted that the big-bang theory requires much more faith than the evidences of science since they pose many problems for the theory.

Dating the Earth

There are numerous evidences[30] both beyond the earth and from the earth, which Drs. Walker, Henry, and Vardiman have demonstrated in their respective chapters, which allow one to date the earth as being young indeed. A few will be stated here. According to the law of entropy, the magnetic field of the earth would have produced heat so intense over billions of years that the earth would have been vaporized by now.[31] Atmospheric gases, such as helium and oxygen, should be more plentiful, but the concentration of hydrogen in the atmosphere demonstrates that the earth is young.[32] If the earth had been spinning at the current rate for billions of years, then it would have been turning so fast in the past that the earth would have been flattened.[33] Hovind noted the following:

> If a spinning object breaks apart in a frictionless environment, everything spins the same way. And yet we have

28. Bird, *Species Revisited*, 1:399.

29. Harbin, "Genesis," p. 23.

30. D.R Humphreys, "Evidence for a Young World," *Impact* 384 (June 2005): p. 1–4.

31. D.R. Humphreys, "Physical Mechanism for Reversals of the Earth's Magnetic Field During the Flood," in *Proceedings of the Second International Conference on Creationism*, ed. R. Walsh (Pittsburgh, PA: Creation Science Fellowship, 1990), 2:129–142; D.R. Humphreys, "The Earth's Magnetic Field: Closing a Loophole in the Case For Its Youth," *Creation Matters* (March–April 2002): p. 1–4.

32. L. Vardiman, *Age of the Earth's Atmosphere* (El Cajon, CA: Institute for Creation Research, 1990).

33. J.D. Morris, *The Young Earth* (Green Forest, AR: Master Books, 1994), p. 56–61, 73–88.

Venus, Uranus and possibly Pluto spinning backwards and at least six moons spinning backwards.[34]

Another problem with an old-earth cosmology is that erosion will gradually wear down the land upon the earth, but there are still finely honed geographical features. After billions of years the effects of erosion would be more pronounced. The geological strata would not display distinct layering if the earth's parallel crustal layers of rock fashioned slowly and if at the same time the earth was undergoing wearing down for billions of years. The pressure that causes oil wells to become gushers would have dissipated by now if the earth were billions of years old. Sediments in the ocean are just a few thousand feet thick, which would not be the case if the earth were as old as evolutionists claim.[35] The evidence then for a young earth is quite conclusive and problematic for old-earth creationists.

Death before Sin

The biggest problem with old-earth cosmology is that there is the presence of death in creation before sin. The Hebrew *mûth* is translated "death." The meaning is clearly physical death.[36] The Old Testament appears to draw a distinction between plant life and animal life. The first distinction is that of blood, which animals possess and plants do not possess. The second difference is the Hebrew word *nephesh*, translated "soul." Both animals and humans have souls, an immaterial entity (see Gen. 1:20, 24, 30; 2:7; 6:17; 7:15, 22; 9:10; Lev. 17:11; Eccles. 3:21), but plants do not. Both animals and humans are conscious living beings (consequently, this also means there is more to ontology than just the physical world). Of course, animal souls are different from human souls. The soul of an animal lacks rationality, but God designed the human soul with rational faculties of intellect and volition.

---

34. Comments made by K. Hovind on "Are the Universe and the Earth Billions of Years Old or Thousands of Years Old," *The John Ankerberg Show*, 2000.

35. Morris, *Young Earth*, p. 88–91; L. Vardiman, *Sea-Floor Sediment and the Age of the Earth* (El Cajon, CA: Institute for Creation Research, 1996).

36. A. Richardson, ed., *A Theological Word Book of the Bible* (New York: Macmillan, 1950), p. 60.

Only mankind possesses dignity, having been created in the image of God, so that the immaterial aspect of humanity is soul and/or spirit (depending on whether one believes mankind to be a dichotomy or trichotomy).

According to Leviticus 17:11, there is an obvious connection between the soul and blood. For this reason it would appear that all animal life survived by eating plant life in the initial creation of Genesis 1–2. Therefore, two types of life forms existed: autotrophs and heterotrophs. The autotrophs included plants that produced their own food from sunlight, carbon dioxide, and water. The heterotrophs ate plants as their food source. It would appear that the heterotrophs did not eat the entire plant so that, in this sense, they would not "kill" the plant life. Nevertheless, the Old Testament does not qualify the death of a plant as belonging to the same category as the death of an animal or human.

If Scripture is referring to biological death only, then this further restricts the evolutionary theories. Death could have been a process that God designed that would function through all the ages to evolve gradually from simple life forms to the multitudes of life forms that are present today. However, this would be an extremely wasteful system because God would be micromanaging a process that does not work in and of itself. Based on the following observations, it would be fair to state that there was not any type of biological death prior to the Fall among animals and humans. If the fossil records are considered valid then clearly there was biological death before the fall of mankind. Old-earth creationist Ross even admitted ". . . you can't disconnect that [death before sin] from long creation days."[37]

By introducing death before sin, old-earth creationists have been given to tremendous compromise since Romans 5:12 states, "Through one man sin entered into the world, and death through sin." It was for this reason that Christ died (Rom. 5:15). The theory of long geological ages also makes God to be the Creator of much needless pain and suffering since there was, at least, a billion years of cruel struggles before man evolved as he

---

37. Comments made by H. Ross on *The John Ankerberg Show*, 2000.

is today. In direct contrast, Scripture states that when God created He deemed all things *very good* (Gen. 1:31).

The problem in the evolutionary scenario is that each so-called proof of science against the biblical account of creation requires a more miraculous leap of faith due to the fact that no one knows how the events of creation took place since none was there to observe them. Theologians do not need to check with the scientists before interpreting Scripture. The Bible as inspired by the Holy Spirit assumes quite logically that the text is then free from error in all areas (see 2 Pet. 1:21).

If the Bible is not infallible when it speaks to scientific issues, then why trust it regarding the testimony of God or salvation? The age of the earth is not an insignificant issue. If the Genesis account of creation is not reliable, then neither is the remainder of the Bible, which rests upon it. Henry Morris, founder and president emeritus of Institute for Creation Research, offered a poignant statement regarding this issue:

> . . . Christians who want to harmonize the standard geological/astronomical age system with Scripture must use eisegesis, not exegesis, to do so. That is, they have to try to interpret Scripture in such a way as to make it fit modern scientism. We believe on the other hand, that the only way we can really honor the Bible as God's inspired Word is to assume it as authoritative on all subjects with which it deals. That means we must use the Bible to interpret scientific data, not use naturalistic presuppositions to direct our Bible interpretations.[38]

Interpreting the creation account in Genesis 1–2 literally leads to the unavoidable conclusion that the existence of man is the direct, immediate, and sovereign action of God.[39] The biblical view of origins is in contrast to the dominant, contemporary,

---

38. H.M. Morris, "The Vital Importance of Believing in Recent Creation," *Back to Genesis* (June 2000), p. b.

39. Much of the following information is developed from W.H. Baker, "Survey of Theology II" (class supplement in TH 226, The Moody Bible Institute of Chicago, 1990), p. 45–48.

scientific opinion that decides on various theories of evolution. To substantiate this contrast, the biblical text needs to be carefully noted regarding four truths provided in Genesis 1:26–27; 2:7, 18–23. *First*, each *kind* of creation, including man, was created directly and immediately as a sovereign act of God, and consequently, each *kind* is not the result of various mutations into their present existence. *Second*, since God only *created man in His own image*, both *male and female* are distinct from the animals, that is, possessing dignity. *Third*, man was *formed* from inanimate and lifeless compositions (*dust from the ground*), and *became a living being* at the moment of creation, which means man was not formed by preceding life forms. *Fourth*, God created Adam as a wholly developed, rational being — possessing the "appearance of age" — which means there is no indication of his development from birth to infancy to childhood to adulthood (Gen. 2:8, 15–17).

The phrase *after their kind* occurs repeatedly in Genesis 1 (1:11, 12, 21, 24, 25) and reveals that God has established definite limitations upon His work of creation. Therefore, the phrase excludes any evolutionary theory that man evolved, or mutated, from a certain lower life form. The word מִין (*miyn*), *kind*, sanctions variation among the *kinds*, but clearly restricts any system wherein sea creatures evolved into land animals and eventually into life as man. The biblical usage of מִין (*miyn*) (e.g., Lev. 11:16) demonstrates that it is not to be likened to the term "species" as biologists would use it ordinarily. The biblical word, מִין (*miyn*), is broader and may include many species.[40]

The Preeminence of Biblical Creationism

In contrast to any materialistic evolutionary views, which regard chance as the origin of man, biblical creationism bestows a preeminent foundation for man's dignity since he is a special work of God. The relationship of mankind to the Creator is superior

---

40. See chapter 3 in J. Klotz, *Genes, Genesis, and Evolution* (St. Louis, MO: Concordia Publishing House, 1955). Klotz demonstrated that biologists, as a whole, have not even derived a consistent definition of the word "species."

since "God created man in His own image, in the image of God He created him; male and female He created them" (Gen. 1:26). Man is created with a likeness to God; therefore, he possesses an incomparable dignity among creation. Furthermore, man possesses the ability to discern and commune with God, giving him purpose because of his remarkable design. '

The whole of Scripture supports and presupposes supernatural creationism. If the historicity of Adam is denied, then the trustworthiness of *all* Scripture is drastically minimized. For example, Romans 5:12–21 teaches *through one man* [Adam] *sin entered into the world* which meant grace would necessitate *one Man, Jesus Christ,* to provide salvation *to the many.* Consequently, Paul's argument is based upon the truth of Adam as a literal, historical figure. If the literal historicity of Adam is denied, then Paul's entire argument concerning justification through Jesus Christ is of no value.

Peter Macky, who was associate professor of religion at Westminster College, believed it is not possible to know with certainty whether there was an historical Adam and Eve. Jack Rogers, former professor of philosophical theology at Fuller Theological Seminary, also embraced the view that the Genesis record does not refer to a single, historical individual.[41] Responding to such views, Donald Carson, research professor of New Testament at Trinity Evangelical Divinity School, emphatically declared:

> I would want to argue that the entire structure of Paul's argument, for example on Adam and Christ not only in Romans 5 but also in First Corinthians 15, presupposes the necessity for an historical Adam because if the race is not bound up in Adam as a single individual man, I don't think his entire soteriology, his whole doctrine of salvation,

41. J. Rogers and D. McKim, *The Authority and Interpretation of the Bible: An Historical Approach* (San Francisco, CA: Harper and Row, 1979). For an authoritative negation of such an argument, which also revealed the careless scholarship of the authors, see J. Woodbridge, *Biblical Authority: A Critique of the Rogers/McKim Proposal* (Grand Rapids, MI: Zondervan, 1982). When asked what alerted him to careless and forced interpretations of the Rogers and McKim proposal, Woodbridge replied, "I read the footnotes."

let alone his doctrine of Christ will stand together. That's my judgment. I'd be prepared to defend it. . . .[42]

Some men, such as Macky and Rogers (as examples among others), would teach that to maintain the biblical plan of redemption, it is only necessary to believe in the reality of sin as opposed to the literal and historical events which led to its origin. The reason such thinking is disastrous is that there are no limits for regarding other teachings of Scripture — such as the nature of Jesus, including His death and resurrection — as non-literal and non-historical, if allegory and myth is introduced in the beginning chapters of Genesis. Indeed, many formerly fine Christian universities and seminaries, which are now liberal, have applied such thinking consistently. The Christian faith is entirely literal and historical, and if it is not, "then our preaching is vain, your faith also is vain" (1 Cor. 15:14).

Nevertheless, Vatican Council II declared, "Hence the Bible is free from error *in what pertains to religious truth revealed for our salvation.* It is not necessarily free from error in other matters (e.g., natural science)" [emphasis in original].[43] The official Roman Catholic statement is not to be regarded lightly. As previously stated, if the Genesis record of creation is not trustworthy, then neither is the remainder of Scripture. Furthermore, Christ would have been deceived since He believed the account of Adam and Eve to be historical (Matt. 19:4–5). Apparently, atheists understand these issues more than those who claim to be evangelical Christians as revealed in the following quote: "Destroy Adam and Eve and original sin, and in the rubble you will find the sorry remains of the Son of God and take away the meaning of his death."[44]

Oppositions to Biblical Creationism

In strict terms, evolution — historically and philosophically — has been an atheistic theory in absolute opposition to the

---

42. Commenting on "Evangelicals Debate Bible Inerrancy," *The John Ankerberg Show,* 1982.

43. Vatican II, *Vatican Council II, Divine Revelation* (Knights of Columbus paraphrase edition), p. 3.11e.

44. *The American Atheist* (1978), as cited in *The Christian News* (November 11, 1996), p. 15.

biblical account of creation. Unfortunately, several Christians have attempted to amalgamate the theory of evolution with the biblical account of creation in Genesis. While these Christians have generally rejected philosophical naturalism, they have embraced and developed views that are antagonistic to the Genesis record.

Theistic Evolution

The theistic evolutionist, or evolving creationist,[45] does not believe the Genesis account should be interpreted literally when it instructs in areas of science. Therefore, this view would interpret the Genesis account allegorically as poetic truth. Those who hold the theistic evolution view believe that all of life and the universe was created by God, but do not believe that Scripture records how God actually created all things. Those who advocate this theory will accept the principal scientific theories as fact. The idea is that God used the evolutionary process.

Progressive Creationism

The majority of progressive creationists interpret each of the six creation "days" of Genesis as ages. Variations among advocates include the day-age view ("long periods of time"), intermittent-day view ("literal days separated by long period"), and framework hypothesis view (seeks to answer, "are the days a literary device rather than an actual chronological sequence").[46] All of the varieties of the progressive view embrace an old-earth creationism. At the start of each day-age (threshold evolution), or long period of time, it is believed God created certain things directly, and then permitted them to evolve from that point (microevolution); consequently, when God created, it was not immediate, but He intervened.[47] Progressive creationism, therefore, does not teach evolution between the directly created "kinds" (macroevolution),

---

45. H.J. Van Till, "The Fully Gifted Creation," in *Three Views on Creation and Evolution*, gen. eds. J.P. Moreland and J.M. Reynolds (Grand Rapids, MI: Zondervan, 1999), p. 172.

46. R.C. Newman, "Progressive Creationism," ibid., p. 106.

47. Microevolution, which is adaptation within species, can be observed. However, the contrary notion of macroevolution, which is transformation between species, has never been observed.

or even evolution in the genetic composition (organic evolution). Adherents of the progressive creationism theory favor it because it maintains an appeal for Christians who are overwhelmed by apparent evidence for an old earth.

Pre-Adamic Creatures

To offer some form of evidence for evolution, fossils of human-like beings have been presented. Some explanations for this fossil evidence include belief in a race of creatures, called "pre-Adamites," who existed before God created Adam.[48] The theory seems to have developed in 1655 with the publication of Isaac La Peyrère's *Prae-Adamitae*. As proof for the theory, a gap of time is said to exist between Genesis 1:1 and 1:2 which ended in the destruction of the world by a tremendous catastrophe. The pre-Adamites, who were created in Genesis 1:1 were either completely destroyed or became extinct within the apparent gap between Genesis 1:1 and 1:2. Genesis 1:2 would be the start of creation as is known today.

Responding to Theistic Evolution

As previously stated, some Christians believe in a kind of evolution, and still base their belief upon what is considered a theistic basis. The propositions of such a view are twofold: (1) belief that matter is not eternal but was created by God; and (2) life was initiated by God but at certain moments the personal Creator guided the mechanism of the evolutionary process.

An attempt to maintain respectability as a Christian and give too much authority to ongoing, ever-changing scientific research poses a grave quandary. The hazard may be to acquiesce too much authority upon scientific proclamations and research, meanwhile ignoring the plain testimony of Scripture. Certainly, it is granted the Bible is not a textbook on science, however, when Scripture refers to scientific issues as inspired by God, it is necessary that one gives thorough attention to the biblical assertions.

---

48. Leading progressive creationist H. Ross teaches that creatures with human-like characteristics "went extinct before Adam and Eve came on the scene" [*The Genesis Question* (Colorado Springs, CO: NavPress, 1998), p. 30].

For example, Scripture is incredibly unambiguous to state that God created each organism *after their kind* (a phrase repeated ten times in Genesis 1). Christians must recognize that the Bible is written in the ordinary language of men, and as such, the phrase positively affirms that each life form was a direct creation of God, and not the result of an evolutionary progression from one life form to a higher life form that was merely overseen by God. Furthermore, the theistic evolutionist neglects to provide a reasonable exegetical rationale for teaching that Genesis 1–11 is poetic, or allegorical, but Genesis 12–50 is historical since both divisions were written in the same narrative genre.

Regardless if it is naturalistic or not, science has indeed helped significantly to improve the living conditions of this world. Nevertheless, Christians need to be discerning regarding the supremacy of special revelation (Scripture) to general revelation (creation),[49] especially when non-Christian scientists reject scriptural assertions regarding specific scientific issues. Theistic evolutionary views are oppositions to Scripture when Christians surrender belief to scientific assertions of original life forms in contrast to biblical revelation regarding creation.

Responding to Progressive Creationism

The recurring use of *evening and morning* in Genesis 1 implies a literal 24-hour day. Consequently, this recurrence presents a major interpretative problem for the progressive creationism theory. There are several facts which biblical creationists can use to argue the veracity of a young earth: (1) the apparent age of the earth is best explained by the influences of the Noahic flood, or

---

49. Since both general revelation and special revelation are made known by "the same self-consistent God," B. Ramm believed no conflict exists between the two revelations [*The Christian View of Science and Scripture* (Grand Rapids, MI: Eerdmans, 1956), p. 17–61]. Both revelations are thought to have their own authority, such as the theologian who is *handling accurately the word of truth* in contrast to the scientist who is deemed appointed as God to be the interpreter of His own creation. Science is replete with conflicts and must not be surrendered to misinterpret Scripture with the so-called authoritative declarations of scientists when there are seeming conflicts.

by the "appearance of age" theory (namely, since Adam was created as a mature adult with the appearance of age, the earth was also created with the appearance of age which would mean the earth is relatively young); (2) it is more consistent with the whole of Scripture to interpret *day* and *dust* literally; (3) a literal interpretation allows the central details concerning Adam, the Fall of man, and the genealogies of Genesis (which imply a young earth) to be unbroken; and (4) errors in evolutionary theory are being progressively admitted by numerous scientists as truthful efforts are made to contend with new discoveries.

Generally, progressive creationists defend their view according to the following statements: (1) There is significant evidence for an old earth and some kind of biological evolution which cannot be ignored; consequently, the Christian can acknowledge the evidence by affirming evolution within the *kinds* of Genesis 1 without ignoring the essential details of the biblical narrative; (2) it is legitimate to interpret the *days* of Genesis 1 as "ages" since it is a meaning found elsewhere in Scripture; (3) the purpose of Genesis 1–2 is not to provide a scientific account of origins, but the chapters emphasize the creation action of God and the uniqueness of man within God's creation; and (4) Genesis 1–11 should be understood as a poetic narrative of man's earliest period and should not be interpreted literally in terms of any scientific statements.

How should young-earth creationists respond to progressive creationism? It would appear that the answer is one's concern to rightly divide the creation accounts in Scripture. If one is a scientist who is certain of the fundamental authority of contemporary scientific method and theory, he or she will likely adopt a position as either a theistic evolutionist or progressive creationist. If, however, it is one's interest to rightly divide the biblical revelation both grammatically and historically, according to the authorial intent, then he will likely adopt a position as a biblical or scientific creationist since only this view uses a literal hermeneutic to understand Genesis 1–11.

Diligent, consistent hermeneutics will not support the argument that the word "day" in Genesis 1 indicates a long geologic time in the past when God accomplished the work of creation. The contention of "day-age" theorists, such as Dr. Hugh Ross and other progressive creationists, is that the six days of creation signify six long "ages" of time. Progressive creationists believe the age of the earth is closer to four and a half to five billion years old. They believe firmly that periods of fossil formation were widespread throughout these long "day-ages" and also believe God formed Adam and Eve approximately a million or more years in the past.[50]

It is true that the word "day" may be used to indicate a longer period of time than a 24-hour period (i.e., solar day), but when the Hebrew word is used with a numeral (*first* day, *second* day) it is always a 24-hour period. Furthermore, the use of the terms *evening* and *morning* would give credibility to 24-hour interpretation. In complete contrast to indefinite day-ages of time, *evening* and *morning* designate that each creation day was a literal 24-hour day of the earth's rotation (e.g., time of day) as associated with a light source. Whenever the word *day* is used *to indicate the work of creation* in other passages of Scripture, it always indicates a 24-hour period: "For in six days the LORD made the heavens and the earth, the sea and all that is in them is, and rested on the seventh day; therefore the LORD blessed the sabbath day and made it holy" (Exod. 20:11). It is obvious that God would have created the earth in long individual ages if it was His desire, but as He revealed in Scripture, it is paramount to interpret the days of creation as 24-hour periods.

Responding to the Pre-Adamic Theory

The pre-Adamic theory (cataclysm or restitution/recreation theory) relates to the correspondence of Genesis 1:1 and 1:2. Although this theory does not specifically accept evolutionary views,[51]

---

50. See J. Kruger and C. Wieland, "Crusading against Christianity: A Response to Claassen," article online (August 26, 2005, Answers in Genesis, accessed August 30, 2005) available from http://www.answersingenesis.org/docs2005/0826claassen.asp.

51. It should be recognized that evolutionists do refer to fossils of humanlike beings as evidence for evolution. The "fossil evidence" is interpreted by some as proof of a race of pre-Adamic creatures.

the supposed "gap" is impossible to harmonize with Romans 5:12 which teaches that death came into the world as a result of Adam's sin, which means the belief in extinction of any "creature" before that time is inconsistent with the biblical revelation. Adherents of this theory, nevertheless, argue that a long period of time is indicated between the first verses of Genesis. The theory affirms belief in the creation of a perfect earth by God, but also inserts a gap of time for a catastrophe (generally the fall of Satan; see Isa. 14:12–20) which destroyed the original creation.[52]

Gap theorists contend that the Hebrew words used in the first two verses of Genesis 1 permit interpreting them as indications of an indefinite lapse of time between an original creation and catastrophe followed by a consequent condition when the earth *was formless and void*. Those who advance this theory propose that the verb *was* (1:2) may be translated "became," which would possibly support such an interpretation. In addition to the argument of the verb *was*, Isaiah 45:18 and Jeremiah 4:23–25 are cited to support this theory. Both words which state that the earth *was formless and void* have the same meaning (i.e., emptiness and nothingness). The usage of the two words together means utter confusion and chaos (disorganization), which is merely a description of the heavens and the earth before God arranged them. Genesis 1:1 teaches that God already created all matter. In Genesis 1:2, God reveals the condition of the matter before He arranged it. The text specifically states that God determined to create the world in six days and prepared the seventh day as a day of rest; thereby, God established the "week." Every people, tongue, and nation utilizes a "week" system. Biblical creationism is a remarkable explanation for such a phenomenon.

Certainly, there may have been a gap in the creation process, if God determined the purposefulness of such, but the fact is that there are significant problems concerning the gap theory. *First*, there is no mention of a gap in the creation process mentioned anywhere else in Scripture, which means the theory is based entirely on deduction

---

52. J.S. Baxter, *Exploring the Book* (Grand Rapids, MI: Zondervan, 1960), p. 34–36.

rather than induction. *Second*, there is a connection between Genesis 1:1 and 1:2 in the Hebrew construction that makes both verses a circumstantial clause. *Third*, there is no linguistic support for interpreting the word "was" in verse 2 as "became." The nature of the Hebrew perfect tense and the fact that the Hebrew syntax indicates a descriptive sentence prohibits a verb of action. *Fourth*, there is no legitimate reason to think the language of verse 2 implies a "catastrophe." Although Genesis 1:2 presents God's creative work as incomplete, or a raw material stage, at that moment, the language does not demand an earth which experienced a catastrophe. The two words "formless" and "void" simply portray an unformed, unpopulated earth in a raw material stage. *Fifth*, even if the gap theory was legitimate, there is still no biblical evidence to indicate that a gap would have continued through vast geological ages. If a gap did occur, it may have been an especially short period of time. *Sixth*, there is no reason to presuppose that fossils were formed necessarily during an indefinite period of time or an event such as a gap. Although some gap theories endeavor to argue that the entire fossil record belongs to a gap event, Genesis 1 reveals that God did not create animals and plants until the third, fifth, and sixth days.[53]

Moses recorded that God formed Adam *of dust from the ground*, and then formed Eve from *one of his ribs* (Gen. 2:7, 18–22). It is impossible to reconcile the existence of pre-Adamic ancestors with the Genesis account, and the fact that Jesus authenticated that account (Matt. 19:4–5). Christ confirmed the Genesis account by quoting from it. Furthermore, Paul substantiated the accuracy of the Genesis account when he wrote, *For it was Adam who was first created*, and *then Eve* (1 Tim. 2:13–14). Moreover, Paul taught that *sin entered the world* through Adam, and *death through sin* (Rom. 5:12). If Adam and Eve had ancestors who had lived and died during thousands (or millions) of years of evolution until God humanized them by breathing into their soul, death would have been operative on earth before Adam sinned — a clear contradiction of Scripture.

---

53. H.M. Morris, *The Genesis Record* (Grand Rapids, MI: Baker Books, 1976), p. 37–48.

Conclusion

The Christian world view is quite simple: God, the Creator of all things, did create all things. Although there are some who teach and write books stating God used evolution as a process to create, such a view is a contradiction of terms. Naturalistic evolution is based upon time and chance, that is, natural selection by natural direction rather than supernatural intervention requiring an intelligent Creator, Designer God. The immense complexity that is observed in the world cannot be explained by fortuitous events that accumulate over vast periods of time driven by random chance.

A view of Scripture that tries to dehistoricize the Genesis account creates nonsense of the remainder of Scripture. Such a theory destroys the message of Scripture because every single term in the Scripture is taken to mean something different than a literal signification. It is a fatal disjunction to deny the self-attestation of Scripture that every word, even to every letter, is originally given by God. To claim inspiration and inerrancy for only the salvation parts of the Bible and not in all areas leads one to a partial biblical authority. Such theories have no basis then of how to separate the salvation parts from the uninspired, errant non-salvation parts.

Of course, the Bible is not a textbook on science, yet when Scripture speaks in areas of science, then the theologian cannot surrender these statements and his or her interpretation to that of a scientist, who will be generally biased of the biblical position. All of creation was *after its kind*, which means that each form was immediately created by God. The Bible does not declare that there was an original life form that God directed through its many stages. Obviously, there is a point of tension, and the theologian must affirm what Scripture declares in this and other areas that converge on scientific details.

The Genesis account also teaches that man is truly fallen and separated from His Creator by reason of his sin. The only cure for man's fallen nature is the redemption through the death of Jesus Christ, "the seed of the woman." The blood of Christ cleanses mankind from his sin, and only as man receives Christ as his Savior will he fully begin to assess the real dignity of God's creation.

Ron J. Bigalke Jr., M.Apol., M.T.S., M.Div., Ph.D., the compilation editor of this book, is founder and director of Eternal Ministries, Inc.; a church planter in Port Wentworth, Georgia; and professor of Bible and theology at Tyndale Theological Seminary and Biblical Institute. He is a native Floridian whom God called to salvation from a life of paganism.

Dr. Bigalke is the general editor of *Revelation Hoofbeats: When the Riders of Apocalypse Come Forth*; *One World: Economy, Government, and Religion in the Last Days*; and *Progressive Dispensationalism: An Analysis of the Movement and Defense of Traditional Dispensationalism*. He is a frequent contributor to several Christian publications, and an active lecturer for the Society of Dispensational Theology. He is also a member of several well-known professional societies, an ordained Southern Baptist minister, and an apologetics evangelism partner with the North American Mission Board. Before assuming his present ministries, Dr. Bigalke held other pastorships, served in secondary education as both a teacher and administrator, and was an extension studies adjunct instructor for Moody Bible Institute. He and his wife, Kristin, have two children.

CHAPTER 5

GEOLOGIC EVIDENCE FOR A YOUNG EARTH

Tas Walker

The handwritten note attached to some photocopied pages was typical: "I wonder if you could help with a geological problem?" The writer, who identified himself as a Bible-believing Christian, was confused. He had just encountered some tired old geological arguments attacking the straightforward biblical account of earth history (i.e., denying a recent creation and a global flood on the basis of "geological evidences").

A number of books in recent decades have reawakened these so called "geological problems" and undermined faith in the Bible for many people. Sadly, the ones who cause most confusion and distress are those written by professing "Bible-believers."[1] A curriculum writer with a Christian home school association wrote and stated he was "pretty well wiped out" after reading these books. He wondered if the ministry "might have answers to what these gentlemen say." Indeed, there are answers! Another person who

---

1. A. Hayward, *Creation and Evolution: The Facts and Fallacies* (London: Triangle, 1985); D.E. Wonderly, *God's Time-Records in Ancient Sediments: Evidences of Long Time Spans in Earth's History* (Flint, MI: Crystal Press, 1977); G.R. Morton, *Foundation, Fall and Flood* (Dallas, TX: DMD Publishing, 1995); H. Ross, *The Genesis Question* (Colorado Springs, CO: NavPress, 1998).

had read some of the same books said, "I may have been overlooking information that cast doubts upon the recent creation model." Since the "recent creation model" he referenced is simply what the Bible plainly states, the individual has really been caused to doubt the Bible. The unsuspecting readers of such books, thinking they are getting something from "Bible-believing Christians," expect encouragement and faith-building material. They are generally unprepared for the explosive mixture of heretical theology, poor science, and vehement attacks upon Bible-believers.

For example, the author Alan Hayward claims to be a "Bible-believing Christian." Hayward is a Christadelphian physicist, which means he denies the tri-unity of God and the clear New Testament teaching of the deity of Christ (for example, John 1:1–14, 5:18; Tit. 2:13).[2] Clearly, "Bible-believing" Hayward chose to reinterpret those parts of the New Testament with which he disagreed. He worked the same way with the Old Testament. Instead of accepting the clear teaching of Genesis, he reinterpreted the passages to correspond with his billion-year preference for the age of the earth.[3] Hayward's approach introduced confusion and problems that destabilize readers. Christians are warned to beware of teachers who vandalize the clear teaching of Scripture to correspond with their philosophy (Col. 2:8).

Superficially, Hayward amassed an impressive battery of arguments as to why the Bible cannot mean what it says. Perhaps the single most important lesson from his book is his strategy itself. Each of his attacks on the Word of God elevated some other "authority," whether derived from geology, astronomy, secular history, or theology, above the Bible. Hayward's approach is as old as the Garden of Eden.

---

2. A. Hayward, personal correspondence to D.C.C. Watson, 1986. Also see Watson's review of Hayward's *Creation and Evolution* in *Creation Research Society Quarterly* 22 (March 1986): p. 198–199.

3. Hayward [*Creation and Evolution*, p. 167] "reinterpreted" the Bible to mean that God did not create in six days but only gave the orders to create (fiats). It then took billions of years for His orders to be executed. His idea not only contradicts the Bible but also is inconsistent with evolutionary geology. It achieves nothing but added confusion.

Answering Those "Bible-Believing" Biblio-skeptics

True knowledge begins with the Bible (Ps. 119:160; 138:2; Prov. 1:7), and that is where every Christian needs to start. God was there when He created the world. He knows everything, does not tell lies, and does not make mistakes. It is from the Bible that one learns that the world is "young." Although the Bible is the final authority for determining how all of life came into existence, various evidences from the earth will be presented in this chapter to substantiate that the earth is indeed young. If the Bible teaches that the earth was millions of years old,[4] one is compelled to believe it. However, the concept of millions of years of death and suffering contradicts the Word of God, and destroys the foundation of the Gospel of Christ. Many people find it difficult to accept that scientific investigation should start with the Bible. They think one can answer the question about the age of the earth by coming to the evidence with an "open mind." Indeed, no one has an open mind. Evidence does not interpret itself; rather, everyone views the world through a belief framework. Unfortunately, as humans, we will never have all the information. Therefore, when one starts from the evidence, one can never be certain that the conclusions are accurate. Just as in a classic "whodunit," just one piece of information can change the whole picture. By contrast, when one starts from the Word of God, one can be certain that what it states is true.

Even if some of the apparent problems cannot be answered presently, it is still possible to be confident that there *is* an answer. The answer may not arrive on this side of eternity, but that would simply be the result of not having all the information necessary to reach the right conclusion. Conversely, ongoing research *may* reveal the answer, and it often has, as will be demonstrated in this chapter.

On first appearance, the evidence that Hayward assembled appeared entirely overwhelming. However, the problems he described are easily answered; indeed, many answers were known

---

4. The Hebrew writers could easily have described long ages if necessary; see R. Grigg, "How Long Were the Days of Genesis 1?" *Creation* 19 (December 1996): p. 23–25.

before he wrote his book. Either he was unaware of the answers, or he deliberately ignored them. Let the reader now examine some of the "science" he presented so persuasively.

Varves

A common argument against the Bible involves varves, that is, rock formations with alternating layers of fine dark and coarse light sediment. Annual changes are assumed to deposit bands with light layers in summer, and dark layers in winter. It is reported that some rock formations contain hundreds of thousands of varves, thereby "proving" the earth is much older than the Bible states.[5] Nevertheless, the assumption that each couplet always takes a year to form is wrong. Recent catastrophes show that violent events (as the Flood described in Genesis) can deposit banded rock formations very quickly. The Mount St. Helens eruption in Washington state produced 25 feet (eight meters) of finely layered sediment in a single afternoon![6] Moreover, a rapidly pumped sand slurry was observed to deposit about 3–4 feet (a meter) of fine layers on a beach over an area the size of a football field (photo, following page). Normal silica sand grains are separated by darker layers of denser mineral grains such as rutile.[7]

When sedimentation was studied in the laboratory, it was discovered that fine bands form automatically as the moving water transports the different sized particles sideways into position.[8] Surprisingly, the thickness of each band was found to depend upon the relative particle sizes rather than on the flow conditions.[9] A layered rock (diatomite) was separated into its particles,

---

5. Hayward, *Creation and Evolution*, p. 87–88.

6. K. Ham, "'I Got Excited at Mount St. Helens!'" *Creation* 15 (June 1993): p. 14–19.

7. D. Batten, "Sandy Stripes: Do Many Layers Mean Many Years?" *Creation* 19 (December 1996): p. 39–40.

8. P.Y. Julien, Y. Lan, and G. Berthault, "Experiments on Stratification of Heterogeneous Sand Mixtures," *CEN Technical Journal* 8 (April 1994): p. 37–50.

9. A. Snelling, "Nature Finally Catches Up," *CEN Technical Journal* 11 (August 1997): p. 125–126.

Rock formation
containing varves

Photo: D. Batten

and when rede-
posited in flowing
fluid, identical lay-
ers formed.[10] Much
is often made of
the Green River
varves[11] in Wyo-
ming. However,
these bands cannot
possibly be annual
deposits because
well-preserved fish
and birds are found
all through the
sediments.

It is unthink-
able that these dead
animals could have rested on the bottom of the lake for decades,
being slowly covered by sediment. Their presence indicates catastrophic burial. It is often claimed that the fish and birds remained
in prime condition at the bottom of the lake because the water
was highly alkaline and this preserved their carcasses.[12] Nonetheless, highly alkaline water causes organic material to disintegrate,
and that is why alkaline powder is used in dishwashers![13] Another
problem for the varve explanation is that the number of bands is

10. G. Berthault, "Experiments on Lamination of Sediments," *CEN Technical Journal* 3 (April 1988): p. 25–29.

11. Hayward, *Creation and Evolution*, p. 87–88.

12. Ibid., p. 215.

13. Some skeptics have claimed that alkali merely "cuts grease," evidently
ignorant of the elementary chemistry involved (i.e., base-catalyzed
hydrolysis of polymers which would do the opposite of preserving the
fish).

not consistent across the formation as it should be if they were annual deposits.[14]

Evaporites

Similar bands in some huge deposits containing calcium carbonate and calcium sulphate in Texas are also used to argue the case for long ages.[15] A common explanation is that the deposits were formed when the sun evaporated sea water, hence the term "evaporite deposits." Naturally, to make such large deposits in this manner would take a long time. However, the high chemical purity of the deposits demonstrates they were not exposed to a dry, dusty climate for thousands of years. Instead, it is more likely that they formed rapidly from the interaction between hot and cold sea water during undersea volcanic activity — a hydrothermal deposit.[16]

Too Many Fossils?

Another claim of biblio-skeptics is that there are "too many fossils."[17] If all those animals could be resurrected, it is said, they would cover the entire planet to a depth of no less than 1.5 feet (0.5 meters). Therefore, they could not have come from a single generation of living creatures buried by the Flood.[18] Not surprisingly, the substance disappears when the detail is examined. The number of fossils is calculated from an abnormal situation: the Karroo formation in South Africa. In this formation, the fossils comprise a "fossil graveyard" — the accumulation of animal remains in a local "sedimentary basin."[19] It is certainly improper to apply this abnormally high population density to the entire earth. The calculation also used incorrect

14. P. Garner, "Green River Blues," *Creation* 19 (June 1997): p. 18–19.

15. Hayward, *Creation and Evolution*, p. 89–91.

16. E. Williams, "Origin of Bedded Salt Deposits," *Creation Research Society Quarterly* 26 (June 1989): p. 15–16.

17. Hayward, *Creation and Evolution*, p. 125–126.

18. Creationists accept that some fossils formed post-Flood, but these are relatively few and do not alter the argument.

19. C.R. Froede Jr., "The Karroo and Other Fossil Graveyards," *Creation Research Society Quarterly* 32 (March 1996): p. 199–201.

information on today's animal population densities and took no account of the different conditions that likely applied before the Flood.[20]

Too Much Coal?

Another argument used against the biblical time-line is that the pre-Flood world could not have produced enough vegetation to create all the coal.[21] Again, this argument is based on wrong assumptions. The pre-Flood land area was almost certainly greater before all the Flood waters were released onto the surface of the earth. Additionally, the climate was probably much more productive before the Flood.[22] Furthermore, it has been discovered that much coal was derived from forests that floated on water.[23] Calculations based only on the area of land would be wrong. Finally, the estimates of how much vegetation is needed are based on the wrong idea that coal forms slowly in swamps and that most of the vegetation rots. The Flood would have buried the vegetation quickly, producing a hundred times more coal than from a swamp.[24]

20. J. Woodmorappe, "The Antediluvian Biosphere and Its Capability of Supplying the Entire Fossil Record," in *Proceedings of The First International Conference on Creationism*, ed. R.E. Walsh (Pittsburgh, PA: Creation Science Fellowship, 1986), p. 205–218; and, J. Woodmorappe, "The Karoo Vertebrate Non-Problem," *CEN Technical Journal* 14 (August 2000): p. 47.

21. Hayward, *Creation and Evolution*, p. 126–128.

22. Higher atmospheric CO_2 has been repeatedly shown to cause more luxuriant plant growth.

23. C. Wieland, "Forests That Grew On Water," *Creation* 18 (December 1995): p. 20–24; J. Scheven, "The Carboniferous Floating Forest — An Extinct Pre-Flood Ecosystem," *CEN Technical Journal* 10 (April 1996): p. 70–81; G. Schönknecht and S. Scherer, "Too Much Coal For a Young Earth?" *CEN Technical Journal* 11 (December 1997): p. 278–282. "Old-earth" author H. Ross [*Genesis Question*, 152–153, 220 (n. 17, 21)] actually cited the paper by Schönknecht and Scherer without the question mark, implying that the paper presented a problem for young-earthers, whereas it actually shows a solution!

24. Woodmorappe, "The Karoo Vertebrate," p. 205–218.

Fossil Forests

The petrified forests of Yellowstone National Park have often been used to argue against the biblical chronology.[25] These were once interpreted as buried and petrified in place (as many as 50 successive times), with a brand-new forest growing upon the debris of the previous one. Naturally, such an interpretation would require hundreds of thousands of years to deposit the whole sequence and is inconsistent with the biblical time scale. Nevertheless, this interpretation is also inconsistent with the fact that the tree trunks and stumps have been broken at their base and do not have proper root systems. Furthermore, trees from different layers have the same "signature" ring pattern, demonstrating that they all grew at the same time.[26]

In contrast to 50 successive forests, the geological evidence is more consistent with the trees having been uprooted from another place and carried into position by catastrophic volcanic mudflows, which is similar to what occurred during the Mount St. Helens eruption in 1980, where waterlogged trees were also seen to float and sink with the root end pointing downward.[27]

Pitch

The origin of pitch is also used to ridicule the account of Noah in the Bible.[28] Pitch is a petroleum residue (so goes the story), and creationists say that petroleum was formed by the Flood. Therefore, where did Noah get the pitch to seal the ark (Gen. 6:14)? The old argument is the result of ignorance concerning how pitch can be made. The widespread use of petroleum is a 20th-century phenomenon. How did they seal wooden ships hundreds of years ago before petroleum was available? In those days, pitch was made

25. Hayward, *Creation and Evolution*, p. 128–130.

26. J. Morris, *The Young Earth* (Green Forest, AR: Master Books, 1994), p. 112–117.

27. J. Sarfati, "The Yellowstone Petrified Forests," *Creation* 21 (March 1999): p. 18–21.

28. Hayward, *Creation and Evolution*, p. 185; Ross, *Genesis Question*, p. 153–154.

from pine tree resin.[29] A huge pitch-making industry flourished to service the demand.

Noah's Mud Bath?

Some attempts to discredit the Bible are wildly absurd, such as the idea that there is too much sedimentary rock in the world to have been deposited by the one-year Flood. It is claimed that the ark would have floated on an ocean of "earthy soup" and no fish could have survived.[30] The argument takes no account of how water actually carries sediment. The claim naïvely assumes that all the sediment was evenly mixed in all the water throughout the Flood year, as if thoroughly stirred in a "garden fishpond." Sedimentation does not occur in such a manner. Instead, moving water transports sediment into a "basin" and, once deposited, it is isolated from the system.[31] The same volume of water can raise more sediment as it is driven across the continents, for example, by earth movements during the Flood.

More (Former) Problems, More Answers

Some similar geological problems which were once claimed to be "unanswerable" for Bible-believers, but for which there are now clear answers, include:

- Coral reefs need millions of years to grow.[32] (Actually, what was thought to be "coral reef" is thick carbonate platforms, most probably deposited during the Flood.[33] The reef is only a very thin layer on top. In other cases, the "reef" did not grow in place from coral but was transported there by water.)[34]

---

29. T. Walker, "The Pitch for Noah's Ark," *Creation* 7 (August 1984): p. 20. See also, "Naval Stores," in *The New Encyclopædia Britannica*, 15th ed., (Chicago, IL: Encyclopedia Britannica, 1992), 8:564–565.

30. Hayward, *Creation and Evolution*, p. 122.

31. Julien, et al., "Experiments on Stratification," p. 37–50.

32. Hayward, *Creation and Evolution*, p. 84–87.

33. M. Oard, "The Paradox of Pacific Guyots," *CEN Technical Journal* 13 (April 1999): p. 1–2.

34. A.A. Roth, "Fossil Reefs and Time," *Origins* 22 (1995): p. 86–104.

- Chalk deposits need millions of years to accumulate.[35] (Chalk accumulation is not steady state but highly episodic. Under cataclysmic Flood conditions, explosive blooms of tiny organisms like coccolithophores could produce the chalk beds in a short space of time.)[36]

- Granites need millions of years to cool.[37] (Not when the cooling effects of circulating water are allowed.)[38]

- Metamorphic rocks need million of years to form.[39] (Metamorphic reactions happen quickly when there is plenty of water, just as the Flood would provide.)[40]

- Sediment kilometers thick covering metamorphic rocks took millions of years to erode.[41] (Only at the erosion rates observed today. There is no problem eroding kilometers of sediment quickly with large volumes of rapidly moving water during the Flood.)

The section on (former) problems demonstrates some of the other similar arguments that were once claimed to be "unanswerable." If this chapter had been written some years earlier, one would not have had all those answers. Creationists still do not have all the answers to some others, but this does not mean that the answers do not exist; rather, it merely means no one has yet

35. Hayward, *Creation and Evolution*, p.91–92.

36. A.A. Snelling, "Can Flood Geology Explain Thick Chalk Beds?" *CEN Technical Journal* 8 (April 1994): p. 11–15.

37. Hayward, *Creation and Evolution*, p. 93.

38. A. Snelling and J. Woodmorappe, "Rapid Rocks: Granites . . . They Didn't Need Millions of Years of Cooling," *Creation* 21 (December 1998): p. 42–44.

39. Hayward, *Creation and Evolution*, p. 91–92.

40. A. Snelling, "Towards a Creationist Explanation of Regional Metamorphism," *CEN Technical Journal* 8 (April 1994): p. 51–57. Also see K. Wise, "How Fast Do Rocks Form?" in *First International Conference on Creationism*, p. 197–204.

41. Hayward, *Creation and Evolution*, p. 91–92.

discovered the answers. There may be new arguments in the future alleging to "prove" that the Bible, or one of the previous answers, is wrong. Moreover, when these are answered, there might be new ones again (such is the nature of science). All scientific conclusions are tentative, and new discoveries mean that old ideas must be changed, which is why creationist research is important. However, science ultimately cannot prove or disprove the Bible. Faith — but not a blind faith — is needed. It is not the facts that contradict the Bible, but the *interpretations* applied to them. Since man will never know everything, one must start with the sure Word of God to make sense of the world around him.

Overview of the Biblical Geological Model

The figure on the following page shows an overview of a biblical geological model relating world history to geology. The biblical time scale is shown on the left with the most recent time at the top and the earliest at the bottom.

The scale is divided into four parts, each clearly identified with the biblical record. Two events are shown — the creation event having duration of six days and the Flood event lasting about one year. The 1,700-year period between the creation event and the Flood event is called the Lost-World era, while the 4,300-year period from the Flood event to the present time is called the New-World era. The term "event" conveys the idea of a significant occurrence within a short period, whereas "era" relates to a much longer period. These terms reinforce the idea that, according to the Bible, geologic processes varied in intensity at different times in the past.

The length of the time scale reflects the length of time associated with the events and eras based on the biblical chronology developed by Ussher. Correlated with the time scale is a second scale, a rock-scale, shown to the right with the most recent rocks at the top and the earliest rocks at the bottom; the same manner they occur in the earth. The lengths of the rock scale units conceptually correspond to the quantity of rock material found on the earth today and stand in marked contrast to the length of the units of the time scale.

This concept of time-rock correlation is fundamental to the biblical geologic model and reflects the non-uniform effect of

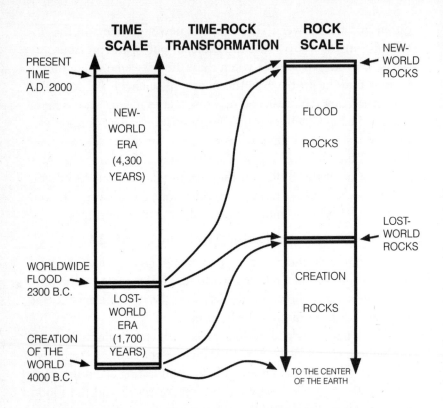

historical events on the geology of the earth. The concept focuses on the geologically significant processes indicating the relative intensity of those processes. The idea is indicated by arrows, which, for example, point from the creation event on the time scale to the rocks on the rock scale formed during this event. Similarly, arrows point from the Flood event on the time scale to the rocks on the rock scale formed during the Flood. Even though the creation and Flood events happened quickly, they were responsible for almost all the rocks present on the earth today. The long eras, which virtually structure the entire time scale, do not contribute significantly to the rock scale. Since these eras have such little impact on the rock scale, the exact dates for the creation and the Flood, within reason, are not critical to the model.

The figure represents the basic framework of the biblical geologic model. The biblical account is clearly explained in the figure together with the underlying concepts that relate that account to the geology of the earth.

Flood Chronology

The basis of a geologic model is a clearly defined history of the earth. Naturally any such history must be an assumed history because no one alive today was present to observe what occurred. Since the propositional revelation of the Bible is true, one must assume that its plain reading gives an accurate understanding of earth history. Biblical chronology is used as the basis for geological investigation.

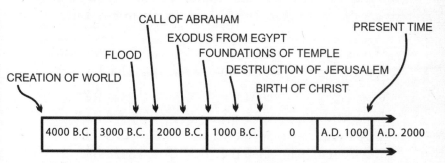

The adjacent time-line illustrates the history of the earth as revealed in the Bible. Various key events are indicated. The dates shown are from Ussher's chronology, which was based on internal evidence from the Bible itself. By adding the years given in the genealogies, and relating these to chronological information in other passages, he determined the dates for the accompanying events. The author uses Ussher's chronology because his chronology is well known. The dates shown on the time-line are:

The creation of the world	4004 B.C.
The worldwide flood	2348 B.C.
The call of Abraham	1921 B.C.
The exodus from Egypt	1491 B.C.
The foundations of temple laid	1012 B.C.
The destruction of Jerusalem	586 B.C.
The birth of Christ	4 B.C.

It is not possible in this chapter to detail here how the dates were determined. It should be noted that biblical chronologies developed by other workers following the same time-line agree with Ussher to within 50 years. Larger differences exist between the various biblical source texts. The following table summarizes the dates for creation and the Flood calculated from the Masoretic (Hebrew) text, the Samaritan text, two LXX (Septuagint) texts, and Josephus (the Jewish historian who lived in the first century A.D.).

The Masoretic text yields the latest date for the creation of the world. Dates calculated from the other sources range from 301 to 1,466 years earlier. Dates calculated for the Flood from the other texts are also earlier than the Masoretic by 650 to 880 years.

Manuscript Source	Date of Creation	Date of Flood
Masoretic	4004 B.C.	2348 B.C.
Samaritan	4305 B.C.	2998 B.C.
LXX Vatican	5470 B.C.	3228 B.C.
LXX Alexandrian	5390 B.C.	3128 B.C.
Josephus	5323 B.C.	3058 B.C.

Many scholars believe the Masoretic text preserved the original numbers, while the numbers in the other texts are somewhat artificially elongated. Nonetheless, the differences are small compared with dates published by secular historians. Additionally, the differences ultimately have no effect on the validity of the geological model because they relate to periods of time when the intensity of geological activity was minimal. For the purposes of the geological model, this author uses the dates published by Ussher, rounded to the nearest 100 years. The Flood is understood to have occurred in 2300 B.C., and creation in 4000 B.C.

Identifying the Geological Dimensions of Biblical History

Since the biblical record has proven itself authentic and accurate, the Bible is the epistemological foundation for determining the broad framework of earth history. As already stated, the chronology developed by Ussher is adopted, rounded to the nearest 100 years. The author understands the earth to have been created by God out of nothing (*ex nihilo*) around 4000 B.C. The Flood, a cataclysm of worldwide extent, occurred around 2300 B.C. Although it is not exactly certain what proportion of the world's sedimentary rocks were deposited during the Flood, the deduction is that it was probably significant. The author will continue to answer the inquiry of the geological dimensions of biblical history throughout this chapter to make these details become clearer.

When one considers biblical history, it is apparent that the creation and Flood events, although of short duration, are the most important times for the earth from a geological perspective. The creation event is preeminent, generating a volume of roughly 1,000,000 x 106 cubic kilometers of material when the earth was formed (this is illustrated by the size of the sphere in the figure on the following page). Of lesser significance was the Flood event, which would have deposited some 300 to 700 x 106 cubic kilometers of material (this is represented by the smaller sphere in the figure). To produce such large quantities of material in such a short time would involve intense geologic processes.

By contrast, the geologic processes observed operating today are orders of magnitude less intense. If the current rates of erosion and deposition are projected over the pre-Flood or the post-Flood era, then the total quantity of material deposited in either era would be less than 0.05 x 106 cubic kilometers. Even if the rates applied during these eras were one or two orders of magnitude different from current rates, the material accumulated during these eras would still be much less than the material generated during the creation or Flood event. The comparatively minuscule volume of material deposited in this time is illustrated by the essentially invisible sphere in the figure.

From a geological viewpoint, therefore, the history of the earth as recorded in the Bible can be divided into four parts which will be referred to as the creation event, the Lost-World era (pre-Flood era), the Flood event, and the New-World era (post-Flood era). The term "Lost-World era" refers to the time between the creation and

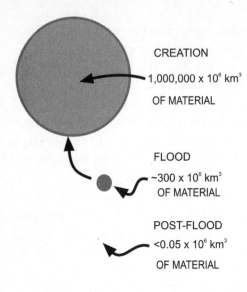

CREATION

1,000,000 x 10⁶ km³

OF MATERIAL

FLOOD

~300 x 10⁶ km³

OF MATERIAL

POST-FLOOD

<0.05 x 10⁶ km³

OF MATERIAL

Flood events. It avoids ambiguity because the term "pre-Flood" includes the creation event. The important conclusion from any consideration of the biblical record is that the intensity of geologic processes was different for each of the four parts of world history. It is because geologic effects were not uniform with time that the quantity of rock material deposited over the history of the earth was not proportional to time. In the creation model, some non-linear transformation must be made between the historical record and the observed geology (this feature is the basic difference between a geological model based on the Bible and a model based on a rigid uniformitarianism).

The Collapse of "Geologic Time"[42]

The age of things is crucial in the debate concerning the authority of the Bible. Most methods that could be used for calculating the earth's age, even though still based on unprovable uniformitarian[43] assumptions, give upper limits much less than the billions of years required for evolution.[44] Evolutionists widely use radioisotope (or radiometric) dating of rocks to support the

---

42. Co-authored with S. Taylor, senior lecturer in electrical engineering at the University of Liverpool, and A. McIntosh, professor in Combustion Theory at Leeds University, U.K.

43. For example, the assumption of constant rates of change.

44 For example, the amount of helium in the atmosphere, the decay and rapid reversals of earth's magnetic field, the salinity of the oceans, lack of continental erosion, and population statistics. A good summary is given by J.D. Morris, *The Young Earth* (Green Forest, AR: Master Books, 1994).

"geologic time" figure of 4.6 billion years. Notwithstanding the inherent unreliability and demonstrated inaccuracy of the radiometric dating techniques (see Appendix 1), ages of rock formations in the millions (and billions) of years are presented as fact in schools, universities, and the media.

However, there is spectacular but little-known evidence that is completely inconsistent with the evolutionary time scale, but entirely consistent with the biblical record of a young earth and a catastrophic global flood. The evidence is provided by radiohalos in coalified wood. The evidence has been published in some of the best peer-reviewed scientific journals, and its strong case against evolution's millions of years is currently unanswered by the evolutionary community.

What Are Radiohalos?

Radiohalos are spherical, microscopic-sized discolorations in crystals. They are found abundantly in certain minerals in earth's rocks, especially micas from granites. In cross-section on a microscope slide, they appear as a series of tiny concentric rings, usually surrounding a central core (Figure 1, this chapter).[45]

The central core is (at least initially) radioactive. High energy alpha particles, emitted from the core during radioactive decay, damage the mineral and discolor it, with most of the damage occurring where the particle stops. How far this particle travels depends on its energy. Since all the alpha particles from a particular type of decay reaction have the same energy, and the particles are fired in all directions, a spherical shell of discoloration will form, appearing circular in cross-section.

For sake of illustration, imagine shooting a bullet into a huge lump of cork.[46] Eventually, the bullet will stop, resulting in a "trail" of damage, the length of which depends on the speed of the bullet.

45. Primary polonium-218 radiohalos command attention because they provide a record of extinct radioactivity in minerals constituting some of earth's most ancient rocks. See R.V. Gentry, *Creation's Tiny Mystery*, 3rd ed. (1986; Knoxville, TN: Earth Science Associates, 1992).

46. Obviously not a perfect analogy — despite being useful — since a bullet into cork would leave equivalent damage all along its path, unlike the alpha particles, which do most damage at the end, as stated.

Different radioactive substances shoot alpha particles ("bullets") at different (though specific) speeds, so it is possible to identify the substance from the diameter of the "sphere of damage." The higher the energy of decay, the faster will be the speed of the "bullet."

Uranium Radiohalos

Radioactive uranium generates a beautiful, multi-ringed halo (Figure 1) because it decays in a number of steps. Of the 15 isotopes (or varieties of elements) in this "decay chain" (see Appendix 2), eight emit alpha particles when they decay, forming eight rings.[47] It is somewhat like a sequence of guns, each of different power, firing an eight-gun salute. When this salute, or decay chain, is fired millions of times in every direction, the bullets from the different guns make eight concentric rings.

If, instead of radioactive uranium, the core were composed of an isotope along the chain, there would be fewer rings. Omitting the first few isotopes in the decay series would be like removing the first few guns in the "salute." Consequently, it is quite simple to determine which isotope was originally in the core by counting the rings. Polonium-218 forms three rings, polonium-214 forms two, and polonium-210 forms only one.

Radiohalos in Coalified Wood

Radiohalos have also been discovered in logs recovered from uranium mines on the Colorado Plateau of the western United States. The logs, partially turned to coal, were found in uranium-rich sedimentary rocks from three different geological formations. Some of these formations had previously been assigned radiometric "dates" ranging from 55–80 million years.[48] Scientists Jedwab[49] and

---

47. The others decay by beta decay (b), not alpha (a). Note that due to overlap, only five of the eight rings of a ^{238}U halo are normally visible.

48. L.R. Steiff et al., "A Preliminary Determination of the Age of Some Uranium Ores of the Colorado Plateau by the Lead-Uranium Method," *US Geological Survey Circular* 271 (1953).

49. J. Jedwab, "Significance and Use of Optical Phenomena in Uraniferous Caustobioliths," in *Coal Science*, ed. Peter H. Given (Washington DC: American Chemical Society, 1966).

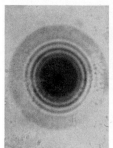 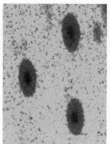 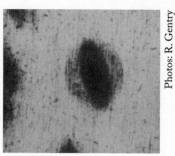

Figure 1
A fully developed uranium radiohalo in biotite (dark mica). Field of view is about 80 μm (0.08 mm). A uranium halo comprises eight rings, but some rings are of similar size and cannot easily be distinguished.

Figure 2
Elliptical polonium-210 halos in compressed coalified wood. Length of ellipse is about 50 μm (0.05 mm).

Figure 3
Combined circular and elliptical halos indicate that polonium-210 continued to decay after the wood was compressed. Diameter of halo is about 50 μm.

Breger[50] described these halos, and Dr. Robert Gentry, a world authority on radiohalos, revisited their work. Following extensive investigation, Gentry published his results in the prestigious journal *Science*,[51] as a book,[52] and as a video.[53]

Most of the halos found in the wood had only one ring, indicating that the radioactive cores once contained polonium-210

50. I.A. Breger, "The Role of Organic Matter in the Accumulation of Uranium: The Organic Geochemistry of Coal-Uranium Association," in *Formation of Uranium Ore Deposits* (Vienna: International Atomic Energy Agency, 1974), p. 99-124.

51. R.V. Gentry et al., "Radiohalos and Coalified Wood: New Evidence Relating to the Time of Uranium Introduction and Coalification," *Science* 194 (15 October 1976): p. 315–318.

52. Gentry, *Creation's Tiny Mystery*, p. 51–62.

53. R.V. Gentry, "The Young Age of the Earth" (Cleveland, OH: Alpha Productions, 1996).

— the last radioactive isotope in the uranium-238 decay chain. Clearly, the wood had been saturated in uranium-rich solutions, and certain spots attracted polonium atoms (also present in these solutions), allowing small cores of polonium-210 to form. As they decayed, these cores left the characteristic polonium-210 halo.

Nevertheless, the solutions must have penetrated the logs relatively quickly (certainly within a year or so). How is that conclusion determined? It is determined since the half-life of polonium-210 is only 138 days. Specifically, within 138 days, half the polonium-210 present would have decayed into the next "daughter" isotope in the chain. The solution had saturated the wood within two or three half-lives (about a year). It could not have taken very long, because in 10 half-lives (less than four years) virtually all of the polonium-210 would have disappeared.

Only one of the three radioactive isotopes of polonium was deposited in the tiny radioactive specks in the logs (which is certain because only one ring formed). The other isotopes from the decay chain (polonium-214 and polonium-218) were missing. Why? They had already decayed; their half-lives are very short (164 millionths of a second and three minutes respectively). Therefore, all polonium-214 would have disappeared within a thousandth of a second, and all polonium-218 would have disappeared in an hour (long before the uranium-rich solutions could saturate the logs).

Significantly, the halos were mainly elliptical, not circular (Figure 2, previous page). Obviously, after the halos formed, the wooden logs were compressed, squashing the originally circular halos into ellipses.

Sometimes a circular halo could be seen with an elliptical halo (Figure 3, previous page). The circular halo indicated that radioactive polonium-210 continued to decay from the same core after the wood was compressed. Therefore, because of the 138-day half-life of polonium-210 as previously mentioned, there was less than four years between the time that the solution

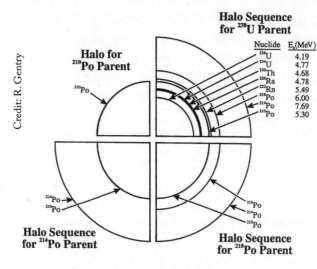

Credit: R. Gentry

Halo for ²¹⁰Po Parent

²¹⁰Po

Halo Sequence for ²³⁸U Parent

Nuclide	E_α(MeV)
²³⁸U	4.19
²³⁴U	4.77
²³⁰Th	4.68
²²⁶Ra	4.78
²²²Rn	5.49
²¹⁸Po	6.00
²¹⁴Po	7.69
²¹⁰Po	5.30

Halo Sequence for ²¹⁴Po Parent

²¹⁴Po
²¹⁰Po

Halo Sequence for ²¹⁸Po Parent

²¹⁸Po
²¹⁴Po
²¹⁰Po

Characteristic ring configurations for
different parent elements

(Left) Different radiohalos have a different number of rings. (Below) Diameter of largest ring is about 70 µm (0.07 mm) in biotite. All four isotopes are from the uranium-238 decay series.

first infiltrated the wood and when it was compressed. The presence of the second halo at the same spot shows that much less than four years had passed before the compression event, as there was still time to produce another halo afterward.[54]

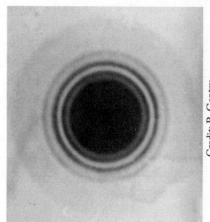

Credit: R. Gentry

An Amazing Event

The wood in which the tiny elliptical halos were found speaks of a devastating flood that uprooted and smashed huge trees, depositing the debris with an enormous volume of

---

54. Gentry demonstrated that the second halo could have formed from the decay of an isotope two steps prior along the "chain." Since the intermediary isotope undergoes beta, not alpha decay, the two possibilities cannot be distinguished from the halo. However, this would stretch things from a maximum of around 4 years to some 22 years (a trivial matter).

sediment over a large area. The halos themselves tell the story of an unusual geologic event. They speak of uranium-rich solutions saturating the logs in less than a year or so, forming tiny specks of polonium, which decayed to produce circular radiohalos, which were, in much less than four years, compressed and deformed.

The story is one of exceptional geological conditions (a highly unusual sequence of events). For instance, in the usual "slow and gradual" scenarios, it would take much longer for sufficient sediment to accumulate on top to deform the wood in such a manner. What is really amazing and significant, however, is the fact that this elliptical halo situation had been found in three different geological formations in the same general region. Evolutionists believe these formations represent three different geological periods ranging from 35 to 245 million years.[55] To believe the millions-of-years time scale, one would need to believe that this amazing sequence of events (with all its precise timing) occurred three different times, separated by more than 200 million years. Clearly this is an incredible scenario. It makes more sense to believe that the sequence occurred once, and that all the sedimentary formations were deposited in the same catastrophe, followed by the same earth movement causing deformation. These polonium halos collapse the "long ages" of geology, and point to the unique, catastrophic Flood recorded in the Bible. Additionally, by the same reasoning, these halos leave little consideration for numerous layers of post-Flood sedimentation as suggested by some authors.[56]

More Confirming Evidence

Further confirmation of this spectacular collapse of geologic time is provided by careful analysis of the tiny cores of some

55. The ages are as follows: Eocene (supposedly 35 to 55 million years ago), the Jurassic (140 to 205 million years ago), and the Triassic (205 to 245 million years ago). See Gentry, *Creation's Tiny Mystery*, p. 56.

56. See A.C. McIntosh, T. Edmondson, and S. Taylor, "Genesis and Catastrophe: The Flood As the Major Biblical Cataclysm," *CEN Technical Journal* 14 (April 2000): p. 101–109.

uranium halos found in the same wood samples.[57] The samples revealed a large amount of uranium-238 but almost no lead-206.[58] If the halos were millions of years old, much more "daughter" lead should have been present. The scarcity of the daughter element, using the same assumptions upon which radiometric dating is based, would indicate that the halos are only several thousand years old, not millions. Similar results were obtained for halos from all three geological formations, indicating that all are approximately the same age. Again, the supposed millions of years of geologic time collapse into only a few thousand.[59]

Dinosaur Tracks

Fossilized dinosaur footprints have been found in various Colorado mines. In Cyprus Plateau Mine (Utah), a fossilized dinosaur footprint was found in the coal seam next to one of the many coalified logs of the plateau. In Kenilworth Mine, eight different types of dinosaur tracks were found.

The pattern of tracks suggests that the animals were fleeing from an imminent catastrophe. Many fossilized dinosaur track patterns suggest that the creatures that made them were fleeing from something; in some cases this may have been a predator. A soft surface which is capable of receiving foot imprints would be unlikely to retain those prints unless covered relatively quickly by further sediment, such as in a flood catastrophe. Nearby, a huge dinosaur graveyard has been found at Dinosaur National Monument (Vernal, Utah) in Jurassic sediments.

Obviously, the dinosaurs that made these tracks did not escape. The catastrophe overtook them. The collapse of geologic time and the young age for the rock formations confirm that

---

57. Samples were discerned using x-ray fluorescence (EXMRF) and the more sensitive ion microprobe mass analysis (IMMA).

58. The ratios of uranium to lead rose to 64,000, indicating the halos are only thousands of years old. Halos millions of years old would have a far lower uranium-to-lead ratio. For further details, see Gentry, *Creation's Tiny Mystery*, p. 61–62, and Gentry, "Radiohalos and Coalified Wood."

59. It is chemically implausible to believe that lead could be leached and leave uranium (the reverse is far more likely).

these dinosaurs lived on earth at the same time as man, only a few thousand years ago. Such scientific evidence, presented in leading journals, is a major problem for the idea of "millions of years." It is, however, consistent with the vast fossil-bearing, sedimentary rock deposits of the Colorado Plateau having been laid down rapidly by the catastrophic global flood described in the Bible, some 4,300 years ago. The dinosaurs that left footprints on the plateau, and were then buried and fossilized in the nearby rocks also lived then at the same time as man.

Conclusion

It cannot be overstated that earth history is important for geology. Geologists have long recognized that history is fundamental to their discipline. Traditionally, the science has been split into two parts: physical geology and historical geology. To understand the rocks properly, one needs a geological model of how the rocks formed. Moreover, to understand how rocks formed, one needs a reliable history of the earth.

Christian geologists have an advantage when it comes to history. Since they believe in the authenticity and accuracy of biblical history, they do not need to speculate about history. By taking the biblical account as an eyewitness record of past events, Christians only need to speculate about how these affected geology. The pioneers of geological science used this approach and saw nothing unscientific about it. Indeed, there are compelling reasons why all geologists should treat the biblical data seriously.

Nevertheless, how do those who do not accept biblical history proceed? Without an eyewitness account, they need to invent their own history. They need to use their imagination, similar to the way Niels Bohr imagined the internal structure of the atom.[60] Geologists who do not accept the Bible invent their

---

60. In the early 1900s, N. Bohr used his imagination to make the first model of the atom. He wanted to understand the electromagnetic radiation that atoms emit. By combining his knowledge about atoms and electricity with his creative imagination, he speculated that atoms were like miniature solar systems.

history by assuming that past geological processes were much the same as the geological processes observed today. In other words, they assume that present geological processes can be extrapolated indefinitely into the past. One direct consequence of this assumption is the idea that earth history extends for billions of years.

Consequently, there are two geological approaches to obtaining earth history which is the essential component of many geological models. One can assume the biblical account is accurate or assume geological processes continued unchanged for millions of years. However, if the Bible is accurate and geologists do not regard it as the epistemological foundation, they will not obtain the correct answers. Furthermore, when they do not begin with the Bible, it is not surprising that they reach a history conflicting with biblical history.

Appendix 1

Radiometric Dating Relies on Assumptions

Radiometric dating relies on three unprovable assumptions about the past:

1. The amount of "daughter" isotope in the rock at the start is known

2. No loss of "parent" or gain of "daughter" since the rock formed (closed system conditions)

3. Constant decay rate of "parent" to "daughter"

If these conditions could be guaranteed, the radiometric dating method would be correct. However, unless eyewitnesses observed the rock when it formed, and checked it constantly thereafter, it is impossible to guarantee that these assumptions are correct. Indeed, there are many cases in the scientific literature where assumptions one and two, though made in good faith, have been shown to be unreliable.

Constancy of decay rate (assumption three) implies that a parameter, which scientists have been measuring for only a century, has been constant for millions of alleged years of earth's history; of course, this is not only unproven but also unprovable. Decay rates (which can vary greatly today under special conditions) may have been much faster in the past; evidence suggesting this is now being analyzed by a creationist consortium.[61] A good summary of the documented inconsistencies and inaccuracies of radiometric dating is given by Woodmorappe.[62]

Appendix 2

Radioactive Decay Series

Radioactive isotopes have an intrinsically unstable atomic structure which makes them disintegrate so that particles escape. One manner in which a parent radioactive atom can decay into a daughter atom is by ejecting an alpha particle from its nucleus. Sometimes the daughter element is also unstable and subsequently decays into another unstable isotope, and continues in a series of steps (a "decay chain").

The isotope uranium-238 begins a decay chain that disintegrates step-by-step into a stable form of lead. It involves 15 isotopes and 14 steps (see diagram on following page). Different isotopes of the same element (e.g., uranium-238 and uranium-235) have a different mass but nearly identical chemical behavior. An alpha particle is a helium nucleus with a mass of four atomic mass units. Therefore, radioactive decay by emission of an alpha particle (e.g., uranium-238) produces a daughter isotope (thorium-234) which is four atomic mass units lighter.

The half-life of a radioactive isotope is the time required for half its atoms to decay. Different isotopes have different half lives (e.g., the half-life of uranium-238 is 4.5 billion years and of polonium-218 is three minutes).

---

61. L. Vardiman, A.A. Snelling, and E.F. Chaffin, eds., *Radioisotopes and the Age of the Earth: A Young-Earth Creationist Research Initiative* (El Cajon, CA: Institute for Creation Research, 2000).

62. J. Woodmorappe, *The Mythology of Modern Dating Methods* (El Cajon, CA: Institute for Creation Research, 1999).

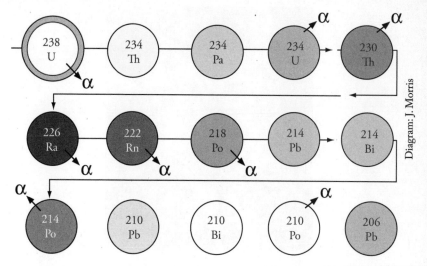

The uranium-238 decay (238U) series. Eight of the 15 isotopes emit an alpha particle when they decay. Letters signify the name of the element (e.g., U for uranium and PO for polonium) and the numbers indicate the mass of the atoms (e.g., 238 atomic mass units).

Our appreciation to Creation Ministries International for permission to use some of the material in this chapter.

Tas Walker, Ph.D., is lecturer and researcher with Creation Ministries International (Australia), Eight Mile Plains, Queensland. He has a bachelor of science degree (geology) with first class honors, a bachelor of engineering degree also with first class honors, and a doctorate in mechanical engineering. Dr. Walker also helped organize conferences, including one of the Simulation Society of Australia. One of his contributions has been to develop models for various aspects of the power industry such as the coordinated operation of the system and construction of power stations.

Dr. Walker has also set up BiblicalGeology.net about geology and the Bible. A biblical framework of geology leads to a new appreciation of the environments and processes of different geological phases. The site describes the basis of this model and a practical application to the Great Artesian Basin of Australia.

CHAPTER 6

EVIDENCE FROM BEYOND THE EARTH FOR A YOUNG EARTH

Jonathan Henry

C onventional theory dates the solar system at 4.6 billion years, and the universe at more than 10 billion.[1] Long chronologies exist for the earth and other planets, the sun and other stars, the solar system, Milky Way Galaxy and other galaxies, and the universe. The chronological array is often taken as irrefutable confirmation of old age. However, these chronologies are based ultimately on the earth's presumed evolutionary age, which in the final analysis derives from the geological chronology of Charles Lyell. Partly for political reasons,[2] Lyell discredited the Mosaic chronology, and the chronology resulting from a century

---

1. The author read earlier drafts of this chapter at the second annual regional meeting of the Conservative Theological Society on February 20, 2004, at Lakeside Community Chapel, Clearwater, Florida; and at the third annual regional meeting of the Conservative Theological Society on April 29–30, 2005, at Clearwater Christian College, Clearwater, Florida.

2. G. Grinnell, "Catastrophism and Uniformity: A Probe into the Origins of the 1832 Gestalt Shift in Geology," *Kronos* 1 (Winter 1976): p. 68.

of radiometric studies is not substantially different from Lyell's chronology.[3] Positive evidence also exists for a short chronology and "recent" creation. The phenomena discussed in the following severely constrain the age of the solar system and thus of the earth, implying an age of order as low as millennia.

Rapid Decay of Planetary Magnetic Fields

Physicist Thomas Barnes showed that the geomagnetic field is decaying with a half-life of 1,400 years.[4] Recent data confirm a half-life of about 1,465 years.[5] This implies a young earth, since the earth at 4.6 billion years would have no magnetic field left. Anti-creationists fault Barnes with inferior credentials,[6] but this charge discounts his earned master's degree and his authorship of a text on electricity and magnetism published by a major press.[7]

Old-age advocates theorize that geomagnetism comes from molten minerals circulating in the earth. High temperature makes the minerals ionize, and circulation of the ions produces a non-decaying magnetic field. Man-made electric current from a generator or "dynamo" also produces magnetism, so by analogy a "dynamo effect" causes geomagnetism.[8] Barnes demonstrated that this is not true, and that geomagnetism is from a decaying electric current.

3. J. Henry, "An Old Age for the Earth Is the Heart of Evolution," *Creation Research Society Quarterly* 40 (December 2003): p. 165, 167–170.

4. T.G. Barnes, "Decay of the Earth's Magnetic Field and the Geochronological Implications," *Creation Research Society Quarterly* 8 (June 1971): p. 24.

5. D. Humphreys, "The Earth's Magnetic Field: Closing a Loophole in the Case for Its Youth," *Creation Matters* 7 (March–April 2002): p. 3–4.

6. B. Vickers, "Some Questionable Creationist Credentials" [article online] (The Talk Origins Archive, 1998, accessed June 24, 2005) available from http://talkorigins.org/faqs/credentials.html.

7. T.G. Barnes, *Foundations of Electricity and Magnetism* (New York: Heath, 1965; reprint, El Paso, TX: Thomas Barnes, 1975), p. 1–413.

8. J. Bloxham and D. Gubbins, "The Evolution of the Earth's Magnetic Field," *Scientific American* 261(December 1989): p. 68; C. Carrigan and D. Gubbins, "The Source of the Earth's Magnetic Field," *Scientific American* 240 (February 1979): p. 119–120.

This current presumably was installed in the earth during creation week and began decaying because of the curse on the ground.[9]

The Earth's Magnetic Field Is Weakening Rapidly

Magnetic field decay implies an earth lifetime of the order of 10,000 years,[10] since much further back than that, core heating associated with the high level of magnetism would destabilize the earth's interior. Overall, the geomagnetic field has lost about 15 percent of its energy since the first measurements in the early 1800s,[11] with a decay of roughly 1 percent per decade.[12] From 1970–2000, the net loss was about 1.41 percent, confirming Barnes' earlier claim,[13] and contradicting descriptions of the field as "self-sustaining" with no energy loss.[14] "In the next two millennia, if the present rate of decay is maintained, the [strength] of the field should reach zero."[15]

Old-age advocates respond that though the field is decaying now, it has been regenerated in the past by "field reversals." However, these reversals are associated with intense seismic activity during the Flood[16] (Humphreys, 1990, p. 129). The article, written by Coe and Prevot[17] and Coe and others,[18] confirmed that magnetic

---

9. T.G. Barnes, *The Origin and Destiny of Earth's Magnetic Field* (El Cajon, CA: Institute for Creation Research, 1983), p. 14, 27–28, 38, 130–131.

10. Ibid., p. 53–54; Carrigan and Gubbins, "Source of the Earth's Magnetic Field," p. 123, 125.

11. Humphreys, "The Earth's Magnetic Field," p. 1.

12. Bloxham and Gubbins, "Evolution of the Earth's Magnetic Field," p. 70.

13. Humphreys, "The Earth's Magnetic Field," p. 3.

14. Carrigan and Gubbins, "Source of the Earth's Magnetic Field," p. 119, 120.

15. Bloxham and Gubbins, "Evolution of the Earth's Magnetic Field," p. 71.

16. D. Humphreys, "Physical Mechanism for Reversals of the Earth's Magnetic Field During the Flood," in *Proceedings of the Second International Conference on Creationism*, ed. R. Walsh (Pittsburgh: Creation Science Fellowship, 1990), 2:129.

17. R. Coe and M. Prevot, "Evidence Suggesting Extremely Rapid Field Variation During a Geomagnetic Reversal," *Earth and Planetary Science Letters* 92 (April 1989): p. 292.

18. R.S. Coe, M. Prévot, and P. Camps, "New Evidence for Extraordinarily Rapid Change of the Geomagnetic Field during a Reversal," *Nature* 374 (April 20, 1995): p. 687.

reversals have occurred rapidly rather than over hundreds of millions of years. Furthermore, such reversals were superimposed on the secular decay trend studied by Barnes. Evidence for reversals does not change the conclusion that magnetic field decay severely constrains the earth's age.

Planetary Magnetic Fields Point to a Millennial Age for Creation

The dynamo theory circumvents this age constraint, but has not led to real understanding of the earth's field or other planetary fields. Before the Voyager flybys of Uranus and Neptune, "the terrestrial case [with the assumption of a dynamo] seemed to serve as a good guide to how planetary interiors should work."[19] These planets were found to have a magnetic axis severely inclined to the rotational axis, making it virtually impossible that the magnetic field of either planet could be from a dynamo. Theorists then proposed that Uranus and Neptune had suffered relatively recent catastrophes to produce their unexpected features, but this idea has been discredited.[20] Presumably, the Uranian and Neptunian fields, like that of the earth, are due to rapidly decaying electric currents.

Naturalistic models for Mercury's origin lead to the conclusion that its core is now solid, leaving no possibility of a dynamo.[21] However, Mercury has an "intrinsic" magnetic field,[22] that is, a field existing with no dynamo. By conventional theory, Mercury should therefore have no magnetic field,[23] and its discovery was a "surprise."[24] Nevertheless, if Mercury has a dynamo, then "the planet has a liquid metallic core,"[25] a contradiction of theory.

Mercury's field is predicted to decay about 5 percent between the Mariner 10 mission in 1975 and the Messenger mission flyby

19. R. Kerr, "The Neptune System in Voyager's Afterglow," *Science* 245 (September 29, 1989): p. 1450.

20. Ibid.

21. J. Fix, *Astronomy* (Boston, MA: WCB/McGraw-Hill, 1999), p. 204.

22. W. Hubbard, *Planetary Interiors* (Reinhold, NY: Van Nostrand, 1984), p. 203.

23. Ibid., p. 207.

24. L. Morrow, "Mercury Unveiled," *Time* 103 (April 8, 1974): p. 52.

25. Fix, *Astronomy*, p. 204.

in 2011.[26] If this prediction is true, Mercury's field is decaying faster than the earth's, implying a Mercury lifetime, and a lifetime for the solar system and the earth, of the order of millennia.

Rapid Dissipation of Planetary Rings

A puzzle for evolutionary chronology began with the Voyager 1 flyby past Saturn's rings in 1980. Before then, earth-bound telescopes provided little ring detail, and planetary rings were assumed to have endured virtually changeless since the emergence of the solar system from the solar nebula — a vast cloud of gas and dust — some 4.6 billion years ago.[27] "Everyone had expected that collisions between particles in Saturn's rings would make the rings perfectly uniform."[28]

Jeffreys[29] had claimed that "the frequency of collision [of ring particles] is very great, and . . . on account of the loss of relative motion at every collision, the rings must long ago have reached a state in which all the particles are moving in very accurate circles, all in the same plane."[30] This view arose from belief in the rings' great age,[31] but Voyager 1 showed that the rings are

26. D. Humphreys, "Mercury's Messenger," *Creation Matters* 9 (July–August 2004): p. 9.

27. T. Northrup and J. Connerney, "A Micrometeorite Erosion Model and the Age of Saturn's Rings," *Icarus* 70 (1987): p. 124; J. Pollack and J. Cuzzi, "Rings in the Solar System," *Scientific American* 245 (May 1981): p. 117, 125–126, 127, 129; L. Soderblom and T. Johnson, "The Moons of Saturn," *Scientific American* 244 (January 1982): p. 101.

28. J. Pasachoff, *Contemporary Astronomy* (Philadelphia, PA: Saunders, 1985), p. 429.

29. H. Jeffreys, "On Certain Possible Distributions of Meteoric Bodies in the Solar System," *Monthly Notices of the Royal Astronomical Society* 77 (1916): p. 84.

30. H. Jeffreys, "Transparency of Saturn's Rings," *Journal of the British Astronomical Association* 30 (1920): p. 295; A. Alexander, *The Planet Saturn*, (London: Faber and Faber, 1962; reprint, New York: Dover, 1980), p. 320.

31. R. Kerr, "Making Better Planetary Rings," *Science* 229 (September 13, 1985): p. 1377.

highly structured and probably young.[32] There was more structure than could be expected to persist over 4.6 billion years, unless all ring-binding forces were accounted for. Efforts to locate
sufficient binding forces have failed, and a "growing number [of
astronomers] believe that the rings of Saturn are constantly . . .
changing due to fragmentation of moonlets and input of new
ring particles."[33]

However, there remains a reluctance to associate ring change
with ring dissipation,[34] since this could imply a young solar system.
This reluctance did not exist before the ascendancy of evolutionary
chronology.[35] Then Saturn's rings were acknowledged to be
rapidly changeable and possibly dissipating. Space probes have
rediscovered rapid ring change and dissipation. For Jupiter's rings,
"[ring] particles should last only a very short time — perhaps only
a few thousand years. . . ."[36] Of Saturn's rings and planetary rings
generally, "It now appears that the length of time for planetary rings
to dissipate is relatively short."[37] Regarding Uranus's rings, "The
thin outer atmosphere of Uranus extends into the rings, so it should
slow down very tiny dust particles and cause them to sink into the
inner atmosphere in a few thousand years or less. . . . Collisions
between ring particles . . . slowly [make] the ring wider."[38]

32. J. Burns, D. Hamilton, and M. Showalter, "Bejeweled Worlds," *Scientific American* 286 (February 2002): p. 73.

33. W. Hartmann, *Astronomy* (Belmont, CA: Wadsworth, 1991), p. 253; NASA, "Do Saturn's Rings Change?" [article online] (Jet Propulsion Laboratory, 2000, accessed April 15, 2005) available from http://learn. jpl.nasa.gov/projectspacef/bkg450b.html; Burns, et al., "Bejeweled Worlds," p. 73.

34. Hartmann, *Astronomy*, p. 252–253.

35. S. Brush, C. Everett, and E. Garber, *Maxwell on Saturn's Rings* (Cambridge, MA: MIT Press, 1983), p. 7.

36. Fix, *Astronomy*, p. 270; Pollack and Cuzzi, "Rings in the Solar System," p. 129.

37. Fix, *Astronomy*, p. 274; J. Eberhart, "Saturn's 'Ring Rain,'" *Science News* 130 (1986): p. 84.

38. Fix, *Astronomy*, p. 289–290; L. Esposito, "The Changing Shape of Planetary Rings," *Astronomy* 15 (September 1987): p. 15.

Saturn's Rings Have Been Widening Rapidly

Since Jupiter's rings have dissipation times of a few millennia, and Uranus's rings maybe less, could Saturn's rings be dissipating this fast? Saturn's rings have little matter, "only about a millionth of the mass of our moon,"[39] similar to that of smaller asteroids such as 243 Ida or 253 Mathilde.[40] Their small mass suggests that the rings could "empty out" fairly quickly. Indeed, Jupiter's rings are thought to be in part the product of the dissolution of two moons, Adrastea and Metis,[41] both with masses comparable to the mass of Saturn's rings.[42]

Alexander[43] documented 350 years of widening in Saturn's A and B rings.[44] In the 1850s, Otto Struve assessed observations from the previous two centuries which indicated ring-spreading into Saturn at a rate of some 60 miles per year.[45] However, with hypothetical assumptions from the increasingly popular nebular hypothesis which claimed a naturalistic origin, an old age, and little change in the solar system presently, Struve's analysis was considered questionable.[46] So strong had belief in the nebular hypothesis

39. T. Snow, *Essentials of the Dynamic Universe* (St. Paul, MN: West Publishing, 1984), p. 157.

40. D. Williams, "Asteroid Fact Sheet" [online] (National Aeronautics and Space Administration, 2000, accessed April 27, 2005) available from http://nssdc.gsfc.nasa.gov/planetary/factsheet/asteroidfact. html.

41. D. Goldsmith, *The Evolving Universe* (Menlo Park, CA: Benjamin Cummings, 1985), p. 461.

42. D. Williams, "Jovian Satellite Fact Sheet" [online] (National Aeronautics and Space Administration, 1999, accessed December 7, 2004) available from http://nssdc.gsfc.nasa.gov/planetary/factsheet/joviansatfact. html.

43. Alexander, *The Planet Saturn*, p. 84–441.

44. W. Corliss, ed., *Mysterious Universe* (Glenn Arm, MD: Sourcebook Project, 1979), p. 466–471.

45. Alexander, *The Planet Saturn*, p. 184; H. Slusher, *Age of the Cosmos* (El Cajon, CA: Institute for Creation Research, 1980), p. 71; O. Struve, "Planets with Rings," *Sky and Telescope* 20 (January 1960): p. 21.

46. S. Brush, C. Everett, and E. Garber, *Maxwell on Saturn's Rings* (Cambridge, MA: MIT Press, 1983), p. 5.

become that Taylor[47] inconsistently claimed ring spreading was compatible with it. However, Maxwell had shown that Saturn's rings are particulate and not rigid disks or liquid. Maxwell's theoretical predictions were confirmed by observation,[48] and Maxwell[49] considered Struve's analysis consistent with theory.

Nevertheless, Struve[50] had failed to measure continued ring spreading, and Lewis[51] concluded that ring observations were not "accordant" due to "the great difficulty in making these measures." However, he also stated that Saturn's rings were "certainly" not undergoing long-term change, even though his data[52] showed C-ring spreading. Lewis thus laid the groundwork for Jeffreys's concept of very old rings.

Saturn's C Ring Formed Recently

Saturn's most prominent rings are the A, B, and C rings.[53] However, the C ring was not visible until the 1800s: "William Herschel, the foremost astronomical observer of his time (1738–1822), makes no mention of the [C ring] in any of his writings, and it is inferred that it was not then a conspicuous object. If this inference be correct, we must conclude that this ring is rapidly growing, and that the rings of Saturn are probably comparatively

---

47. W. Taylor, "Rings of Saturn," *Science* 2 (1883): p. 660.

48. Brush et al., *Maxwell on Saturn's Rings*, p. 24; Alexander, *The Planet Saturn*, p. 187.

49. J. Maxwell, *On the Stability of the Motion of Saturn's Rings* (London, Macmillan, 1859), in *The Scientific Papers of James Clerk Maxwell*, ed. W. Niven (London: Cambridge University, 1890; reprint, New York: Dover, 1965), 2:353, 373–374.

50. O. Struve, "Neue Messungen an den Saturnsringen," *Astronomische Nachrichten* 105 (1883): p. 17–20.

51. T. Lewis, "The Dimensions of Saturn's Ring," *Observatory* 18 (1895): p. 385.

52. T. Lewis, "Measures of Saturn's Rings," *Observatory* 19 (1896): p. 203.

53. L. Horn, M. Showalter, and C. Russell, "Detection and Behavior of Pan Wakes in Saturn's A Ring" *Icarus* 124 (1996): p. 663; T. Snow, *Essentials of the Dynamic Universe* (St. Paul, MN: West Publishing), p. 156.

recent introductions to the solar system."[54] Nevertheless, the C ring now can be seen "with telescopes of moderate size."[55] Since Herschel's telescopes were among the best of his day, with Saturn a "favourite object of study,"[56] one is led to conclude that he missed the C ring because it was absent. The first recorded observation was in 1848.[57] *Consequently one of the three prominent rings of Saturn has evidently developed since the early 1800s.* The inner edge of the C ring is approaching the planet,[58] and Napier and Clube[59] calculated the rate of approach as 60 miles per year.

The history of C ring observations implies rapid ring spreading and dissipation. The inner edge of the B ring is now 57,150 miles (91,975 km) from the center of Saturn, and the inner edge of the C ring is at 46,390 miles (74,658 km).[60] Thus, the width of the C ring is 10,760 miles (17,317 km), or about 9,320 miles (15,000 km), a width which developed since about 1850. This implies an infall of ring particles over some 60 mi/yr, or 100 km/yr, in agreement with the in-spreading computation of Napier and Clube. Like Jupiter's and Uranus' rings, Saturn's rings appear to be decaying in a millennial time frame. Ring dissipation does not require millions of years. When planetary rings were thought to be old, they were taken as evidence for an old solar system.

54. N. Dupuis, *The Elements of Astronomy Principally on the Mechanical Side* (Uglow and Company, 1910), as quoted in H.L. Armstrong, "An Examination Of Theistic Evolution," *Creation Research Society Quarterly* 13 (September 1976): p. 120.

55. R. Baker, *Astronomy* (New York: Van Nostrand, 1950), p. 222.

56. H. King, *The History of the Telescope* (London: Griffin, 1955; reprint, New York: Dover, 1979), p. 133.

57. Fix, *Astronomy*, p. 270; Baker, *Astronomy*, p. 222.

58. T. Lewis, "Measures of Saturn's Rings," *Observatory* 19 (1896): p. 203.

59. W.M. Napier and S.V.M. Clube, "A Theory of Terrestrial Catastrophism," *Nature* 282 (November 29, 1979): p. 457.

60. D. Williams, "Saturnian Rings Fact Sheet" [online] (National Aeronautics and Space Administration, 1999, accessed March 10, 2005) available from http://nssdc.gsfc.nasa.gov/planetary/factsheet/satring-fact.html.

Intimation of their youth therefore obliterates a prop of the conventional chronology.

Have New Saturnian Rings Formed Since the C Ring?

Baum[61] reported "dusky nebulous matter in the form of an additional ring" beyond ring A, with "a diffuse fringe [extending] the ring system beyond its normal limits." Baum may have been seeing one or more of the now-recognized tenuous outer rings (the F, G, and E rings). Alternatively, he may have been seeing dissipation of A ring material outward, and if ring particles "reach the outer edge of the rings, they leave the ring system."[62] Feibelman[63] likewise reported "an extension or at least a gradual tapering of the outer edge of the A ring." Therefore, it appears that the A ring is losing particles to the outer F, G, and E rings, and eventually to space beyond. How trustworthy are such ground-based observations? Dismissing them as subjective phenomena would be premature. Indeed, existence of the F ring had been theorized before the Voyager flybys,[64] though Jeffreys discounted this prediction.

Further, inside the C ring, "the possibility of a faint ring . . . was raised some time ago [from ground-based observations], and this D ring was actually found."[65] Ground-based discovery of the D ring before its Voyager detection shows validity for ground-based ring-spreading observations. Like the outer F, G, and E rings, the D ring seems to be composed of small particles. These particles are spiraling into Saturn: ". . . individual ring particles work their way slowly inward. . . . If they move inward far enough, they encounter the tenuous outer layers of the planet's

61. R. Baum, "On the Observation of the Reported Dusky Ring outside the Bright Rings of the Planet Saturn," *Journal of the British Astronomical Association* 64 (1954): p. 194.

62. Fix, *Astronomy*, p. 274.

63. W. Feibelman, "Concerning the 'D' Ring of Saturn," *Nature* 214 (May 20, 1967): p. 793.

64. H. Jeffreys, "The Effects of Collisions on Saturn's Rings," *Monthly Notices of the Royal Astronomical Society* 107 (1947): p. 267.

65. Snow, *Essentials of the Dynamic Universe*, p. 156; Alexander, *The Planet Saturn*, p. 196–197, 235.

atmosphere and are destroyed."[66] Ring particles of Jupiter and Uranus also show this behavior.[67] To summarize, particles in outer rings dissipate into space; those in innermost rings fall toward the planet.

Efforts to Save Long Ring Chronologies Have Failed

The Uranian and Jovian ring systems were discovered shortly before the Voyager views of Saturn's rings, and according to NASA appeared too young to exist in an old solar system: "The theory that explained how Saturn's rings could persist through 4.6 billion years of solar system evolution also explained why Saturn was the only planet that could have a ring. Then those theories had to be revised to account for the rings of Uranus. The revisions implied that Jupiter would not have a ring. Now Jupiter has been found to have a ring and we have to invent a theory to explain it."[68] The older unworkable theory was the orbital resonance hypothesis.[69]

When Saturn was the only known ringed planet, orbital resonances, due to moons of Saturn gravitationally acting on ring particles, could account for the limited ring structure visible from earth. The resonance hypothesis "had been worked out with fewer than a half-dozen rings [of Saturn] known. The ring structure the Voyagers discovered is too complex to . . . explain thousands of rings."[70] "A thousand rings seemed a monumental problem for theorists. They had run out of resonances long ago."[71] NASA concluded, "No theory has yet been developed that explains how all

---

66. Fix, *Astronomy*, p. 274.

67. Hartmann, *Astronomy*, p. 243; Fix, *Astronomy*, p. 289.

68. M. Tippets, "Voyager Scientists on Dilemma's Horns," *Creation Research Society Quarterly* 16 (December 1979): p. 185.

69. H. Alfvén, "On the Structure of the Saturnian Rings," *Icarus* 8 (1968): p. 75, 76–77.

70. Pasachoff, *Contemporary Astronomy*, p. 430.

71. J. Elliot and R. Kerr, *Rings: Discoveries from Galileo to Voyager* (Cambridge, MA: MIT Press, 1984), p. 137; W. Thompson, "Catastrophic Origins for the Asteroids and the Rings of Saturn," *Creation Research Society Quarterly* 13 (September 1976): p. 84.

three of these planets could have rings for so long" (i.e., 4.6 billion years).[72]

The "shepherd moon hypothesis" was then proposed to give planetary rings a long lifetime. As originally proposed, shepherd moons were supposed to corral ring particles, keeping entire ring systems together over eons.[73] The shepherd moon theory was once used to account for all ring structures of Saturn, Jupiter, and Uranus.[74]

After the Voyager 2 flyby of Uranus's rings in 1986, NASA scientist Bradford Smith stated, "We are assuming [the existence of shepherds], because we don't know any other way to do it [i.e., preserve the rings]."[75] Since then, conventional opinion on the antiquity of planetary rings has changed due to difficulties in the shepherd moon theory. Rings are no longer viewed as debris from the solar nebula with an age of billions of years.[76] Instead, the rings have formed by the fracturing of one or more moons, and therefore must have formed "recently."[77] "Recently," however, is a relative term, and may signify millions of years.[78]

Nevertheless, shepherd moons continue to be presented as reason for the existence of planetary rings.[79] Though ring decay occurs, it is still not acceptable to allow this fact to imply

72. Tippets, "Voyager Scientists," p. 185.

73. Alfvén, "Structure of the Saturnian Rings," p. 77; J. Trulsen, "On the Rings of Saturn," *Astrophysics and Space Science* 17 (1972): p. 333, 335, 336.

74. Hartmann, *Astronomy*, p. 250-251, 263; Goldsmith, *Evolving Universe*, p. 461; Pasachoff, *Contemporary Astronomy*, p. 441.

75. J. Eberhart, "Voyager 2's Uranus: 'Totally Different,'" *Science News* 129 (1986): p. 73.

76. J. Cuzzi, "Ringed Planets — Still Mysterious II," *Sky & Telescope* 69 (January 1985): p. 22.

77. Fix, *Astronomy*, p. 275; M. Podolak, W. Hubbard, and J. Pollack, "Gaseous Accretion and the Formation of Giant Planets," in *Protostars and Planets III*, eds. E.H. Levy and J.I. Lunine (Tucson, AZ: University of Arizona, 1993), p. 1120.

78. Esposito, "Changing Shape of Planetary Rings," p. 15; D. Sobel, "Secrets of the Rings," *Discover* 15 (April 1994): p. 88.

79. Burns et al., "Bejeweled Worlds," p. 70.

a young solar system, and shepherds are invoked to extend a ring's chronology. Therefore, rings must be simultaneously decaying, yet confined by shepherds: "[Planetary rings] tend to spread. . . . Sometimes planetary rings are kept in place by the gravitational force of shepherd moons. Saturn has a very intricate ring system with lots of moons helping to keep its rings together."[80] This is false — "lots" of shepherds have not been found. Another false claim is that the "'shepherding' effect has been found to confine a number of rings in the solar system."[81] Out of hundreds of thousands of ringlets in planetary ring systems, only a few have been found with nearby moonlets interpreted as shepherds. Most notable are the F ring of Saturn, Jupiter's ring system, and Uranus's thick ring. As mentioned above, the last two are now viewed primarily as rapidly decaying, despite putative shepherding effects.

Where Are the Shepherd Moons?

"Shepherd moons" such as Prometheus and Pandora, moons of Saturn near the F ring, have been photographed,[82] but mere existence does not confirm they are acting as shepherds. Further, moons once described as "shepherds" seem to be disintegrating into the ring structure. This is acknowledged for Jupiter and Uranus.[83] During the 1995 Saturn-ring plane crossing, the Hubble Space Telescope looked for new satellites. Two were announced as new in a press release and were designated 1995S1 and 1995S2. They turned out to be the already known moons Atlas and Prometheus. Even more interesting, five other bodies,

---

80. N. Masetti and K. Mukai, "What Keeps Planetary Rings in Place?" [article online] (Goddard Space Flight Center, 2000, accessed April 15, 2005) available from http://imagine.gsfc.nasa.gov/docs/ask_astro/answers/981027a.html.

81. NASA, "Ring Node Glossary" [article online] (Planetary Rings Node, 1997, accessed February 27, 2005) available from http://ringmaster.arc.nasa.gov /glossary.html.

82. A. Rubin, "Exploring Saturn's Rings," *Astronomy* 30 (December 2002): p. 53.

83. Fix, *Astronomy*, p. 270, 289.

1993S3 to S7, were observed, but were later "hypothesized to be shattered moonlets" in the F ring.[84] Conclusion: bodies perceived as "shepherd" moons of Saturn are undergoing disintegration within the ring structure.

Discussing these fragmented satellites, Philip Nicholson of Cornell University said, "[O]ne scenario for the origin of Saturn's ring system is that it is made up of countless fragments from several pulverized moons.... [T]he new objects orbit Saturn near the narrow F ring, which is a dynamic transition zone between the main rings and the larger satellites. [Fragmented moons would eventually] spread around the moon's orbit to form a new ring."[85] Showalter[86] surmised that Saturn's narrow G ring, thought to be composed of very fine dust, may in fact be "the 'decaying corpse' of a moon destroyed by meteoroid impact." Since the F ring is a "dynamic transition zone" where satellite fragmentation is likely to occur, what is the possibility that the so-called "shepherds," Prometheus and Pandora, could be undergoing the same type of dissolution?

A stunning observation answered this question. The reason the previously mentioned satellite 1995S2 was not initially recognized as Prometheus is that its location did not match the position expected. Prometheus had "slipped in its orbit by 20 degrees from the predicted position . . . a consequence of a 'collision' of Prometheus with the F ring, which is believed to have occurred in early 1993."[87] Thus, Prometheus is not so

84. D. Williams, "Saturn Ring Plane Crossing" [article online] (National Aeronautics and Space Administration, 1997, accessed June 20, 2005) available from http://nssdc.gsfc.nasa.gov/planetary/satmoons_pr.html.

85. D. Isbell and R. Villard, "Saturn Moon Mystery Continues: Could Hubble Have Discovered Shattered Satellites?" [article online] (National Aeronautics and Space Administration, 1995, accessed October 5, 2004) available from http://nssdc.gsfc.nasa.gov/planetary/text/satrpx1095.txt.

86. M.R. Showalter, "A Survey of the Narrow Planetary Rings," Eos 73, supplement, 177 [online] (The Planetary Rings Nodes) available from http://ringside.arc.nasa.gov/www/showalter/1992_montreal.html.

87. Isbell and Villard, "Saturn Moon Mystery Continues" [article online].

much "shepherding" the F ring as mutually interacting with it, sometimes colliding with it, and likely disintegrating as a result. It is doubtful that the so-called shepherds of the F ring ever fulfilled that function. In 1980, Voyager 1 detected a twisting or "braiding" in the F ring attributed to Prometheus and Pandora, but Voyager 2 in 1981 detected "no signs of braiding in the F ring."[88] Therefore, the "shepherds" Prometheus and Pandora are not shepherds after all.

Since the F ring is a "dynamic transition zone," it is most likely that Prometheus and Pandora are fragments of larger bodies en route to further disintegration, the same process thought to have produced the moonlets 1995S3 to S7. Prometheus and Pandora are not spherical and have an irregular shape.[89] They seem either to be captured asteroids or fragments of a larger moon. The F ring itself is expected to widen over time, eventually dissipating altogether.[90]

The Voyager missions demolished the belief that planetary rings must be old. The Cassini probe began orbiting Saturn in 2004. What additional evidence is it returning of rapid ring dissolution and youth?

Lunar Recession

According to Genesis 1:14–18, God spoke the moon into existence as a unique celestial body on day 4 of the creation week. Opposing the Genesis account are naturalistic theories of lunar origin: (1) the fission theory (the "spouse" theory), popularized first by George Darwin,[91] son of Charles Darwin;

---

88. Pasachoff, *Contemporary Astronomy*, p. 430; Pollack and Cuzzi, "Rings in the Solar System," p. 119.

89. D. Williams, "Saturnian Satellite Fact Sheet" [online] (National Aeronautics and Space Administration, 1999, accessed November 8, 2004) available from http://nssdc.gsfc.nasa.gov/planetary/factsheet/saturniansatfact.html.

90. JPL, "Chaos Seen in Movement of Ring-Herding Moons of Saturn," [article online] (*Science Daily*, 2002, accessed October 14, 2004) available from http://www.sciencedaily.com/releases/2002/10/ 021014072923.htm.

91. G. Darwin, *The Tides* (Boston, MA: Houghton Mifflin, 1898), p. 278–286.

(2) the capture theory ("daughter" theory); (3) the accretion theory ("sister" theory); and (4) the impact theory. The impact theory is now most favored because the other theories "have serious flaws."[92]

The capture theory has been discredited because of the improbability of earth's capturing an approaching moon-size object. Rather than explaining the origin of the moon itself, this theory merely displaces the problem of lunar origin to an indeterminate point far from earth.

The accretion theory claims that the moon coalesced from debris remaining from the solar nebula in close orbit about the earth. The accretion theory, sometimes called the "double planet theory," says that the earth and the moon formed in tandem from the solar nebula. If this theory were true, the earth and the moon should have similar structure and composition. As might be expected from the creation of the moon as a unique heavenly object, its composition does not match the earth's. Indeed, the accretion theory has been discredited because of difficulty in explaining how debris can coalesce, and also because of the problem of "explaining why the abundance of iron in the earth and the moon is so different."[93]

The fission theory claims that the moon coalesced from debris spinning off the presumably molten earth eons ago. The impact theory claims that a Mars-size asteroid once impacted the earth, with debris being thrown upward by the impact and eventually coalescing into the moon. The fission and impact theories both require that the debris forming the moon begin coalescing at or near earth's Roche limit. The Roche limit is the distance from a central body, such as a planet, inside of which orbiting debris cannot coalesce. The gravitational force of the central body on an orbiting particle is stronger on the particle's near side than on its far side. Within Roche's limit, this differential gravitational force is greater than the particle's own self-gravitation, and particles break apart rather than joining.

---

92. Fix, *Astronomy*, p. 190, 192.

93. Ibid., p. 191; A. Hammond, "Exploring the Solar System III: Whence the Moon," *Science* 186 (November 22, 1974): p. 911.

An artificial satellite can exist within Roche's limit if non-gravitational cohesive forces hold the object together, but once torn apart into smaller pieces, the pieces cannot rejoin. Saturn's rings are evidently fragments of moons once orbiting Saturn. Forces due to collisions, or disruptive forces within the moons, tore the moons apart. Before they fragmented, cohesive forces held the moons together, but once the moons disintegrated, they could not re-form. Similarly, earth's moon could never form inside the Roche limit out of debris due to fission. Even the impact theory leaves moon's origin "still unresolved," and it was adopted "not so much because of the merits of theory as because of the . . . shortcomings of other theories."[94] Lunar origin theories have a history of being accepted with fanfare, then being quietly dropped as unworkable. Indeed, Hartmann[95] quipped, "The moon seems a highly unlikely object. Theoreticians have been led by frustration on more than one occasion to suggest facetiously that it does not exist."[96]

The Moon's Maximum Age Is Less Than 4.6 Billion Years

The moon was never at Roche's limit, but was positioned or "set" in the firmament (Gen. 1:17) at approximately its present distance from earth. The moon is very slowly receding from the earth. Below is computed the time which would hypothetically be required for the moon to recede from Roche's limit to its present position. The recession rate dr/dt of the moon[97] is:

---

94. A. Ruzicka, G. Snyder, and L. Taylor, "Giant Impact and Fission Hypotheses for the Origin of the Moon: A Critical Review of Some Geochemical Evidence," *International Geology Review* 40 (1998): p. 851; J. Lissauer, "It's Not Easy to Make the Moon," *Nature* 389 (September 25, 1997): p. 328.

95. W. Hartmann, *Moons and Planets* (Belmont, CA: Wadsworth, 1972), p. 127.

96. Lissauer, "It's Not Easy to Make the Moon," p. 327.

97. Darwin, *Tides*, p. 274; D. DeYoung, "The Earth-Moon System," in *Proceedings of the Second International Conference on Creationism* (Pittsburgh, PA: Creation Science Fellowship, 1990), 2:81.

$$\frac{dr}{dt} = \frac{k}{r^6} \qquad (1)$$

where r is the semimajor axis of the moon's orbit about the earth, t is time, and k is a proportionality constant. When $t = 0$, $r = r_0$.

To compute the moon's recession time to its present orbit, we first integrate equation (1). Over the time interval 0 to t, the moon's distance from the earth increases from Roche's limit r_0 to its present orbit at distance r. Integrating t and r over these intervals gives:

$$t = \frac{1}{7k} (r^7 - r_0^7) \qquad (2)$$

in which t is the maximum age of the earth-moon system. The present value of r is 3.844×10^8 m. For an object orbiting a planet, Roche's limit r_0 is

$$r_0 = 2.4554 \, R \left[\frac{\rho_p}{\rho_m} \right]^{1/3} \qquad (3)$$

where R is the radius of the central body (the earth in this case); ρp is the density of the central body; and ρm is the density of the orbiting body, in this case the moon.[98] With $R = 6.3781 \times 10^6$ m for the earth; $\rho_p = 5515$ kg/m^3; and $\rho_m = 3340$ kg/m^3, we find that $r_0 = 1.84 \times 10^7$ m. This is less than 5 percent of the moon's current orbital radius.

---

98. J. Whitcomb and D. DeYoung, *The Moon: Its Creation, Form, and Significance* (Winona Lake, IN: BMH Books, 1978), p. 42.

From equation (1), the proportionality constant k is the product of the sixth power of the distance r, and the current recession rate. The present value of the recession rate is 4.4 ± 0.6 cm/yr, or $(4.4 ± 0.6) \times 10^{-2}$ m/yr.[99] Therefore, $k = 1.42 \times 10^{50}$ m⁷/yr. With this value for k, the right hand side of equation 1 equals the present recession rate dr/dt, when r = the moon's current orbital radius.

From equation (2), the time for the moon to recede from r_0 to r is 1.3 billion years. Without introducing tidal parameters, this is the moon's highest allowable evolutionary age, and is similar to DeYoung's[100] estimate. Though long relative to biblical chronology, it is a serious challenge to the belief that the moon is 4.6 billion years old,[101] as Baldwin[102] noted: "Jeffreys' early studies of the effects of tidal friction [the cause of lunar recession] yielded a rough age of the Moon of 4 billion years. . . . Recently, however, Munk and MacDonald have interpreted the observations to indicate that tidal friction is a more important force than had been realized and that it would have taken not more than 1.78 billion years for tidal friction to drive the Moon outward to its present distance from any possible minimum distance. This period of time is so short, compared with the age of the earth, that serious doubts have been cast upon most proposed origins and histories of the moon."

Efforts to Save a Long Lunar Chronology Have Failed

One response to the chronological challenge of recession has been the impact theory, in which lunar material originates within Roche's limit but is quickly ejected beyond it. The impact theory in turn is grounded in an older concept, the "resonance theory," which claims that the moon was never actually at Roche's limit. According to this theory, the moon is currently

99. K. Lang, *Astrophysical Data: Planets and Stars* (Berlin: Springer-Verlag, 1992), p. 31.

100. DeYoung, "Earth-Moon System," p. 82.

101. W. Munk and G. MacDonald, *The Rotation of the Earth* (London: Cambridge University, 1960), p. 202.

102. R. Baldwin, *A Fundamental Survey of the Moon* (New York: McGraw-Hill, 1965), p. 40.

receding, but was once approaching the earth as part of a series of alternating recession/approach events as old as the moon's conventional age.[103] The resonance theory, however, presumes conventional age rather than proving it, so is no support for evolutionary chronology.

Another response has been to minimize the lunar recession rate. The current recession rate is 3.8 cm/yr according to NASA,[104] which is the lower end of the range of lunar recession rates discussed above, and Fix[105] cites a value of only 3 cm/yr. A third response is to employ adjustable tidal parameters to stretch recession chronology into harmony with the conventional solar system lifetime.[106]

Naturalistic lunar origin theories assume the moon to have been once close to the earth. If the moon's distance r had ever been much smaller than presently, equation (1) shows that the recession rate dr/dt "must have been much larger in earlier times."[107] George Darwin stated, "Thus, although the action [rate of lunar recession] may be insensibly slow now, it must have gone on with much greater rapidity when the moon was nearer to us."[108] Using equations 2 and 3 above, together with the conventional age of 4.6 billion years for the earth-moon system, we can compute how far the moon should have receded from Roche's limit over that time. Using $r_0 = 1.84 \times 10^7$ m, $k = 1.42 \times 10^{50}$ m^7/yr, and t = 4.6 x

103. K. Hansen, "Secular Effects of Oceanic Tidal Dissipation on the Moon's Orbit and the Earth's Rotation," *Reviews of Geophysics and Space Physics* 20 (1982): p. 457; S. Brush, "Ghosts from the Nineteenth Century: Creationist Arguments for a Young Earth," in *Scientists Confront Creationism*, ed. L. Godfrey (New York: Norton, 1983), p. 78.

104. D. Williams, "Moon Fact Sheet [online] (National Aeronautics and Space Administration, 2000, accessed January 27, 2005) available from http://nssdc.gsfc.nasa.gov/planetary/factsheet/moonfact.html.

105. Fix, *Astronomy*, p. 182.

106. D. Finch, "The Evolution of the Earth-Moon System," *Moon and Planets* 26 (1982): p. 113–114; G. Dalrymple, *The Age of the Earth* (Stanford, CA: Stanford University, 1991), p. 51–52.

107. J. Verhoogen, *Energetics of the Earth* (Washington, DC: National Academy of Sciences, 1980), p. 22.

108. Darwin, *Tides*, p. 274.

10^9 yr, we find that r = 4.7 x 10^8 m. This is 20 percent higher than the actual distance of the moon from the earth. Conclusion: the earth-moon system cannot be 4.6 billion years old.

The Age of Planetary Heat

The planets did not evolve from a common source, but were individually or "specially" created (as wandering "stars," see Gen. 1:16). Special creation therefore permits the possibility of diversity among the planets, but naturalistic origins theory leads to the expectation of overriding commonalities. One point of diversity involves the heat output of the giant planets — the "Jovian planets" Jupiter, Saturn, Uranus, and Neptune. All planets give back into space the heat they receive from the sun, but most of the giant planets give off much more heat than this. The excess is 67 percent for Jupiter, 78 percent for Saturn, and 170 percent for Neptune.[109]

Naturalistic origins theory envisions solar system development from the solar nebula over 4.6 billion years. As high-energy nebular material collected into planets, planets became molten, and the giant planets, because of their huge size, continue to give off this primordial heat.[110] This theory is questionable.[111] Further, there is no reason to assume that the moon or planets initially had hot interiors.[112] Radiohalo evidence shows that the earth was not molten originally.[113]

---

109. J. Henry, "The Energy Balance of Uranus: Implications for Special Creation," *CEN Technical Journal* 15 (December 2001): p. 87.

110. J. Trefil, *Space Time Infinity* (New York: Pantheon/Smithsonian, 1985), p. 125; Hartmann, *Astronomy*, p. 267; R. Robbins and W. Jeffreys, *Discovering Astronomy* (New York: Wiley, 1988), p. 158.

111. Podolak et al., "Gaseous Accretion and Formation of Giant Planets," p. 1112.

112. H. Urey, "Was the Moon Originally Cold?" *Science* 172 (June 11, 1971): p. 403.

113. R. Gentry, "Fossil Alpha-Recoil Analysis of Variant Radioactive Halos," *Science* 160 (June 14, 1968): p. 1230; R. Gentry, S. Cristy, J. McLaughlin, and J. McHugh, "Ion Microprobe Confirmation of Pb Isotope Ratios and Search for Isomer Precursors in Polonium Radiohalos," *Nature* 244 (August 3, 1973): p. 282; R. Gentry, *Creation's Tiny Mystery* (Knoxville, TN: Earth Science Associates, 1992), p. 29–33.

Other explanations for excess heat are gravitational contraction[114] and separation of materials (phase separation) in planetary interiors. However, models of planetary interiors are "theoretical,"[115] representing conditions that "cannot be replicated in laboratories."[116] The Voyager flybys confirmed that Jupiter is in "strict hydrostatic equilibrium," so cannot be contracting.[117] Since Jupiter is the most massive planet, there is virtual certainty that other giant planets cannot be gravitationally contracting. Jovian "global oscillation" data confirm that phase separation is a minor process if occurring at all,[118] so phase separation is "unlikely."[119] Ouyed and others[120] concur that "gravitational settling by diffusion" cannot "account for Jupiter's excess heat." In summary, "existing models for the jovian interior need to be revised,"[121] and "all the models of Jupiter (and Saturn) . . . are basically incorrect."[122]

Furthermore, the three Jovian planets emitting extra heat cannot have been doing so for 4.6 billion years. Bishop and de Marcus[123] observed that even if Jupiter had begun with an

114. Pasachoff, *Contemporary Astronomy*, p. 417.

115. W.J. Nellis, M. Ross, and N.C. Holmes, "Temperature Measurements of Shock-Compressed Liquid Hydrogen: Implications for the Interior of Jupiter," *Science* 269 (September 1, 1995): p. 1249.

116. R. Ouyed, W. Fundamenski, G. Cripps, and P. Sutherland, "D-D Fusion in the Interior of Jupiter?" *Astrophysical Journal* 501 (1998): p. 368.

117. Hubbard, *Planetary Interiors*, p. 263; Podolak et al., "Gaseous Accretion and Formation of Giant Planets," p. 1114.

118. Nellis et al., "Temperature Measurements of Shock-Compressed Liquid Hydrogen," p. 1251.

119. W. Nellis, "Making Metallic Hydrogen," *Scientific American* 282 (May 2000): p. 89.

120. Ouyed et al., "D-D Fusion," p. 369.

121. A. Alavi, M. Parrinello, and D. Frenkel, "Ab Initio Calculation of the Sound Velocity of Dense Hydrogen: Implications for Models of Jupiter," *Science* 269 (September 1, 1995): p. 1252.

122. T. Guillot, G. Chabrier, D. Gauthier, and P. Moriel, "Effect of Radiative Transport on the Evolution of Jupiter and Saturn," *Astrophysical Journal* 450 (1995): p. 470.

123. E. Bishop and W. de Marcus, "Thermal Histories of Jupiter Models," *Icarus* 12 (1970): p. 317.

unreasonably high surface temperature of 20,000°C when it first formed, the cooling time to its present temperature would have been too brief to satisfy conventional chronology. The reason is that huge convection currents in Jupiter dissipate heat rapidly.[124] Likewise for Saturn, "All cooling calculations to date . . . indicate an age about half the age of the solar system."[125]

Uranus Has Little or No Excess Heat

A more serious difficulty for conventional chronology is Uranus's unique thermal behavior. It gives off little or no excess heat,[126] thus disproving conventional explanations of excess heat output for other giant planets. "Ground-based and spacecraft observations have revealed large excess energy fluxes from Jupiter, Saturn, and Neptune but a very small excess from Uranus," and there may be "no energy excess."[127] Nevertheless, contrary claims exist: "Uranus and Neptune release more energy than they receive from the sun. . . . [T]hey glow with internal heat."[128] This type of claim is false and arises from the expectation that the giant planets have evolved toward a similar condition. Naturalistic origins theory considers Uranus and Neptune to be "sister planets," though thermally speaking, "Uranus and Neptune are different."[129]

124. Hubbard, *Planetary Interiors*, p. 267–268.

125. D. Saumon, W. Hubbard, G. Chabrier, and H. van Horn, "The Role of the Molecular-Metallic Transition of Hydrogen in the Evolution of Jupiter, Saturn, and Brown Dwarfs," *Astrophysical Journal* 391 (1992): p. 828.

126. Podolak et al., "Gaseous Accretion and Formation of Giant Planets," p. 1112, 1113; J. Pearl, B. Conrath, R. Hanel, J. Pirraglia, and A. Coustenis, "The Albedo, Effective Temperature, and Energy Balance of Uranus, As Determined from Voyager IRIS Data," *Icarus* 84 (1990): p. 26, 27.

127. J. Pearl and B. Conrath, "The Albedo, Effective Temperature, and Energy Balance of Neptune, as Determined from Voyager Data," *Journal of Geophysical Research* 96 (supplement, 1991): p. 18,921.

128. Anonymous, "Diamond Hail in Uranus and Neptune," *Sky & Telescope* (April 2000): p. 24.

129. G. Abell, D. Morrison, and S. Wolff, *Exploration of the Universe* (Philadelphia, PA: Saunders, 1987), p. 333.

Before the Voyager 2 flyby of Uranus in 1986, Uranus was assumed to be thermally similar to the other giants, emitting as much as 30 percent excess heat.[130] However, "there has been no evidence of an internal heat source (unlike the other gaseous planets)."[131] Indeed, "Uranus is different from the other giant planets in that it is not radiating a substantial amount of excess internal heat. . . . It is not clear why Uranus has such a low internal heat output compared to the other Jovian planets."[132] Uranus's thermal behavior is a serious challenge to conventional solar system chronology. Its lack of excess heat implies that the conventional heat-producing theory of planetary formation cannot be true, leaving open the possibility that the solar system could be young. "[T]o preserve the billion-year age" of the solar system,[133] Ouyed and others[134] proposed deuterium fusion in the giant planets to produce the excess heat. Ouyed[135] has since acknowledged that this model does not work.

Uranus and Neptune Are Not "Sisters"

Of the Jovian planets, Neptune has the highest ratio of energy emitted to energy absorbed, yet Uranus has the lowest. Until the 1989 Voyager 2 flyby past Neptune, a mixing model explained the thermal differences between Neptune and Uranus. According to this scenario, "Neptune . . . suffered a collision late in its formation that stirred the ice and rock of its interior all the way to the center. That mixing helped break down

130. A. Ingersoll, "Uranus," *Scientific American* 256 (January 1987): p. 39–40.

131. "Uranus: The Seventh Planet" [article online] (Perth Observatory, 2001, accessed January 22, 2005) available from http://www.wa.gov.au/perthobs/hpc2ura.htm.

132. "Uranus" [article online] (Encyclopædia Britannica, 2001, accessed January 22, 2005) available from http://www.britannica.com/bcom/eb/article/printable/2/0,5722,118802,00.html.

133. R. Samec, "The Age of the Jovian Planets," *CEN Technical Journal* 14 (April 2000): p. 3.

134. Ouyed et al., "D-D Fusion," p. 367.

135. R. Ouyed, personal correspondence to the author, May 18, 2001.

the stratification that would otherwise have greatly inhibited the heat-driven vertical circulation that now carries heat to the surface.

"Uranus' late hit, on the other hand, was way off center, as evidenced by the way it is lying on its side. That kind of collision might have failed to stir up the deep interior, leaving its heat largely trapped there. Because the rotation period provides one indication of how well mixed the interior is, a Neptunian day of 17 hours [versus 17.2 hours for Uranus] would have implied just the difference in mixing between the two planets . . . to explain the difference in heat leaking out."[136] This theory was discredited when Voyager 2 found that Neptune's rotational period is only 16 hours, a period too small to imply the mixing which would explain why Neptune radiates significant excess heat but Uranus does not. There is no firm evidence that Uranus suffered the catastrophe this model proposes, and now, "The substantial difference between the energy balance of Uranus and Neptune is still not completely understood."[137]

For Neptune, in addition to Jupiter and Saturn, radioactivity may be a heat source. After all, radioactivity is thought to supply most of the earth's internal heat, though "nobody knows just how much this heat source produces."[138] Knowledge of radioactivity in Neptune is even scarcer. Aside from the thermal difference between Uranus and Neptune, these planets differ from the other Jovian planets in at least six other ways.[139] Rather than being revealed as more like each other, the Jovian planets are emerging as increasingly dissimilar, and Uranus's unique thermal behavior continues as a challenge to conventional chronology.

---

136. Kerr, "Neptune System in Voyager's Afterglow," p. 1450.

137. Pearl and Conrath, "Albedo, Effective Temperature, and Energy Balance of Neptune," p. 18,930.

138. D. Normille, "Experiment Uses Nuclear Plants to Understand Neutrinos," *Science* 284 (April 2, 1999–June 25, 1999): p. 1911.

139. T. Guillot, "Interiors of Giant Planets Inside and Outside the Solar System," *Science* 286 (October–December 1999): p. 74.

Other Challenges to Conventional Chronology

1. Mercury's Atmosphere

Mercury has an atmosphere less than one-trillionth as substantial as earth's. Even this rarified atmosphere should not exist on Mercury after 4.6 billion years, and its discovery by the Mariner 10 probe was a "surprise."[140] At one time this atmosphere, especially the helium gas, was believed to be atoms of "solar wind" captured from the sun.[141] However, hydrogen is the most common element in the sun, whereas on Mercury "the sparsity of detected hydrogen argues against this origin."[142] Mercury's high surface temperatures, peaking at about 430°C (800°F), should have driven its rarified atmosphere away over eons. Conclusion: Mercury is younger than 4.6 billion years.

2. Venus' Heat

Venus has the hottest surface of any planet, but it should have cooled much more over 4.6 billion years.[143] The earliest explanation of Venus' heat was that the substantial Venusian atmosphere blankets the planet, keeping the heat in for eons. However, an atmosphere substantial enough to insulate the planet for so long would exist only if Venus had been so hot originally that "its atmosphere would have been lost" into space, being driven off by the heat.[144] Sagan[145] proposed an atmospheric "greenhouse effect" trapping heat over eons, and this idea was refined into the "runaway" greenhouse concept.[146] However, water is one of the most powerful greenhouse

---

140. Morrow, "Mercury Unveiled," p. 52.

141. B. Murray, "Mercury," *Scientific American* 233 (September 1975): p. 64.

142. N. Short, *Planetary Geology* (Englewood Cliffs, NJ: Prentice-Hall, 1975), p. 289.

143. Anonymous, "The Mystery of Venus' Internal Heat," *New Scientist* 88 (November 13, 1980): p. 437.

144. V. Firsoff, *The Interior Planets* (London: Oliver and Boyd, 1968), p. 103.

145. C. Sagan, "The Surface Temperature of Venus," *Astrophysical Journal* 65 (1960): p. 352.

146. S. Rasool and C. de Bergh, "The Runaway Greenhouse Effect and Accumulation of CO_2 in the Venus Atmosphere," *Nature* 226 (June 13, 1970): p. 1037.

gases, and observations showed "no evidence of water vapor in the lower atmosphere of Venus,"[147] so the Venusian greenhouse was disproved.[148] Venus appears too hot to be old.

3. Mountains of Venus

Venus's average surface temperature is about 460°C (950°F), hotter than the melting point of lead (328°C or 622°F). At this temperature, rocks are not rigid but slightly "plastic." Over billions of years, the crust could not support high mountains, and the mountains could not maintain their steep slopes. However, the Magellan probe found that Venus has fresh-looking mountain slopes and some of the tallest peaks in the solar system, for example, the 26,000-foot (8,000 m) Maat Mons.[149] Of 75 craters mapped, only one showed signs of aging. One theory to account for the lack of expected aging is that recent lava flooding destroyed the old craters, but why would a planet's volcanism turn off so abruptly and completely? When planetary geologists view the Venusian surface, "they see a newborn babe," a surface "too pristine" to be 4.6 billion years old.[150]

4. The Moon's Heat

Based on the idea that the moon started out molten 4.6 billion years ago and has cooled since, opinion used to be that the moon must now be cold throughout.[151] Lunar mapping by the Clementine satellite showed, "Most likely, part of the rock is still molten."[152] Indeed, the first lunar astronauts measured a higher heat

---

147. M. Janssen, R. Hills, D. Thornton, and W. Welch, "Venus: New Microwave Measurements Show No Atmospheric Water Vapor," *Science* 179 (March 9, 1973): p. 994.

148. Short, *Planetary Geology*, p. 284.

149. R. Kerr, "A New Portrait of Venus: Thick-Skinned and Decrepit," *Science* 263 (February 11, 1994): p. 759; Fix, *Astronomy*, p. 214.

150. R. Kerr, "Venus Is Looking Too Pristine," *Science* 250 (November 9, 1990): p. 912.

151. G. Gamow, *A Planet Called Earth* (New York: Bantam Books, 1965), p. 41–42.

152. R. Kerr, "Geophysicists Celebrate Two Satellites, Mourn A Third," *Science* 264 (June 17, 1994): p. 1666.

flow from the moon than expected, indicating "the moon's interior is much hotter than most thermal models had anticipated."[153] Though the moon's heat flow "is 1/3 of that of the earth, [t]his is surprisingly large for such a small body, which should have cooled more rapidly than the larger earth."[154] Radioactive decay of lunar elements could explain this unexpected heat, but such elements have not been detected as required. The straightforward explanation is that the moon has not had time to cool.

5. Transient Lunar Phenomena

A 4.6-billion-year-old moon should be "essentially dead" with no geological activity,[155] and "most scientists have concluded that lunar volcanism has not been possible for some time."[156] Yet through the centuries observers have reported "transient lunar phenomena" (TLP), momentary flashes of light due to eruption of gases.[157] Many TLP have been sighted "near the crater Aristarchus and around the edges of many of the circular maria," showing that the moon "is not completely dormant."[158] Prior to the first Apollo moon landing, NASA concluded "the number of [TLP reporting] errors [was] not high."[159] Conclusion: TLP sightings are genuine and not illusions. Nevertheless, in 1964 when NASA organized a network of amateur lunar observers which reported a TLP in progress, professional opinion was that, "It is far easier to believe that misinterpretations of mundane atmospheric and instrumental effects are responsible" for TLP sightings.[160] But in

153. Short, *Planetary Geology*, p. 184.

154. Fix, *Astronomy*, p. 190.

155. Short, *Planetary Geology*, p. 332.

156. M. Kitt, "Sculpting the Moon," *Astronomy* 15 (February 1987): p. 87.

157. B. Middlehurst, J. Burley, P. Moore, and B. Welther, *Chronological Catalog of Reported Lunar Events* (Washington, DC: NASA, 1968), p. 5–45.

158. Kitt, "Sculpting the Moon," p. 87; Short, *Planetary Geology*, p. 171.

159. B. Middlehurst and P. Moore, "Lunar Transient Phenomena: Topographical Distribution," *Science* 155 (January 27, 1967): p. 449.

160. W. Sheehan and T. Dobbins, "The TLP Myth: A Brief for the Prosecution," *Sky & Telescope* 98 (March 1999): p. 123.

1994, about 100 amateur astronomers noticed a 40-minute darkening near the edge of Aristarchus crater; the Clementine lunar satellite was mapping the area, and Aristarchus had really turned redder after the TLP reported by the amateurs.[161] However, after correcting the Clementine data for lighting geometry and other effects, the evidence for the 1994 TLP faded.[162] Nevertheless, in another reversal, TLP sightings were vindicated in late 1999 when Leonid meteors crashing on the moon were also sighted as flashes of light.[163] TLP observers seem to be observing the activity of a "young" moon.

6. Mountains of the Moon

On an old moon, tall mountains should not have survived. However, in places not visible from earth, the Clementine satellite measured elevation ranges as high as 15.5 miles (25 km).[164] Actually, this "lack of isostatic adjustment" has been known for decades[165] and is characteristic of a young moon.

7. The Asteroid Belt

Asteroids are chunks of rock and dust mostly between the orbits of Mars and Jupiter. Conventional theory says that asteroids are debris that did not coalesce into a planet when the solar system formed. Jupiter's gravitational tug supposedly kept the debris from coalescing. This theory does not really work, and to theorists the asteroid belt is a "problem," with current theory "headed towards the dustbin of history."[166] These difficulties have led theorists to speculate that "asteroid belts might not

---

161. C. Seife, "Moon Mystery Emerges from the X-Files," *New Scientist* 163 (October 23, 1999): p. 22.

162. Anonymous, "Lunar Surface Change: A False Alarm," *Sky & Telescope* (March 2000): p. 22.

163. R. Talcott, "Leonid Meteors Strike the Moon," *Astronomy* 28 (March 2000): p. 30.

164. Kerr, "Geophysicists Celebrate Two Satellites," p. 1666.

165. Short, *Planetary Geology*, p. 73, 75.

166. J. Lissauer and G. Stewart, "Growth of Planets from Planetesimals," in *Protostars and Planets III*, p. 1061, 1080, 1081, 1088.

be a common feature among planetary systems otherwise much like our own."[167]

Even if formation of the primordial asteroid belt could be explained, there is the problem of how a Jovian protoplanet could clear the belt of debris so as to make it appear as it is today. Though the asteroid belt was once more massive,[168] early space age probes showed that it is emptying faster than expected.[169] Opinion used to be that collisions among asteroids are rare, but the 1991 discovery of impact grooves on Gaspra showed that collisions are more frequent than once believed.[170] Asteroidal collisions form dust which spirals into the sun or, in the case of very small particles, is ejected from the solar system.[171] This implies relatively young age for the asteroid belt.

Further, the Yarkovsky effect, a non-gravitational force that sunlight exerts on asteroids, moves them into near-earth orbit faster than had been expected.[172] The maximum expected lifetime of near-earth asteroids is of the order of a million years, after

167. Ibid., p. 1081–1082.

168. C. Chapman and D. Davis, "Asteroidal Collisional Evolution: Evidence for a Much Larger Early Population," *Science* 190 (November 7, 1975): p. 553.

169. Lissauer and Stewart, "Growth of Planets," p. 1081; Robbins and Jeffrey, *Discovering Astronomy*, p. 124; J. Beatty, "'Secret' Impacts Revealed," *Sky & Telescope* 87 (February 1994): p. 26.

170. J. Veverka, P. Thomas, D. Simonelli, M. Belton, M. Carr, C. Chapman, M. Davies, R. Greeley, R. Greenberg, J. Head, K. Klassen, T. Johnson, D. Morrison, and G. Neukum, "Discovery of Grooves on Gaspra," *Icarus* 107 (1994): p. 72; E. Asphaug, "The Small Planets," *Scientific American* 282 (May 2000): p. 53; Hartmann, *Astronomy*, p. 289.

171. M. Kerker, "Movement of Small Particles by Light," *American Scientist* 62 (January–February 1974): p. 97.

172. S. Chesley, S. Ostro, D. Vokrouhlicky, D. Capek, J. Giorgini, M. Nolan, J.L. Margot, A. Hine, L. Benner, and A. Chamberlin, "Direct Detection of the Yarkovsky Effect by Radar Ranging to Asteroid 6489 Golevka," *Science* 302 (October 3, 2003–December 19, 2003): p. 1739, 1741.

which they collide with the sun.[173] This raises doubts that asteroids originated 4.6 billion years ago, 4,600 times more than the near-earth asteroid lifetime. Asteroid "moons" pose an even more serious age constraint. Tidal effects limit the lifetime of an asteroid's moon to about 100,000 years.[174] This fact and the difficulties of "moon" capture led some astronomers to doubt the existence of asteroidal moons.[175] The Galileo probe sighted Ida's moon Dactyl in 1993,[176] confirming this age constraint.

8. Io's Heat

Jupiter's moon Io was believed to be cold and dead before the 1979 flyby of Voyager 1. Then Voyager 1 observed active volcanoes on Io. This was unexpected; Io had been thought "to have an ancient cratered surface much like that of the earth's moon."[177] The volcanism means that Io has lots of internal heat. Tidal-heating accounts for "at most 40% of the estimated heat flow," and this is about 200 times larger than the contribution from radioactivity.[178] There is thus no known source of the heat; apparently Io is losing heat generated at some earlier time. This heat cannot be from the solar nebula, since over 4.6 billion years the accumulated heat would have been lost long ago. The heat accumulation must be recent. This conclusion challenges conventional chronology, since it implies that the internal heat of moons and planets could not have originated 4.6 billion years ago.

173. P. Farinella, Ch. Froeschlé, C. Froeschlé, R. Gonczi, G. Hahn, A. Morbidelli, and G. Valsecchi, "Asteroids Falling into the Sun," *Nature* 371 (September 22, 1994): p. 315.

174. R. Binzel and T. van Flandern, "Minor Planets: The Discovery of Minor Satellites," *Science* 203 (March 2, 1979): p. 905.

175. E. Tedesco, "Binary Asteroids: Evidence for Their Existence from Lightcurves," *Science* 203 (February 23, 1979): p. 905.

176. Asphaug, "Small Planets," p. 51–52.

177. L. Soderblom, "The Galilean Moons of Jupiter," *Scientific American* 242 (January 1980): p. 91.

178. A. Showman and R. Malhotra, "The Galilean Satellites," *Science* 286 (October 1, 1999–December 24, 1999): p. 82, 83.

9. Europa's Heat

Jupiter's moon Europa was believed to be a frozen world until the Voyager views, which showed smooth plains between craters evidently filled in with liquid water from below. Over the conventional time scale, the heat necessary to melt the ice would have disappeared long ago. Tidal heating and "all known mechanisms" fail to account for the heat still present.[179] Conclusion: Europa appears to be young.[180]

10. Ganymede's Magnetic Field

Jupiter's moon Ganymede has a magnetic field, but the core is too hot for permanent magnetism to exist. The field is conventionally theorized to result from a dynamo,[181] but a dynamo requires a very hot interior, and Ganymede is so small it would have cooled in a small fraction of 4.6 billion years. Either (1) Europa is old, cold, has no dynamo, and its magnetic field is from some other (non-dynamo) source; or (2) its magnetism is from a dynamo, which requires that it be hot, and therefore young. The first conclusion violates the conventional dynamo theory of magnetic fields; the second conclusion violates the conventional chronology.[182]

11. Titan's Atmosphere

Saturn's moon Titan has an atmosphere rich in methane gas, CH_4. Methane molecules are large enough that, according to planetary scientist Tobias Owen,[183] Titan's atmosphere "should

---

179. Anonymous, "Cozy Nights," *New Scientist* 162 (June 5, 1999): p. 27; J. Spencer, L. Tamppari, T. Martin, and L. Travis, "Temperatures on Europa from Galileo Photopolarimeter-Radiometer: Nighttime Thermal Anomalies," *Science* 284 (April 2, 1999–June 25, 1999): p. 1514.

180. Showman and Malhotra, "The Galilean Satellites," p. 81; T. Johnson, "The Galileo Mission to Jupiter and Its Moons," *Scientific American* 282 (February 2000): p. 43.

181. G. Sarson, C. Jones, K. Zhang, and G. Schubert, "Magnetoconvection Dynamos and Magnetic Fields of Io and Ganymede," *Science* 276 (April 4, 1997–June 27, 1997): p. 1106.

182. Johnson, "Galileo Mission," p. 47.

183. T. Owen, "Titan," *Scientific American* 266 (February 1982): p. 98.

not have escaped from Titan over the history of the solar system." The Cassini probe flew by Titan in 2004, however, and detected less methane than expected.[184] The methane is not stable, breaking down to produce hydrogen gas which escapes rapidly into space, as confirmed by the Huygens probe which landed on Titan in 2005. In a reversal of his 1982 statement, Owen now states that, were Titan 4.6 billion years old, the methane "would have all disappeared," unless replenished from an internal source.[185] No internal source is known, and Titan appears to be young.

Conclusion

The phenomena discussed herein limit the age of the solar system, and thus of the earth and the universe, to much less than 4.6 billion years. Decay rates for planetary magnetic fields and planetary rings constrain the age to a millennial time frame. Other age-limiting phenomena exist, such as Mercury's youthful surface,[186] Io's magnetic field decay,[187] and Neptune's moon Triton's youthful surface.[188]

---

184. R. Kerr, "Hydrocarbon Seas of Titan Gone Missing," *Science* 306 (October 1, 2004–December 24, 2004): p. 1676; R. Kerr, "Titan, Once a World Apart, Becomes Eerily Familiar," *Science* 307 (January 7, 2005–March 25, 2005): p. 330.

185. J. Leicester, "Methane Rain Falls Hard on Titan's Plains, Scientists Say," *Tampa Tribune*, January 22, 2005, p. 7.

186. Fix, *Astronomy*, p. 202–203.

187. Sarson et al., "Magnetoconvection Dynamos and Magnetic Fields," p. 1106.

188. R. Naeye, "Neptune's Triton a Mere Babe," *Astronomy* 28 (March 2000): p. 33.

Jonathan F. Henry, M.S.Ch.E., Ph.D., earned his doctorate from the University of Kentucky in chemical engineering. He is now chairman of the science division and professor of natural science at Clearwater Christian College in Florida. He became an active creationist after reading Dr. Henry Morris's book, *Many Infallible Proofs*.

In 1987, he began speaking and writing in defense of biblical creation. He has authored *The Astronomy Book* for Master Books, as well as publishing in other outlets, including *Creation Research Society Quarterly, Creation Ex Nihilo Technical Journal, Journal of Creation*, and *Creation Matters*. Jonathan has engaged in debates and conferences in venues such as the Georgia Humanist Society, the Conservative Theological Society, and churches and educators' conventions.

Since 1992, Jonathan and his wife, Sharon, have home-schooled their four children. The two oldest, Faith and David, completed homeschooling through high school, and the two younger, Daniel and Charity, are presently being homeschooled.

CHAPTER 7

EVIDENCE FOR A YOUNG EARTH FROM THE OCEAN AND ATMOSPHERE

Larry Vardiman

The earth was created by God as the most beautiful planet in our solar system. Why? It is because God is a god of beauty and design and He desired to prepare a special home for His highest creature, man. The first Apollo astronauts on the way to the moon peered out the window of their spacecraft and were enthralled by the beauty of the earth framed against the blackness of the heavens. They stated, "Earth is like a Christmas tree ornament hung in space."

What makes the earth so beautiful? The interplay between the light from the sun and the white, blue, green, and brown colors from the earth produce incredible vistas from mountaintops and space. The ocean and atmosphere, the grasses and forests, the mountains and deserts, and the clouds and snow reflect, absorb, and scatter various colors of the rainbow. For example, during the day, blue light is selectively scattered by the atmosphere to form a beautiful, blue canopy of light. The stars are eclipsed and the atmosphere is visible. Nevertheless, at night, only a minor amount of light from the moon and stars is scattered, permitting one to see through the atmosphere to the stars in space. The reflected light from clouds and glaciers contrasts strongly with the blue of the atmosphere and ocean. God has truly given mankind a beautiful place to call home.

However, in today's skeptical culture, in which many deny the existence of God or question His declarations in Scripture that He created the atmosphere on the second day of creation and the ocean on the third day just a few thousand years ago, it is not enough to refer to beauty and design as evidence of His creative power and refer to the Bible as the record of His activities. Many now demand that independent evidence of a recent origin must be gleaned from the ocean and atmosphere directly to validate what Scripture states. Fortunately, a resurgence of quality research grounded on biblical revelation has developed over the last 20 years or so. A number of Ph.D. scientists — with training in the atmosphere and ocean sciences and committed to a young earth — have devoted full- and part-time efforts to understanding processes that reveal estimates of rates and timing. The intent of this chapter is to survey the current status of evidence of a few of the arguments for a young ocean and atmosphere.

Water on the Earth

About two-thirds of the surface of the earth is covered by an ocean of water. The water fills the deepest trenches on earth to about 35,000 feet below sea level. Only the mountains and higher terrain extend above sea level. The amount of water in the ocean is sufficient to cover the entire earth to a depth of about 8,000 feet if the surface of the earth were completely smooth. Earth is unique among the planets of the solar system because it currently exhibits the only liquid water on any planet at the surface. A small amount of water exists on a few of the other planets in either gaseous or frozen form, but only the earth has liquid water. The temperature of the other planets is either too cold or too hot to maintain water in liquid form. Liquid water is necessary for most life processes on the earth and explains why the planet is so fertile. Some of the other planets like Mars may have contained liquid water in the past, as evidenced by erosional features, but this water has either evaporated and escaped to space or is trapped in the crust in frozen form.

Liquid water is a unique substance. It makes life processes possible, it is a universal solvent, it stores large amounts of heat, it absorbs or releases large quantities of heat during phase changes, and it is denser than the solid state. Each of these properties is important, but probably the most significant property for a discussion of the interplay between the ocean and the atmosphere is the massive influence the ocean has on the atmosphere. The ocean's mass is almost 2,500 times greater than that of the atmosphere and its specific heat is about 4 times greater, so the ocean contains approximately 10,000 times more energy than the atmosphere. Consequently, long-term thermodynamic processes in the ocean essentially "drive" those in the atmosphere.

For example, the current concern about *global warming* is focused on changes in the temperature of the atmosphere caused by measured increases in carbon dioxide over the past 50 years approximately. Modeling studies assume the increase in concentration of carbon dioxide since 1958 will lead to an increase in the average global temperature of some 10°F over the next 100 years. Such a large increase in average temperature would be of concern if it were to happen. However, models used to generate this dire prediction assume the increase in carbon dioxide is due to man's activities and that the atmosphere is not coupled to the ocean. Indeed, it is likely that the ocean is releasing a large percentage of the increased concentration of carbon dioxide due to the ocean's ability to dissolve and store carbon dioxide. A very small increase in ocean temperature will release a massive amount of carbon dioxide and overwhelm any variation introduced by industrial processes. Additionally, the ocean will act as a massive thermostat to modulate temperature change in the atmosphere. The ocean is like a giant flywheel in the earth-atmosphere system. Neither of these effects has been seriously considered in the global-warming debate.

A Warmer Ocean in the Past

Nevertheless, there is evidence that the ocean was dramatically warmer in the past than it is today. It is commonly believed that during the Cretaceous Period (some 65 million years ago, according to the conventional evolutionary time frame) the average ocean temperature was much warmer than today — possibly as warm as 100°F on the average. The temperature estimate is based on numerous methods including climate models and various paleothermometers (estimates of historical temperatures from proxy variables). However, the primary justification for this estimate is derived from sea-floor sediment data.[1] Small microscopic organisms called formanifera grow in the ocean and produce calcium carbonate shells (testes) which settle to the ocean floor when the organism dies. The shells contain different ratios of the stable oxygen isotopes ($^{18}O/^{16}O$) depending on the temperature of the ocean in which they grew. Therefore, by analyzing the ratio of these two isotopes as a function of depth in sea-floor sediments an estimate of the average ocean temperature as a function of time can be made.

Unfortunately, the conventional method for estimating how fast sea-floor sediments accumulate ignores the global flood described in Genesis and seriously overestimates the amount of time during which the sediments formed. The conventional method dates the Cretaceous Period at 65 million years and older giving a cooling trend for the average ocean temperature which is extremely slow (i.e., 1.5°F per million years or less). Conversely, if the majority of the sea-floor sediments were assumed to have accumulated following the Genesis flood some 5,000 years ago, the cooling trend would be much faster (i.e., 8°F per thousand years). There is even a hint of more rapid cooling immediately following the Flood, followed by a decline in the cooling rate. The more rapid cooling trend is more realistic than the conventional interpretations because actual cooling trends

---

1. L. Vardiman, *Sea-Floor Sediments and the Age of the Earth*, ICR Technical Monograph (San Diego: Institute for Creation Research, 1996).

typically exhibit an exponentially declining cooling curve as a function of the temperature differential between a hot object and a cold thermal sink. As the temperature difference decreases, the cooling rate decreases, as shown in Figure 1.

Therefore, the evidence for a warmer ocean in the past argues for recent, rapid cooling of young earth. Indeed, the Genesis flood also provides an explanation for why the ocean was warmer during the Cretaceous Period. The warm ocean was a result of heat released during the catastrophic processes of the Flood. If the Genesis flood was as catastrophic as the Genesis account implies and direct geologic evidence supports, tremendous quantities of heat would have been released from all the geologic activity which occurred during the year of the Flood. Hot, molten magma would have been released to form the 40,000-mile long mid-ocean ridges on the ocean floor all around the globe. Continents would have been separated and moved thousands of miles.

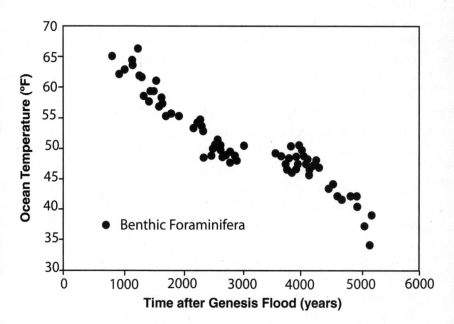

Figure 1. Temperature decrease with time following the Genesis flood derived from $^{18}O/^{16}O$ ratios in the shells of microscopic marine organisms.

Tens of thousands of volcanoes would have erupted. The entire crust of the earth would have been buckled to form mountains, mountain chains, and trenches over the surface of the earth. Hot water would have been released from *the fountains of the great deep* and *the windows of heaven*. The heat from all this geologic work would have been mixed throughout the depth and horizontal extent of the ocean by the water covering *all the high mountains* during the early stages of the Flood and then retreating off the continents at the end. Therefore, the Cretaceous Period would probably have been the result of the catastrophic Flood processes. The conventional model for the Cretaceous Period has no generally accepted explanation for the source of heat that would cause the oceans to be as warm as 100°F.

If the ocean temperature were warmer following the Genesis flood than it is today, as indicated by these data, it is likely that a massive *El Niño* effect would have been present for several thousand years after the Flood. An *El Niño* event is a periodic warming of the ocean along the West Coast of the North and South American continents during which increased evaporation and heat flow from the surface of the ocean into the atmosphere energizes storms traveling across the Pacific onto the continents. The energetic *El Niño* storms produce severe weather along the coasts and redistribute precipitation patterns around the world. More snow typically falls in the mountains and rain falls at lower elevations causing local floods. Typically, *El Niño* events occur today with a periodicity of 7–10 years and produce a warming of the sea-surface temperature by 1–3°F.

Following the Genesis flood, the average ocean temperature may have been initially as warm as 100°F worldwide throughout the depth of the ocean. Of course, this is considerably warmer than the average temperature of about 40°F today. The heat generated by the Flood would have been mixed throughout the ocean from the poles to the equator and from the sea surface to the sea floor. Today the sea-surface temperature only approaches 100°F near the equator. The sea-surface temperature in the polar regions and the water at the bottom of the ocean from the poles to the equator can actually be colder than 32°F because the water is salty and can be cooled below the normal melting temperature of pure ice.

The Ice Age

The current distribution of ocean temperature was produced since the Flood by the movement of hot water at the equator toward the poles, cooling to the atmosphere and space by radiation, sinking to the bottom of the ocean, and moving back toward the equator along the ocean floor. A tremendous quantity of heat was removed from the ocean in this process. Large quantities of water were also evaporated from the warm ocean and transported onto the continents where it was recondensed as rain and snow. The snow preferentially fell in the polar regions and on mountaintops over a period of less than 1,000 years. Glaciers and ice sheets formed quickly in this process, producing the Ice Age, which is conventionally thought to have occurred multiple times and taken about 100,000 years each time. The equivalent of 200–300 feet of water over the entire ocean is believed to have been removed from the ocean to the continents, lowering the average sea level and exposing continental shelves worldwide. Shallow land bridges between Asia and Alaska and between Southeast Asia and Australia were exposed, permitting easier migrations of people and animals from one continent to another following the Flood.

Conventional scientists have proposed dozens of explanations for the cause of the Ice Age, but all of them have excluded the Genesis flood. The explanations vary from a reduction in the solar output of the sun to bursts of meteorite bombardment, increased volcanic activity, to periodic fluctuations in the heating by the sun due to minor changes in orbital parameters. None of the conventional explanations have been successful in fully explaining the Ice Age. A primary reason for this is that none of them have included an adequate explanation for transferring such large quantities of water needed to form the ice sheets from the ocean to the continents under cold, Ice Age conditions. Cold air present during the Ice Age would not have been able to hold sufficient water vapor to produce large amounts of snow and ice. An old adage is often applied by old-timers to the lack of snow on really cold days in the winter: *It is too cold to snow!* A catastrophic solution, which provides a source of water to form snow, is needed to explain the Ice Age. A hot ocean following the Genesis flood solves this problem.

Giant Hurricanes

Surprisingly, a hot ocean also produces another effect which was only recently discovered. Large, intense hurricanes, called *hypercanes*, may have formed during the millenium following the Genesis flood when the sea-surface temperature was very hot. A sea-surface temperature warmer than 90°F is often stated as one of the conditions for a tropical depression to grow into a hurricane. Today, this condition only occurs in the tropics during late summer. The warmer the sea-surface temperature, the faster a tropical storm will intensify and the stronger it will become. Emanuel[2] has proposed that at even higher temperatures a hurricane will continue to grow and intensify into a *hypercane*. The author of this chapter[3] found that for sea-surface temperatures as high as 120°F, *hypercanes* can grow to hundreds of miles in diameter, produce horizontal winds of over 300 miles per hour, vertical winds of 100 miles per hour, and precipitation rates greater than ten inches per hour. Figure 2 shows an example of such a hypercane simulated in the Gulf of Mexico when the ocean surface was artificially maintained at a high temperature.

Hypercanes following the Genesis flood would have contributed to the accumulation of snow and ice in polar regions and on mountaintops and produced massive erosion of the bare unconsolidated landscape of the continents following the Genesis flood. It is because the low-level atmospheric winds which steer a hurricane generally flow from east to west in the tropics, as they do today, most of the erosion would have occurred on the eastern coasts of the continents at low latitudes. Few hurricanes affect the

---

2. K. Emanuel, *Divine Wind: The History and Science of Hurricanes* (New York: Oxford University Press, 2005).

3. L. Vardiman, *Climates before and after the Genesis Flood: Numerical Models and Their Implications,* ICR Technical Monograph (San Diego: Institute for Creation Research, 2001).

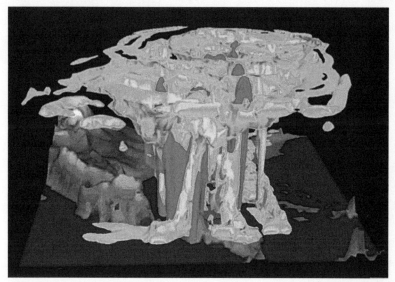

Figure 2. Numerical simulation of a giant hurricane (hypercane) in the Gulf of Mexico which grew when sea-surface temperature was artificially maintained at 120°F.

mid-latitudes today because the oceans are too cold poleward of about 30° latitude. However, immediately after the Flood the oceans would have been hot enough worldwide to support hurricanes and even *hypercanes* for hundreds of years. In mid-latitudes where the low-level winds flow from west to east, the erosional features would have occurred on the western coasts of continents. In high latitudes where the low-level winds also flow from east to west, the erosion would have occurred on the eastern coasts of the continents.

Salt in the Ocean

Temperature changes are not the only window on the history of the ocean. Another piece of evidence arguing for a young ocean relates to the amount of salt it contains and the rate at which it was added. Austin and Humphreys[4] conducted an inventory of

---

4. S.A. Austin and D.R. Humphreys, "The Sea's Missing Salt: A Dilemma for Evolutionists," in *Proceedings of the Second International Conference on Creationism* (Pittsburgh: Creation Science Fellowship, 1990), p. 17–33.

the amount of Na^+ in the ocean (the positive ion from salt) and found that by making assumptions most favorable to an old-age, evolutionary model, such as no initial Na^+, minimum input rates, and maximum output rates, the oldest ocean calculated was 62 million years. Such calculations are almost 75 times less than the 4.5 billion years for the conventional estimated age of the earth. The calculated age can easily be accommodated into a young, creationist model when non-zero initial concentrations of Na^+ and the likely affects of the Genesis flood are considered.

Na^+ is the most common dissolved metal in the ocean. The worldwide delivery of Na^+ to the ocean by rivers has been recognized by scientists for hundreds of years.[5] Until the early 1900s, salt in seawater was thought to be a legitimate method for estimating the age of the earth. However, with the discovery of radioisotope dating, which gives age estimates of 4.5 billion years, the concentration of Na^+ was believed to give an estimate of *residence time* rather than the age of the earth. *Residence time* is the average length of time the sodium ion would survive in the ocean before being removed. This steady state model of salt in the ocean says that Na^+ is removed from the ocean about as fast as it enters, causing the amount of Na^+ in the ocean to remain roughly constant with time.[6]

Austin and Humphreys[7] compared the magnitude of the input and output rates of Na^+ to determine if the model is close to being in steady state. They computed the minimum input from 11 sources of Na^+ to the ocean including rivers, sediments, atmospheric and volcanic dust, glaciers, ground water, and hydrothermal vents, and seven sinks of Na^+ from the ocean including sea spray, cation

5. E. Halley, "A Short Account of the Cause of the Saltness of the Ocean, and of the Several Lakes that Emit No Rivers; with a Proposal, by Help Thereof, to Discover the Age of the World," in *Philosophical Transactions of the Royal Society of London*, 30 vols., ed. H. Oldenburg (London: 1665–1715), 29:296–300.

6. W.W. Rubey, "Geologic History of Seawater: An Attempt to State the Problem," *Bulletin of the Geological Society of America* 62 (1951): p. 1111–1148.

7. Austin and Humphreys, "The Sea's Missing Salt."

exchange, pore water, halite deposition, basalt alteration, and albite and zeolite formation. They found a minimum input rate today of 457 billion Kg/year and a maximum output rate of 122 billion Kg/year. Only 27 percent of the Na^+ going into today's ocean can be accounted for by known output processes. A separate study by Drever and others[8] demonstrated that the negative ion Cl^- is also being added to the ocean at a much faster rate than it is being removed. Therefore, the ocean is not presently in a *steady state* condition and the age of the earth must be less than 62 million years.

A maximum age of 62 million years still seems like an extremely long period of time compared to a biblical age of thousands of years. However, it must be remembered that the study by Austin and Humphreys[9] went to extremes to give the evolutionary time scale the benefit of the doubt. The estimated age still falls far short of the assumed conventional age of the earth. However, if one were to factor in biblical arguments, this number would be reduced significantly, likely down to only thousands of years.

For example, there is no reason to assume the ocean did not already have dissolved salts when it was formed. Many of the fish and other creatures which live in the ocean today require salt water to survive. They would likely have been able to adapt to a more salty environment, but probably not to the level of concentration observed today if it was originally fresh water. Therefore, a major reduction in the estimated age of the ocean could be due to the ocean's initial condition already containing large concentrations of Na^+. There may be methods for estimating the initial concentration of salt in sea water by analyzing fossil fish or other organizations which died during the Genesis flood. Their bodies may exhibit mechanisms or residual evidence of antediluvian conditions. There may also be other techniques for analyzing samples of pre-Flood conditions, such as fluid inclusions in vesicles of pillow lava (vesicles are small glass bubbles formed when magma

8. J.I. Drever, Y.H. Yi, and J.B. Maynard, "Geochemical Cycles: the Continental Crust and the Oceans in Gregor," in *Chemical Cycles in the Evolution of the Earth*, eds. R.M. Garrels, F.T. Mackenzie, and J.B. Maynard (New York: John Wiley, 1988), p. 17–53.

9. Austin and Humphreys, "The Sea's Missing Salt."

cools). Pillow lava formed under water would likely capture small samples of sea water which would have retained the characteristics of the water when it was trapped.

Of even more importance is the likely addition of major quantities of salts during the Genesis flood. If the Flood is as catastrophic as the Bible states, in which *all the high mountains that were under the whole heaven were covered*, it is probable that the Flood would have caused global devastation of unimaginable magnitude. There was no such thing as a calm worldwide Flood. Moreover, the geologic record exhibits evidence for an incredible global catastrophe in which the earth's entire ocean and the crust were involved. About three-fourths of the earth's land surface is covered with sedimentary rock formed during the Genesis flood when material from the crust was pulverized and mixed into the ocean, finally settling to the bottom to form sediments which turned into rock when the water retreated off the land. During the process in which rocks, gravel, sand, and muds rained through the ocean to form sediments on the ocean floor, the ocean was leaching salts and minerals from the materials. Dissolved salts and minerals were left in the water after the Flood contributing to the load of Na^+ and other ions one finds in the ocean today. Therefore, it is easy to understand that the ocean must be much younger than the conventionally assumed age and very likely supports an age of thousands of years, if earth history as recounted in the Bible is taken literally.

Minor Gases in the Atmosphere

Like the ocean, the atmosphere contains evidence of past geophysical processes. Instead of dissolved solids, like the ocean, the atmosphere contains concentrations of minor permanent gases which help one understand past chemical and nuclear processes. The atmosphere is composed mostly of nitrogen ($\sim$78 percent) and oxygen ($\sim$21 percent). It also contains much smaller concentrations of many other chemically active gases, such as carbon dioxide and the noble gases argon ($\sim$1 percent), neon, helium, krypton, and xenon which are inert.[10] These noble gases are

---

10. J.C.G. Walker, *Evolution of the Atmosphere* (New York: Macmillan, 1977).

particularly useful because they do not participate in chemical reactions and their concentrations can help to quantify the types and rates of nuclear processes.

For example, the radioactive element uranium-238 is commonly present in many crustal rocks and forms helium when it disintegrates by nuclear decay. As the helium leaks from the rocks in the crust of the earth it escapes into the atmosphere where its concentration has been used to estimate how long the rocks have been decaying. Helium is a relatively light gas and a small amount can escape earth's gravitational field when it is ionized and accelerate upward by what is called the *polar wind*. For several years before the magnitude of the polar wind was determined, this author reported that the lack of helium in the atmosphere argued for a young earth.[11] Based on the measured and computed escape rate of helium to space in the polar wind, that argument is no longer valid. However, the large concentrations of helium remaining in crustal minerals is still a strong argument. Humphreys[12] has presented an unassailable case that the earth is 6,000 ± 2,000 years based on the residual concentration of helium in zircon grains of granites and the rapid diffusion rate of helium from them.

Another gas that could be used for this calculation is argon; it is produced by the decay of uranium in the rocks of the earth. Argon contributes the largest amount of any of the minor gases to the atmospheric composition; it is also massive enough that it will not escape to space by any conceivable mechanism. Argon's concentration should then be directly related to the amount of nuclear decay in the rocks of the earth. However, quantifying the amount of time based on the amount of argon in the atmosphere has several complexities which make it difficult to use.

---

11. L. Vardiman, *The Age of the Earth's Atmosphere: A Study of the Helium Flux through the Atmosphere*, ICR Technical Monograph (San Diego: Institute for Creation Research, 1990).

12. D.R. Humphreys, "Young Helium Diffusion Age of Zircons Supports Accelerated Nuclear Decay," in *Radioisotopes and the Age of the Earth: Results of a Young Earth Creationist Research Initiative*, eds. L. Vardiman, A.A. Snelling, and E.R. Chaffin (San Diego: Institute for Creation Research, 2005).

First, the rate of escape from the crust to the atmosphere is uncertain. It is because argon is such a massive atom that it is also relatively large compared to other gases like helium. It is harder for such a large atom to diffuse from the crystalline structure in rocks where it is formed and, thus, should have a slower escape rate from the crust. Diffusion rates of argon from various minerals need to be validated. *Second*, this author and others[13] found that nuclear processes in rocks of the earth have been accelerated during episodes in earth history, which make invalid a simple calculation of the age of the earth based only upon the concentration of argon in the atmosphere divided by an assumed constant production rate. The large amount of argon in the atmosphere argues for a large amount of nuclear decay, but not necessarily a long time period. *Third*, like most geochronometers, the problem of the initial concentration of argon needs to be undertaken. Once again, it is not necessary to assume a zero concentration of argon in the atmosphere at its origin.

Conclusions

It is becoming more and more evident that many geophysical arguments from the ocean and atmosphere support a young earth. Indeed, conventional explanations for an old earth must often employ the *petitio principii* fallacy ("begging the question") by special pleading and ignoring conflicting data. Many processes, like heat and salt in the ocean, and helium and argon in the atmosphere, argue directly for a young earth. Some of the estimates for the age of the earth can even be quantified when catastrophic processes revealed in the Bible are considered. Therefore, the age of the earth problem is not so much one of forcing science and the Bible to agree, but rather, one of believing the Bible to establish the proper scientific questions. The future of creation science is bright due to so many highly trained scientists who have confidence in the Bible now working on such problems.

---

13. Vardiman, Snelling, and Chaffin, *Radioisotopes and the Age of the Earth*.

Larry Vardiman, M.S., Ph.D., is professor of atmospheric science at the Graduate School of the Institute for Creation Research, Santee, California. He holds a B.S. in physics from the University of Missouri, a B.S. in meteorology from St. Louis University, and an M.S. and Ph.D. in atmospheric science from Colorado State University. He is a member of the American Meteorological Society and has authored numerous research papers in the area of cloud physics and meteorology.

Chapter 8

The Genesis Flood

John C. Whitcomb

E specially since the publication of *The Genesis Flood* with co-author Dr. Henry M. Morris in 1961,[1] there seems to be an increasing interest in this fascinating topic among Christians worldwide. Is it possible that the vast majority of secular geologists and paleontologists are in deep error concerning the origin and history of this planet? Even more astonishing is the possibility that the majority of Old Testament scholars and theologians have vastly underestimated the magnitude and significance of the Flood described in Genesis 6–9. The present writer has greatly matured in his thinking, by the mercy of God, from being a uniformitarian evolutionist at Princeton University (1942–43), to being a Christian who allowed for millions of years from the original creation in Genesis 1:1 to the situation described in Genesis 1:2 (1943–53), to being a recent-creation global catastrophist (1953 to the present). The positional shifts did not occur without great mental and spiritual struggles.[2]

The ultimate issue of the credibility of the Genesis account of the flood resides, of course, upon the credibility of the words

---

1. J.C. Whitcomb and H.M. Morris, *The Genesis Flood: The Biblical Record and Its Scientific Implications* (Philadelphia: Presbyterian and Reformed Publishing Company, 1961).

2. J.C. Whitcomb, "The Conversion of an Evolutionist" [audiotape] (Indianapolis, IN: Whitcomb Ministries).

of our Lord and Savior, Jesus Christ. He said, "As the days of [Noah] . . . before the flood they were eating and drinking, marrying and giving in marriage, until the day that [Noah] entered into the ark, and knew not until the flood came, and took them all away . . ." (Matt. 24:37–39). Stop a moment and ponder those words. Our Lord said a man named Noah survived *the Flood* by entering *the ark* when *the Flood came, and took them all away.* Could this possibly mean that a regional deluge, which did not need any kind of an ark for Noah to survive, took away only some people? Could it be, as many Christian men of science believe, that all mankind was confined to just one region so a regional flood could indeed take *them all away?* Nevertheless, even in such a highly unlikely scenario (i.e., not one person venturing beyond Mesopotamia or climbing a high hill in 1,656 years!), would *the ark* really be needed? Could not Noah and his family, given even a two-month warning (to say nothing of 120 years!), have escaped a regional flood? Would all birds, mammals, and reptiles in the world have been destroyed by a regional flood (especially since God created the animal kingdom with tremendous ability to migrate, sense danger, and move away from a potentially hostile environment)?

The *sine qua non* is whether the Son of God is a dependable source of information about the Flood. Could He ever deceive people or be deceived? Was He serious when He said, "Heaven and earth shall pass away, but my words shall not pass away" (Matt. 24:35)? He said to the Jews, "But if you believe not his [Moses'] writings, how shall ye believe my words?" (John 5:47). Today, however, Bible-believing Christians are facing new and enormous challenges.

In spite of God's evident blessing upon the biblical and scientific creation movement worldwide,[3] two new movements began to appear in the late 1980s, which were totally opposed

---

3. H. Morris, *History of Modern Creationism*, rev. ed. (Santee, CA: Institute for Creation Research, 1993); J.C. Whitcomb and H.M. Morris, "Fireside Chats" [DVD] (Santee, CA: Institute for Creation Research, 2003) available from Whitcomb Ministries, 6147 Hythe Rd., Indianapolis, IN 46220, (317) 849-2166, www.whitcombministries.org.

to naturalistic Darwinism, but were opposed concurrently to biblical and scientific creationism. From a biblical perspective, this was sadly predictable. The apostle Paul, for example, confronted the church at Corinth with these words: "For there must be also heresies among you, that they which are approved may be made manifest among you" (1 Cor. 11:19). The presence of false teaching can be, in God's mysterious providence, a healthy process. God's people must not adopt a view on ultimate origins solely based on a human authority figure, regardless of brilliance or eloquence. Each Christian needs to be as the Bereans who "received the word with all readiness of mind, and searched the scriptures daily, whether those things were so" (Acts 17:11). Conversely, large numbers of Christians have been deceived into abandoning biblical creationism and catastrophism, thereby reenacting what happened in early 19th century England (even before Darwin).[4]

Progressive Creationism

The first of these movements is called "progressive creationism," represented mainly by Dr. Hugh Ross, a Christian astronomer who founded the ministry "Reasons to Believe." He believes that creation began many billions of years ago with a so-called "big bang." Ross also believes plants and animals were supernaturally and periodically created (not evolved) through millions of years; Adam's rebellion against God did not cause death in the animal kingdom; and the Flood was local in extent. He believes the Bible is fully inspired, but thinks it needs to be reinterpreted in the light of a 67th book which God has now provided for man, namely, modern science.[5]

Dr. Henry M. Morris and others had written numerous books and articles dealing with various objections to biblical and scientific creationism, especially after the publication of the coauthored volume, *The Genesis Flood*. The present author's own effort to pro-

---

4. T. Mortenson, *The Great Turning Point: The Church's Catastrophic Mistake on Geology—Before Darwin* (Green Forest, AR: Master Books, 2004).

5. M.D. Rasche, "The 67th Book of the Bible? The Slippery Slope of Progressive Creationism," *Acts and Facts* 32 (June 2003).

vide a biblical response to 23 leading critics of the concept of the global Flood is found in *The World That Perished*.[6] However, it was not until January 2003 that the Institute for Creation Research in Santee, California, responded thoroughly to "progressive creationism" and to Dr. Hugh Ross particularly. The author was invited to join three scientists and another theologian to participate in eight panel discussions and responses to his published positions. The recordings are available through the Institute for Creation Research in an audio format entitled *After Eden: Understanding Creation, the Curse and the Cross*. The author was especially amazed at the futile effort of the "progressive creationists" to reduce the Flood to a Mesopotamian deluge to justify millions of years of sedimentation and fossilization before the creation of mankind.

Soon after the Institute for Creation Research project, Dr. Jonathan Sarfati wrote a 410-page volume entitled, *Refuting Compromise: A Biblical and Scientific Refutation of "Progressive Creationism" (Billions of Years) As Popularized by Astronomer Hugh Ross*.[7] An entire chapter of his book is devoted to the question of how a global flood best harmonizes the Bible and true science. Another powerful response to the local Flood view has been provided by John Woodmorappe, in his masterpiece, *Noah's Ark: A Feasibility Study*.[8]

The Intelligent Design Movement

The second countermovement is even more amazing to behold. It is called "the intelligent design movement" (IDM), and is dedicated to the proposition that atheistic naturalism and neo-Darwinian evolutionism have completely failed to explain the nearly infinite, irreducible complexity of living things[9] and can

6. J.C. Whitcomb, *The World That Perished*, 3rd rev. ed. (Grand Rapids, MI: Baker, 2005).

7. J. Sarfati, *Refuting Compromise: A Biblical and Scientific Refutation of "Progressive Creationism" (Billions of Years) As Popularized by Astronomer Hugh Ross* (Green Forest, AR: Master Books, 2004).

8. J. Woodmorappe, *Noah's Ark: A Feasibility Study* (El Cajon, CA: Institute for Creation Research, 1996).

9. See M. Behe, *Darwin's Black Box: The Biochemical Challenge to Evolution* (New York: The Free Press, 1996).

be defeated by scientific, philosophical, and rationalistic arguments alone without any appeal to the Bible or to the Creator of the world, our Lord Jesus Christ. Among the most prominent members of this movement are Michael Behe; William Dembski; Michael Denton of New Zealand; Phillip E. Johnson, former professor of law at the University of California, Berkeley; Stephen Meyer; Paul Nelson; Charles B. Thaxton; Jonathan Wells; and Thomas Woodward.

Every true Christian should applaud legitimate efforts to restore sanity and reality to the study of ultimate origins. Our schools, especially, need to be purged of evolutionary perversions presented in the name of "science."[10] Most of the argumentation of IDM books is, to this extent, on target. *The tragedy of the movement*, however, is that it deliberately stops short of honoring God's written revelation on the creation of the world. Donald A. Knapp, former professor at William Tyndale College, added, "and, more seriously, the identity of the 'intelligent' Designer at least in terms of an all-powerful, infinite (to correspond with irreducible complexity), and omniscient personal Being whose attributes must include all elements of personality (wisdom, purpose, sovereign care, etc.)."[11] Indeed, the Book of Genesis as literal history seems to be *an embarrassment* and *an unwanted and unnecessary burden to bear* in the debate with evolution-oriented scientists. Dr. Phillip E. Johnson, considered by many to be the leading spokesman for the movement, while claiming to be a Christian, stated the matter as follows:

> Get the Bible and the Book of Genesis out of the debate, because you do not want to raise the so-called Bible-science dichotomy [which is the heart of the debate]. Phrase the argument in such a way that you can get it heard in the secular academy and in a way that tends to unify the religious dissenters. That means concentrating on, "Do you need a Creator to do the creating, or

---

10. J. Wells, *Icons of Evolution: Science or Myth?* (Washington, DC: Regnery Publishing, 2000).

11. D.A. Knapp, personal correspondence to the author, July 26, 2005.

can nature do it on its own?" and refusing to get side-tracked onto other issues, which people are always trying to do. They'll ask, "What do you think of Noah's flood?" or something like that. Never bite on such questions because they'll lead you into a trackless wasteland and you'll never get out of it.[12]

Indeed, to assert that the universe is the direct result of an Intelligent Designer is *an essential foundation for origins study*. However, it is only the very bottom rung of the ladder that leads upward toward full creation truth. It is vastly insufficient! To honor God fully and to bring genuine light into the enormously important question of how our world began, one must also believe in the divinely inspired account of cosmic and biologic origins in Genesis 1 and 2, including God's record of the magnitude and duration of the Flood in Genesis 6–9. True Christians should be deeply shocked to learn that *the Son of God*, by whom "all things were created that are in heaven and that are on earth" (Col. 1:16), the One "in whom are hidden all the treasures of wisdom and knowledge" (2:3), the ultimate Designer of all life, matter, energy, space, and time *has been practically ignored* by those who write so profoundly and so eloquently of "the intelligent design" of plants, animals, and people.

In response, this author humbly insists that *it is essential to believe the Genesis record of origins in order to please God*. Believing the Genesis record obviously includes *the manner* in which living things were created ("full-grown" with a superficial appearance of history; e.g., Adam and Eve); *the order* in which things were created (e.g., the earth before the sun and moon; trees before marine life; and flying creatures and whales before reptiles and land mammals); and *the duration* of creation events (six 24-hour days only a few thousand years ago). Our Lord explained that Adam and Eve were created "at the beginning" — not billions of years after the earth came into existence (Matt. 19:4). Therefore, it is also essential to believe that *death in the animal kingdom* (and

---

12. "Berkeley's Radical: An Interview with Philip E. Johnson," *Touchstone* 15 (June 2002): p. 41.

massive fossilization) *did not occur before the creation of mankind*, but was *an effect of Adam's rebellion* (Gen. 1:31; see also Rom. 5:12 with 8:20–23). Trillions of fossilized plants and animals throughout the world — in the vast majority of cases — can only be explained in terms of *the global catastrophism of the Genesis flood*.

The Pharisees, of course, believed in a literal creation week and a universal flood. They also accepted the entire Old Testament as being inspired of God. Its acceptance was essential as a foundation of faith, as our Lord repeatedly taught (e.g., Matt. 5:18; 22:29; John 5:46); however, it was not sufficient to please God! Our Lord said to them: "Search the scriptures [i.e., the Old Testament]; for in them ye think ye have eternal life: and they are they which testify of me. And ye will not come to me, that ye might have life" (John 5:39–40). Many Pharisees could quote the entire Hebrew Bible, beginning with Genesis 1:1, but were blind to the Light of the world (8:12–19).

In the creation/evolution debate today, there is a truly frightening element that is sadly neglected and can lead to someone's eternal loss. Our Lord said, "For whosoever shall be ashamed of me and of my words, of him shall the Son of man be ashamed, when he shall come in his own glory, and in his Father's, and of the holy angels" (Luke 9:26; see also Mark 8:38). If one divorces Christ himself from the discussion, how can he truly help people who are walking in the darkness of materialistic evolutionism?

It is granted that discussions and debates concerning intelligent design can (in God's providence) temporarily grasp and hold the attention of unbelieving minds. Nevertheless, *saving faith* can only come through the acceptance of the "living and powerful" Word of God (Heb. 4:12) and its witness to the finished work of Christ upon the cross and His bodily resurrection from the dead (see Rom. 10:9–10). For this reason, the apostle Paul ended his powerful presentation of intelligent design to the Athenian philosophers on Mars Hill by asserting that the true and living God of creation "now commandeth all men every where to repent: because he hath appointed a day, in the which he will judge the world in righteousness by that man whom he hath ordained" (namely Jesus, concerning whom he had been preaching in the marketplace for several days; Acts 17:30–31). He has given assurance of this to all by raising Him from the dead (Acts 17:31). It was because he honored the Lord Jesus in this address that "certain men clave unto him, and believed" (Acts 17:34).

On another occasion, Paul wrote, "For I am not ashamed of the gospel of Christ: for it is the power of God unto salvation to every one that believeth" (Rom. 1:16). Moreover, to the intellectuals at Corinth he declared, "Yea, woe is unto me, if I preach not the gospel!" (1 Cor. 9:16). The burning question, then, that modern proponents of intelligent design must answer is: are people believing in Christ as Lord and Savior and experiencing a profound renewing of the heart/mind as a result of hearing their message?

The apostle Peter did not command each Christian to "be ready always to give an answer to every man that asketh you a reason of the hope that is in you" exclusively through intellectually sophisticated, rationalistic argumentation. To the contrary, he introduced his command with words that are frequently ignored in modern apologetic systems: "but sanctify [set apart, honor, reverence] the Lord God in your hearts" (1 Pet. 3:15). It is, therefore, God's Word, not man's word, which can change unbelievers into believers. "Saving faith," which every human being desperately needs, "cometh by hearing, and hearing by the word of God" (Rom. 10:9, 17). Hearing the Word of God is the only "wedge" that can separate evolutionists from the blindness of sin and bring them to *a full knowledge of Christ the Creator of the world and the only Savior of men* just as this inspired, infallible, and thus inerrant "wedge," authored by the third Person of the triune godhead, did for this author, a former evolutionist at Princeton University 65 years ago.

Consequently, while Dr. Hugh Ross and his followers are attempting to reduce the mountain-covering, year-long Deluge to a local flooding in Mesopotamia, the intelligent design scientists and philosophers officially *ignore* not only the Genesis record of the flood, but also the entire Book of Genesis and the 65 subsequent God-inspired books.[13]

The Framework Hypothesis

At least two other theories (which one trusts will never become "movements") have been proposed by theologians who claim to believe the Bible, but who, at the same time, reject biblical and scientific creationism. One theory, called "the framework hypothesis," has been promoted by Dr. Meredith G. Kline, formerly professor of Old Testament at Westminster Theological Seminary in Philadelphia, Dr. Henri Blocher of France, and others.

The basic thesis of this position is that the seven-day scheme of Genesis 1:1–2:3 is simply *a figurative framework*. Therefore:

> The total picture of God's completing His creative work in a week of days is not to be taken literally. Instead, it functions as a literary structure in which the creative works of God have been narrated in a topical order. The days are like picture frames. Within each day-frame, Moses gives us a snapshot of divine creative activity. Although the creative fiat-fulfillments . . . refer to actual historical events that actually occurred, they are narrated in a nonsequential order within the literary structure or framework of a seven-day week.[14]

13. E. Blievernicht, "The Rhetoric of Design: A Review of *Doubts About Darwin: A History of Intelligent Design* by Thomas Woodward," *TJ* 18 (December 2004): p. 46–47; K. Ham, "AIG's Commentary on the ID (Intelligent Design) Movement" [article online] (Answers in Genesis, August 28, 2002, accessed July 23, 2005) available from http://www.answersingenesis.org/docs2002/0828id.asp; H.M. Morris, "Design Is Not Enough!" *Back to Genesis* 127 (July 1999); T. Mortenson, "Philosophical Naturalism and the Age of the Earth: Are They Related?" *The Master's Seminary Journal* 15 (Spring 2004): p. 71–92; C. Wieland, "AIG's Views on the Intelligent Design Movement" [article online] (Answers in Genesis, August 30, 2002, accessed July 23, 2005) available from http://www.answersingenesis.org/docs2002/0830_IDM.asp; also see, the highly significant correspondence between Henry M. Morris and William Dembski [typescript] (2005) available from the Institute for Creation Research.

14. L. Irons with M.G. Kline, "The Framework View," in *The Genesis Debate: Three Views on the Days of Creation*, ed. D.G. Hagopian (Mission Viejo, CA: Crux Press, 2001), p. 219.

Consequently, according to this theory, Genesis 1–2 gives no indication as to the timing or order of creation events! In response, J. Ligon Duncan III and David W. Hall, two Reformed theologians, concurred, "this view is curiously selective . . . incorrect, eccentric, and thinly supported. . . . Never before in the history of the Christian church has this denial [of the timing, duration, and order of the actual creation] been so comprehensively stated. . . ."[15] Duncan and Hall concluded:

> If the crowning glory of the framework view is that it "liberates" the text from apologetical and harmonistic considerations to speak to these theological matters, then . . . it does so at an enormous cost. This is the fundamental problem with the whole approach. The exegetical discussion is just a sideshow compared to the real issue. The framework hypothesis gets rid of a perceived apologetical problem by denying that the Genesis protology speaks to cosmogony or chronology. But in the end, the hypothesis buys us far more difficult and momentous theological questions about the perspicuity of Scripture, the historicity of Genesis 1–11, and most significantly, the goodness of the original creation and the causal connection between sin and death in the created order. . . . *Thus, many evangelicals who favor figurative interpretations of Genesis 1-2* (including many framework proponents) *also argue for a limited flood that only appeared to be universal.* . . . In the end, this approach seriously endangers our ability to honestly claim that we hold to the historicity of Scripture.[16]

The Divine Accommodation Theory

One more opposing theory needs to be mentioned: "the divine accommodation theory" of Paul H. Seely, as defended in an article

---

15. J.L. Duncan and D.W. Hall, "The 24-Hour Response," in *Genesis Debate*, p. 257–59.

16. Ibid., p. 263–64. See also the strong refutation of the "framework hypothesis" by D.F. Kelly, *Creation and Change: Genesis 1:1–2:4 in the Light of Changing Scientific Paradigms* (Great Britain: Christian Focus Publications, 1997), p. 107.

for *Westminster Theological Journal*.[17] Seely, who has been identified as "an independent scholar specializing in biblical history and the relationship of science to Scripture,"[18] rejects both the local flood view and the global flood view! He wrote, "Both camps believe they are following the description of the Flood given in the Bible. As we shall see, however, neither camp is completely following the biblical description of the Flood, and both fail to harmonize the account with modern science. A third approach is needed."[19]

What, then, is this "third approach"? Seely argued that Genesis 6–9 presents a universal flood but not a global flood! "The biblical account is not describing a flood limited to Mesopotamia or to an area as small as the Black Sea, but rather one that covered the entire earth as it was then conceived, the area we might now call the greater Near East."[20] However, if the Flood was that enormous, why could it not have been global? It is because "glaciology and geology agree that there was no global flood at any time in the last 100,000 years and more. Geology, glaciology, and archaeology thus falsify the extent of the Flood as it is described in Genesis 6–9."[21]

Seely, like many secular scientists, has evidently made an idol of geologic uniformitarianism. How does he know, for example, that an ice core from Greenland shows "annual layers going back tens of thousands of years"?[22] Is he aware of the fact that many layers could have been formed in one year?[23] In his book *Frozen in Time: The Woolly Mammoth, the Ice Age, and the Bible*,[24] Michael

---

17. P.H. Seely, "Noah's Flood: Its Date, Extent, and Divine Accommodation," *Westminster Theological Journal* 66 (Fall 2004): p. 291–311.

18. Ibid., p. 291.

19. Ibid.

20. Ibid., p. 298.

21. Ibid., p. 303.

22. Ibid., p. 299.

23. M.J. Oard, "Ice Cores vs the Flood," *TJ* 18 (August 2004): p. 58–61; also see previous issues dealing with this question: *TJ* 15 (December 2001) and *TJ* 16 (April 2002).

24. M. Oard, *Frozen in Time: The Woolly Mammoth, the Ice Age, and the Bible* (Green Forest, AR: Master Books), 2004.

Oard demonstrated that "uniformitarian scientists may be counting 100 layers that they think are annual. These layers in the creationism model may represent only one year."[25] Even today, since the end of the Ice Age:

> The precipitation of the southeast Greenland ice sheet is surprisingly high. During World War II, six P-38 Lightning fighters and two B-17 Flying Fortress aircraft were forced to ditch [in that region]. A team went back to recover them in the late 1980s and discovered that the planes were buried under 260 feet (80 m) of ice and snow that had accumulated since 1942! . . . Such high precipitation . . . gives us a hint of the possibilities when the ice sheet was much lower and the climate much different in the Ice Age.[26]

So much, then, for Seely's claim that the Flood could not have covered the entire globe because of Greenland's ice core measurements. His deep commitment to radiometric dating schemes (carbon-14, etc.), which is informed by uniformitarian perspectives, have also been totally invalidated by the R.A.T.E. (Radioisotopes and the Age of the Earth) team of the Institute for Creation Research.[27]

Seely concluded, "The Flood account is not trying to educate the Israelites scientifically, but is accommodated to their prior scientific understanding."[28] However, Seely hastily assured his readers, "This does not mean that the story of the Flood is a myth. A comparison to the Mesopotamian accounts of the same flood shows that Genesis 6–9 is a-mythological if not anti-mythological. Nor does it mean that the story is just fiction." By now evangelical readers (including the present writer) are surely in a state of shock. However, the final attack to the historical

---

25. Ibid., 123.

26. Ibid., 125.

27. D. DeYoung, *Thousands . . . Not Billions: Challenging an Icon of Evolution Questioning the Age of the Earth* (Green Forest, AR: Master Books, 2005).

28. Seely, "Noah's Flood," 311.

truth of Scripture follows: "The biblical account is divinely accommodated to and integrally intertwined with the science of the times, and that accommodation to outdated science prevents it from ever being completely harmonized with modern science. Its purpose is not to teach history but theology. . . ."[29] Donald Knapp responded and asked:

> Where have we heard that theory before, that is, accommodation to the terminology and "understanding" of those living at the time? It has taken many forms in Bernard Ramm's book dealing with creation theories such as Concordism, Religious Only, etc. How long will it be before the endless procession of pseudo-scientific unbelief comes to a crashing halt?[30]

Anyone who consistently follows Seely's line of reasoning will inevitably question the historicity of the Tower of Babel judgment, the plagues in Egypt, the crossing of the Red Sea and the Jordan, and all other biblical miracles including the resurrection of our Lord Jesus Christ from the dead on the third day (see Paul's devastating argument in 1 Cor. 15:12–19 against those who believed in Christ's "resurrection" but denied that He literally and physically arose from the dead).

If the Bible "does not teach history but theology," then what kind of theology does it teach? All biblical theology is based upon actual events that God has accomplished in a real world with real angels, real people, real animals, and in real time. Our Lord put it bluntly: "If I have told you earthly things, and ye believe not, how shall ye believe, if I tell you of heavenly things?" (John 3:12). If *the history* one finds in Genesis 1–11 is not believable, how can *the theology* of Genesis be credible or even understandable? This colossal theological blunder has characterized the thinking of all liberal and neo-orthodox theologians for generations, and it is astonishing that *Westminster Theological Journal*, which claims to be an evangelical journal, would publish such an article.

---

29. Ibid.

30. Knapp, personal correspondence, 2005.

Do the opening chapters of the Bible describe real events? Dr. Walter C. Kaiser observed that in the first 11 chapters of Genesis:

> There are sixty-four geographical terms, eighty-eight personal names, forty-eight generic names and at least twenty-one identifiable cultural items (such as gold, bdellium, onyx, brass, iron, gopher wood, bitumen, mortar, brick, stone, harp, pipe, cities, towers). The significance of this list may be seen by comparing it, for example, with "the paucity of references in the Koran. The single tenth chapter of Genesis has five times more geographical data of importance than the whole of the Koran." Every one of these items presents us with the possibility of establishing the reliability of our author. The content runs head on into a description of the real world rather than recounting events belonging to another world or level of reality.[31]

The author's first encounter with Paul Seely was in 1994, when Seely sent to him a 29-page paper, "The Geographical Extent of Noah's Flood: An Answer to Whitcomb and Morris," requesting a response within one month. The response was provided on 15 September 1994. Seely sent the same paper to Dr. John R. Meyer, who was the director of the Van Andel Research Center in Chino Valley, Arizona. Dr. Meyer's five-page response was outstanding.[32] Dr. Meyer and this author found it difficult to regard Paul Seely seriously, for he had written earlier that the effort of Henry Morris and this author to interpret the Genesis record at face value "spreads like a giant cancer . . . making its obscurantism result in disillusionment, debacle, and spiritual death."[33]

---

31. W.C. Kaiser, "The Literary Form of Genesis 1–11," in *New Perspectives on the Old Testament*, ed. J.B. Payne (Waco, TX: Word, 1970), p. 59.

32. J.R. Meyer, personal correspondence to P.H. Seely, 1994 (available from Whitcomb Ministries).

33. P.H. Seely, "Rebuttal 'Adam and Anthropology,'" *Journal of the American Scientific Affiliation* 23 (March 1971): p. 26; see full quote in Whitcomb, *The World That Perished*, p. 136.

Conclusion

One theologian/scientist has written an entire Master of Theology thesis examining the argumentation of *The Genesis Flood*. He demonstrated that some of the arguments in support of a global flood are weaker than others, and confirmed what was stated emphatically in the book, namely, that the work was neither complete nor perfect(!).[34] Nevertheless, he concluded[35] that the strongest biblical evidences for a global flood are: "(1) great depth [Gen. 7:19–20] implies universality by hydrodynamic equilibrium; (2) great ark size [1,396,000 cubic feet] indicates a complete cross-section of living beings were to be saved, strongly implying global destruction; and (3) apostolic [biblical] interpretation in 2 Peter 3:5–7 confirms this exegesis [see his exegetical analysis of this passage in the thesis]."[36] "Unfortunately" he sadly observed, "there has been no interaction with any of these arguments by critics of *The Genesis Flood*."[37]

The final words of Charles Clough's thesis are as follows: "*The Genesis Flood*, it is concluded, presents the most influential case within contemporary [Christian] apologetics for traditional exegesis in the face of modern historical science. It offers to evangelicals as thorough a challenge to their historical thinking as *The Origin of Species* did a century ago."[38]

Even though *The Genesis Flood* was neither complete nor perfect, God has apparently used the book to help thousands of His people around the world take the Bible more seriously in the realms of creationism and catastrophism. It does not require great skills in biblical hermeneutics, exegesis, and theology to understand God's message concerning the depth, extent, and significance of the Flood. Not only has He given the overwhelming and repeated statements of Genesis 6–9, and the specific words of the

---

34. C.A. Clough, "A Calm Appraisal of *The Genesis Flood*" (unpublished Th.M. thesis, Dallas Theological Seminary, 1968).

35. Ibid., p. 67.

36. Ibid., p. 56–57.

37. Ibid., p. 48, 170.

38. Ibid., p. 171.

Lord Jesus Christ in Matthew 24 and Luke 17, and the clear explanation of the apostle Peter (2 Pet. 3:3–7), but also the insights of Job 38:8–11, Psalm 29:10, Psalm 104:6–9, Isaiah 54:9–10, Jeremiah 5:22, Hebrews 11:7, and 1 Peter 3:18–20.[39]

Biblical catastrophism, in the final analysis, stands firmly upon the foundation of divine revelation in Scripture, not on the ever-changing theories of men. By the grace of God, then, may all Christians build their lives and their destinies upon Him, *by the word of God, which liveth and abideth for ever* (1 Pet. 1:23).

---

39. See index in Whitcomb, *The World That Perished*, for discussions of these passages.

John C. Whitcomb, Th.M., Th.D., is president of Whitcomb Ministries, Inc. and founder and professor of Christian Workman Schools of Theology.

Dr. Whitcomb has been a professor of Old Testament and theology for more than 50 years, and is widely recognized as a leading biblical scholar. He taught at Grace Theological Seminary in Winona Lake, Indiana, from 1951–1990, and gained much recognition for his work on *The Genesis Flood* (Presbyterian and Reformed Publishing Co.), which he co-authored with Dr. Henry Morris in 1961. This book has been credited as one of the major catalysts for the modern biblical creationism movement.

Among Dr. Whitcomb's other published works are *The Early Earth* and *The World That Perished* (Baker Book House), and commentaries on Esther and Daniel (Moody Press). Additionally, he has authored six comprehensive Bible charts, numerous multimedia slides, and many biblical and theological articles. Major emphases in his teaching have been biblical creationism, dispensational theology, premillennial eschatology, and presuppositional apologetics.

Dr. Whitcomb's life and ministry may be summed up in this quotation: "I want to be in the full-time business of finding out what God says and telling as many people as I can."

CHAPTER 9

NEOCREATIONISM: A MORE ACCEPTED CREATIONISM?

Henry M. Morris

Creationism is being fitted for new clothes today by a number of very articulate writers and speakers, and it is hoped by many that this will help it gain acceptance in the elite company of academics who have heretofore opposed it. One leader of the opposition to any form of creationism, Dr. Eugenie C. Scott, executive director of the National Center for Science Education, calls this development neocreationism.

Phrases like "intelligent design theory," "abrupt appearance theory," "evidence against evolution," and the like, have sprung up, although the content of many of the arguments is familiar. This view can be called "neocreationism."[1]

Scott noted that the arguments for neocreationism are the same arguments that have been used by traditional creationists for many years. The new clothing is not so much what has been added, but what has been removed.

---

1. E.C. Scott, "Creationists and the Pope's Statement," *Quarterly Review of Biology* 72 (December 1997): p. 403.

> Neocreationists are by no means identical to their predecessors, however.... Neither biblical creationists nor theistic evolutionists. . . . Most of them are "progressive creationists."[2]

This new creationism is really not very new, except perhaps for the terminology. Progressive creationists, in addition to traditional creationists, have been documenting intelligent design (that is, the magnificently organized complexity of every living creature) and "abrupt appearance" (that is, the complete absence of any true transitional forms in the fossil record) for well over 150 years.

However, note what is missing. The neocreationists are not "biblical creationists," Scott said. They may believe that the Bible is the Word of God, but they assume its testimony is irrelevant to their arguments. As Nancy Pearcey said:

> Design theory is also redefining the public school debate. At issue is not the details of evolution versus the details of Genesis; it's the stark, fundamental claim that life is the product of impersonal forces against the claim that it is the creation of an intelligent agent.[3]

Now, this approach is not really new, either. During the past quarter century, the Institute for Creation Research scientists have participated in well over 300 creation/evolution debates with university professors on college and university campuses, and each debate is intentionally framed to deal only with the scientific evidences, never with "the details of Genesis." Other creation lectures have been given on hundreds of campuses and scientific meetings with the same format, dealing only with science.

Indeed, Institute for Creation Research has also published a number of books[4] that present the case for creation strictly from a scientific perspective with no reference to religion. These debates

---

2. Ibid.

3. N. Pearcey, "Debunking Darwin," *World* 11 (March 1, 1997): p. 14.

4. The most recent of these is *Science and Creation*, vol. 2, in *The Modern Creation Trilogy*, H.M. Morris and J.D. Morris (Green Forest, AR: Master Books, 1996).

and books have been successful in winning many individual scientists and others to belief in creation, and frequently as a tool in winning them eventually to saving faith in Christ.

However, what it will not do is displace evolutionism as the reigning paradigm in the intellectual community. One form or another of evolutionism, either atheistic or pantheistic, has been the reigning paradigm in every age since the beginning of human history (with one exception), and the prophetic Scriptures indicate that it will still be so when the Lord Jesus Christ returns at the end of this age to establish His own eternal kingdom.[5] The one exception consists of those small communities in many different nations and times who have believed in a personal Creator God who created all things, and who has revealed His purposes in creation and redemption through His written Word, the Holy Scriptures.

In more modern times, William Paley popularized the design argument with his great book *Natural Theology*, first published in 1802, profoundly influencing the English-speaking world of his day — even including Charles Darwin! The book began with a detailed description of the "irreducible complexity" of a functioning watch, noting that even the most rabid skeptic would acknowledge that the watch — or at least its prototype — must have been designed and made by a skilled watchmaker. Just so, he argued persuasively, the much more complex universe required a universe-maker. These themes of intelligent design are compellingly developed at great length in Paley's 402-page book.

Darwin, however, wanted to find a way to escape Paley's conclusion, not for scientific reasons, but because he refused to accept a God who would condemn unbelievers like his father to hell.[6] Many modern Darwinians now follow him in maintaining that what appear to be evidences of design can also be explained by natural selection.

---

5. For documented evidence of the age-long, worldwide dominance of evolutionism, see H.M. Morris, *The Long War Against God* (Grand Rapids, MI: Baker Book House, 1989).

6. C. Darwin, *Autobiography*, ed. Nora Barlow (New York: Norton, 1969), p. 87.

Richard Dawkins, professor of zoology at Oxford University, is the most articulate present-day advocate of neo-Darwinism, which maintains that evolution proceeds gradually through the preservation of small beneficial mutations by natural selection. Dawkins, a doctrinaire atheist, has published an influential book called *The Blind Watchmaker*. Dawkins comes down hard on "fundamentalist creationists" but even harder on modern anti-Darwinists who try to insert God somehow into the "science" of origins.

This author supposes it is gratifying to have the pope as an ally in the struggle against fundamentalist creationism. It is certainly amusing to see the rug pulled out from under the feet of Catholic creationists such as Michael Behe. Even so, given a choice between honest to goodness fundamentalism on the one hand, and the obscurantist, disingenuous doublethink of the Roman Catholic Church on the other, this author knows which he prefers.[7]

Dawkins gloats over the fact that Pope John Paul II is an evolutionist,[8] but he is also impatient with the pope's insistence that the human soul has been "created." Everything, according to Dawkins and the modern neo-Darwinians, is attributable solely to the action of time and chance on matter, so that what appears to be evidence of design is really evidence of the creative power of random mutation and natural selection. Although Dawkins calls Behe a creationist, Behe himself claimed to be an anti-Darwinian evolutionist.

More and more evolutionary biologists these days, indeed, are rejecting neo-Darwinism, acknowledging that the gaps in the fossil record (which have repeatedly been emphasized by

7. R. Dawkins, "Obscurantism to the Rescue," *Quarterly Review of Biology* 72 (December 1997): p. 399.

8. Ever since the publication of Pope John Paul II's October 1996 message on evolution, there has been controversy over what he actually said. The actual official English translation of his speech appeared in the October 30 edition of *L'Osservatore Romano*, and it does indeed affirm that he said, "the theory of evolution is more than a hypothesis" (Catholic News Service, November 19, 1996). He also spoke of "several theories of evolution," but by this he was referring mainly to the "materialist, reductionist, and spiritualist interpretations."

creationists ever since Darwin's day, especially by the scientists representing the creation revival of the past four decades) make gradual evolution very hard to defend. Very few of these (if any) are becoming creationists, however — not even neo-creationists. The evidence of "abrupt appearance" is interpreted by them as "punctuations" in the "equilibrium" of the natural world. The increasing complexity of organisms in so-called evolutionary history is not interpreted as coming from intelligent design but as order emerging from chaos, probably by the mechanism of so-called "dissipative structures."[9]

Other evolutionists recognize that there is, indeed, evidence of intelligent design in the world, but they take it as evidence of Gaia (the Greek earth goddess, or Mother Nature) or of some "cosmic consciousness." This New Age movement is essentially a return to ancient evolutionary pantheism, a complex of religions now growing with amazing rapidity all over the world. Therefore, Darwinians interpret the evidence of design in nature as natural selection, punctuationists interpret it as order through the chaos of dissipative structures, and New Age evolutionists interpret it as the intelligence of Mother Earth.

Getting people to believe in "intelligent design" is, therefore, neither new nor sufficient. People of almost every religion (except atheism) already believe in it. The only ones who do not, the atheists, have rejected it in full awareness of all the innumerable evidences of design in the world. These cannot be won by intellectual argument, no matter how compelling. As Isaac Asimov said, "Emotionally, I am an atheist. I don't have the evidence to prove that God doesn't exist, but I so strongly suspect he doesn't that I don't want to waste my time."[10]

King David, by divine inspiration, had a comment on the attitude of such atheists: "The fool hath said in his heart, There is no God" (Ps. 14:1; see also Ps. 53:1). Similarly, in Romans 1:21–22, the apostle Paul, discussing such people, said, "Because that,

9. H.M. Morris, "Can Order Come Out of Chaos?" *Back to Genesis* 102 (June 1997).

10. I. Asimov, Interview by P. Kurtz: "An Interview with Isaac Asimov on Science and the Bible," *Free Inquiry* 2 (Spring 1982): p. 9.

when they knew God, they glorified him not as God, neither were thankful; but became vain in their imaginations, and their foolish heart was darkened. Professing themselves to be wise, they became fools."

This is strong language, and "design theorists" might recoil from using it, especially concerning their own academic colleagues, but it was God who said it! And intellectual fools are not won by intellectual arguments; if they are changed at all, it will be through some traumatic experience brought about by the Holy Spirit in answer to prayer.

Such Scriptures are speaking of those who are atheists "in their hearts." Like Asimov (and Dawkins and others), they are "emotional" atheists who have tried to ignore or subvert the real evidence with the pseudo-science of evolutionary speculation. There are, conversly, many "reluctant atheists" — those who have been so influenced by the doctrinaire atheists among their teachers and other intellectuals, that they feel they cannot believe in the God of the Bible even though, in their hearts, they would like to believe.

People like this can be reached by sound evidence and reasoning. In our debates, for example, we know from many personal testimonies that a good number of students and young professionals in the audiences who had felt they had no choice but atheistic evolutionism, have indeed been won to solid creationism and soon to saving faith in Christ, at least in part by the scientific evidence. We hope this will be the experience of those who are now stressing "intelligent design," just as has often been true in the past.

However, it will not be so if they stop with just the evidence for design and leave the Designer — the God of the Bible — out of it. Even though we intentionally limit our debates (and some of our books) to the scientific evidence, everyone in the audience and among our readers is well aware that we are really undergirding biblical creationism (including recent creation and the global flood), because that is the clearly stated position of the Institute for Creation Research.

However, modern "intelligent design theorists" intentionally emphasize that, while they oppose materialism and Darwinian evolutionism, they are not arguing for biblical creationism. At a conference on what was called "Mere Creation," held at Biola University in November 1996, the main speaker, Phillip E. Johnson, said in his concluding remarks:

> For the present, I recommend that we also put the Biblical issues to one side. The last thing we should want to do, or seem to want to do, is to threaten the freedom of scientific inquiry. Bringing the Bible anywhere near this issue . . . closes minds instead of opening them.[11]

In a widely reprinted article, a *New York Times* writer said, "These new creationists avoid one pitfall of their predecessors by not positing, at least publicly, the identity of the creator. 'My decision is simply to put it off,' Mr. Johnson said, 'and I recommend that to others.'"[12]

Now that may be all right as a temporary agreed-on constraint for a particular discussion — as in one of our scientific debates. However, that cannot be the goal, and we need to be honest about this if we really believe the Bible to be the word of God. The innumerable evidences of intelligent design in nature really do not point to theistic evolution or dissipative structures or Gaia, but if we stop our program without arriving at the true God of the Bible as the Creator of all things, then many converts to "design" will gravitate to one of these other beliefs and never come to know Jesus Christ as their Savior.

As faith without works is dead, so is design without the Designer!

---

11. P.E. Johnson, "Separating Materialist Philosophy from Science," *The Real Issue* 15 (November–December 1996). The "Mere Creation" conference involved over a hundred participants, practically all of whom were either theistic evolutionists or progressive creationists. According to E. Scott, "most of them have appointments at secular institutions" (Scott, "Creationists and the Pope's Statement," p. 403).

12. L. Goodstein, "New Light for Creationism," *New York Times* (December 21, 1997).

The Vital Importance of Believing in Recent Creation

Those of us who still believe not only that the Bible is the inerrant Word of God, but also that God intended it to be understood by ordinary people (not just by scholarly specialists in science or theology) have been labeled "young-earth creationists."

We did not choose that name for ourselves, but it is true that, since we believe that God is capable of saying what He means and means what He says, we have to believe that the whole creation is far younger than evolutionists can accept.

It would be much more comfortable for us *not* to believe in a young earth, of course. Not only are the entire scientific and educational establishments committed to "old-earth evolutionism," but so also are the supposedly more intellectual segments of the religious world. The seminaries and colleges of the so-called mainline denominations have almost all capitulated to "theistic evolutionism," and most evangelical colleges and seminaries espouse "old-earth creationism," or what many call "progressive creationism."

So "young-earth creationism" is not a comfortable position to hold, especially for scientists or ambitious students, and it would be tempting either to give it up (as many have, under the persuasive influence of such winsome speakers as Hugh Ross, Robert Gange, and other popular evangelicals) or else just to say it really does not matter how or when God created (as do most modern churches and para-church organizations), as long as we believe that He is our Creator.

But it *does* matter, and that is why Institute for Creation Research was formed in the first place almost 40 years ago. Our very statement of faith specifies this position. In this chapter, therefore, it will be reemphasized once again why it is vitally important to continue to believe, as our Christian forefathers did, that "in six days, the Lord made heaven and earth, the sea, and all that in them is, and rested the seventh day" (Exod. 20:11).

Implications of the Old-Earth Position

It is obvious that belief in a 4.6 billion-year-old earth and a 15 billion-year-old universe did not come from the Bible, for there is not a hint of evolution or long geological ages anywhere in the Bible. The author's book, *Biblical Creationism*, for example, examined every relevant verse in every book of the Bible, and there is no suggestion anywhere of the geological or astronomical ages that are widely assumed today. The concepts of evolution and an infinitely old cosmos are often found in the ancient pagan religions, but never in the original Judaeo-Christian literature.

Therefore, Christians who want to harmonize the standard geological/astronomical age system with Scripture must use eisegesis, not exegesis, to do so. That is, they have to try to interpret Scripture in such a way as to make it fit modern scientism. We believe, on the other hand, that the only way we can really honor the Bible as God's inspired Word is to assume it as authoritative on all subjects with which it deals. That means we must use the Bible to interpret scientific data, not use naturalistic presuppositions to direct our Bible interpretations.

Those who choose the latter course, however, embark on a very slippery slope that ends in a precipice. For if the long geological ages really took place, that means there were at least a billion years of suffering and death in the animal kingdom before the arrival of men and women in the world. Each geological "age" is identified by the types of dead organisms now preserved as fossils in the rocks of that age, and there are literally billions of such fossils buried in the earth's crust. This fact leads to the following very disturbing chain of conclusions, as follows:

1. God is not really a God of grace and mercy after all, for He seems to have created a world filled with animals suffering and dying for a billion years, and He did so for no apparent reason whatever, assuming that His ultimate goal was to create human beings for fellowship with himself.

2. The Bible is not really an authoritative guide, for if it is wrong in these important matters of science and history, which we supposedly can check for ourselves, using the usual criteria of scientific and historical investigation, then how can we trust it in matters of salvation, heaven,

and everlasting life, which we have no means of verifying scientifically? "If I have told you earthly things, and ye believe not," said Jesus, "how shall ye believe, if I tell you of heavenly things?" (John 3:12).

3. Death is not really the wages of sin, as the Bible says, for violence, pain, and death reigned in the world long before sin came in. God is directly responsible for this cruel regime, not Adam. Furthermore, when God observed the completed creation of "everything that He had made . . . the heavens and the earth . . . and all the host of them . . . He pronounced it all to be very good" (Gen. 1:31; 2:1). This seems to imply that God is sadistic, taking pleasure in observing the suffering and dying of His creatures.

4. The Bible teaches that Jesus Christ was our Creator before He became our Savior (John 1:1–3, 10; Col. 1:16; etc.). However, Christ thought that it was "from the beginning of the creation" (not billions of years after the beginning of the creation) that "God made them male and female" (Mark. 10:6), quoting from the record of the creation of Adam and Eve (Gen. 1:27). If He had really been there at the beginning, He would have known better. Furthermore, if God had really created a world of nature "red in tooth and claw," leading to "the survival of the fittest," how is it that His Son later taught His followers that "Whosoever will save his life shall lose it" (Mark 8:35), and that they should love their enemies and "do good to them that hate you" (Matt 5:44)?

5. Still more significantly, if physical human death was not really an important part of the penalty for sin, then the agonizingly cruel physical death of Christ on the cross was not necessary to pay that penalty, and thus would be a gross miscarriage of justice on God's part.

6. This would lead us to conclude further that we have no real Savior. Christ is no longer here on earth, but sin and death are still here, so the promises in the Bible concerning future

salvation seem to have been just empty rhetoric. If God's Word was wrong about creation and about the meaning of Christ's death, it becomes obvious that its prophecies and promises concerning the future are of no value either.

7. Finally, there remains no reason to believe in God at all — at least not in the personal, loving, omniscient, omnipotent, holy, righteous God that the Bible makes Him out to be. If that kind of God really existed, He would never have created the groaning, suffering, dying world implied by the long ages required for evolution. If suffering and death in the world — especially the suffering and death of Christ — are not the result of God's judgment on sin in the world, then the most reasonable inference is that the God of the Bible does not exist. The slippery slope of compromise finally ends in the dark chasm of atheism, at least for those who travel to its logical termination.

Where Christians Must Stand

Therefore, no matter how much more convenient it would be to adopt the old-earth approach or the "does not matter" approach, we cannot do it. We could have more speaking engagements, more book sales, larger crowds, and better acceptance even by the evangelical Christian world if we would just take the broad road, but we cannot do it. The Bible *is* the inerrant, infallible, inspired Word of the living, gracious, omnipotent Creator, and the Lord Jesus Christ *is* our crucified and risen Savior, and all the *real* facts of science and history support these truths.

Conversely, there is *no* genuine scientific evidence for evolutionism. No true evolution from one kind of organism to a more complex kind has ever been observed in all human history, and there is no *recorded* history beyond the six thousand or so years of biblical history. Any alleged earlier ages have to be postulated on the discredited assumption of uniformitarianism. Even if such imaginary ages ever existed, they left no credible fossil records of real evolutionary transitions among the billions of fossils preserved in the rocks.

What the fossils *do* show is *death* — rapid death and burial, indeed, or else they would not have been preserved at all. And death speaks of sin and judgment, not evolution and long ages. Pain and death are not "good" things, and a loving God would not call them good. They are instead, *the wages of sin* (Rom. 6:23). This judgment by our all-holy Creator necessarily fell on Adam and his descendants and on all the "dominion" over which God had placed him in charge.

In the new earth which God in Christ will create after sin is finally purged out of this groaning creation, however, "there shall be no more death, neither sorrow, nor crying, neither shall there be any more pain" (Rev. 21:4). Once again, God's creation will all be *"very good!"*

In the meantime, we do well to continue to believe His Word just as it stands. God forbid that we should ever "love the praise of men more than the praise of God" (John 12:43).

Let the Word of God Be True!

It has now been more than 50 years since a committee of evangelical geologists rebuked this author about a paper he had just presented at the 1953 convention of the American Scientific Affiliation. The paper was entitled, "Biblical Evidence for Recent Creation and a Worldwide Deluge."These men were all graduates of a prominent Christian college, yet took strong exception to my premise that the Bible should govern our interpretation of the geological data, arguing that my position would prove an embarrassment to the Christian community.

Several years later another geologist, then teaching at the same Christian college, spent the summer at Virginia Tech (where this author was a department head at the time) and attended the college Sunday school class he was teaching. He also insisted that science should govern our biblical interpretations, not the other way around. All these men insisted that we could and should stretch the meaning of any Scripture as far as necessary to make it conform to the current majority view of scientists.

That approach, of course, is how earlier compromising religious scientists had arrived at such concepts as theistic evolution, the gap theory, progressive creation, the local flood, and other such adjustments. They assumed that the evidence for an ancient earth was so strong that the plain record of the Bible (six-day creation, the global flood, etc.) simply had to be reinterpreted to accommodate it. This approach soon led to full-blown theological liberalism and worse.

At the Institute for Creation Research, we believe the Bible to be the verbally inspired, fully inerrant Word of God, completely true in science and history as well as in matters of ethics and spirituality. Furthermore, we are confident that God is able to say exactly what He means, so His Word should be taken literally unless the context clearly indicates a metaphorical meaning is intended. This is what the Bible itself teaches concerning itself.

The classic summary text, of course, is 2 Timothy 3:16, in which Paul reminded his readers, "All scripture [not just those parts dealing with religious matters, and not just the 'thoughts' but the actual words written, for that is the very meaning of the word 'Scripture'] is given by inspiration of God [literally 'God-breathed,' not the product of human reasoning]."

This great truth is not based on just one passage, for this is taught throughout the Bible. The Lord Jesus said, for example, "The scripture cannot be broken" (John 10:35). That this principle applies to every word was also confirmed by Him. "For verily I say unto you, Till heaven and earth pass, one jot or one tittle shall in no wise pass from the law, till all be fulfilled" (Matt 5:18).

The same high view of God's words is also found frequently in the Old Testament. Among others, practically every verse of the longest chapter in the Bible (Ps. 119) extols some virtue of the Scriptures. For example, there is the testimony of Psalm 119:160. "Thy word is true from the beginning: and every one of thy righteous judgments endureth for ever."

Then consider the sobering truth that the Bible closes with a warning from Christ not to tamper with its words. "For I testify unto every man that heareth the words of the prophecy of this book [note well, 'the words']. If any man shall add unto these things, God shall add unto him the plagues that are written in this book: And if any man shall take away from the words of the book of this prophecy [again note, 'the words of the book'], God shall take away his part out of the book of life" (Rev. 22:18–19). It is, thus, presumptuous and dangerous for any self-styled modern "prophet" to allege that he has received some new revelation from God, or for any self-appointed modern critic to presume to reject the plain truth of Scripture in favor of some *ad hoc* reinterpretation based on current scientific theory.

Practically all Christian young-earth creationists would agree with the above. They often cite 2 Peter 3:3–6 as precisely relevant to this issue. There the Apostle warns against the uniformitarian approach to the study of earth history. Scoffers of the last time, Peter predicted, would insist "all things continue as they were from the beginning of the creation" (thus presuming that naturalism and uniformitarianism govern all scientific laws and processes), thereby willfully ignoring the divinely revealed facts of the special creation of all things in the beginning and then the global interruption of all processes by the great Flood 1,656 years later. If what Peter said is true, then the uniformist approach to the study of earth history can only be valid back to the time of that worldwide flood at the most.

Although most Bible literalists will agree with that principle in general, we sometimes tend to forget it in practice. For example, the concept of entropy (the second law of thermodynamics) provides a powerful argument against vertical evolution, stating the universally observed fact that all systems tend to disintegrate with time. It seems to correlate perfectly with the implied effects of God's great Curse on Adam's dominion following his sin of disobeying God's Word. Yet there is a temptation to question this correlation because of the assumption that most natural processes must have been operating in accordance with the second law even before sin and the Curse. But that is uniformitarian reasoning! The Genesis record specifically says that processes before the Fall and Curse were different from those after (note Gen. 1:31; 2:3; 3:17–18). We need to remember that we cannot legitimately discuss events and processes in the period between creation and the Curse in terms of present processes.

This particular question might be resolved by assuming that, before the Curse, entropy was conserved just as energy is conserved, but that it began to increase with the Curse. The second law was thus operative before that, but in a slightly different form. As far as the first law is concerned (the principle of energy conservation), that principle seems to have been operating ever since the end of the creation period. Christ the Creator is now "upholding all things by the word of His power" (Heb. 1:3).

Conversely, to assume that the decay aspects of the entropy law were operating before the Curse seems to be a tacit admission (perhaps unintentional) that death was also operating before the Fall, and this clearly contradicts Scripture (e.g., Rom. 5:12; 1 Cor. 15:21). The Bible — not scientism — should govern our interpretation of any such problems.

The question of the firmament (Gen. 1:6) has also generated various interpretations, but we need to keep in mind that the Hebrew word (*raqia*) means simply "expanse," as in "a great expanse of water between California and Hawaii." An essentially synonymous English term would be "space." Moreover, just as "space" can be used to refer to space either as an entity or to a particular space, so likewise for the word "firmament."

There are at least two — probably three — special "firmaments" mentioned in Scripture. The most exalted firmament is under God's throne (Ezek. 1:26). Also, there is an atmospheric firmament, where birds fly, and a stellar firmament, where the stars are (Gen. 1:14, 20). There are likewise three "heavens" (note 2 Cor. 12:2), and it is significant that God called the firmament "heaven" (Gen. 1:8), where the Hebrew for "heaven" is actually a plural noun (*shamayim*), frequently translated "heavens." These distinctions are not often made by creationists when discussing a particular firmament (or space, or heaven), but they are biblical, and it is important to take careful note of the context in each case.

This brings up another controversial subject, the canopy theory, the essential component of which is "the waters which were above the firmament" (Gen. 1:7). If the particular firmament (or space, or heaven) in mind here is the atmosphere, and if the waters were in the vapor state, then many biblical facts and scientific relationships are beautifully explained. However, there are certain scientific difficulties that are still unresolved, and there is again a temptation to abandon the theory because of these.

Although the Bible does not specifically teach the canopy theory in so many words, there are several mysteries at least partially explained by it (the source of the waters for the 40-day rain producing the global flood, the longevity of the antediluvians, the lack of any rain before the Flood, the diurnal mist that watered the antediluvian lands, the origin of the rainbow, the greater size of most animal orders before the Flood, and others), that it can at least be offered as a good possibility. The scientific challenges are not insuperable. This is especially true in light of the fact that so many hitherto scientific "givens" are currently being vigorously reconsidered — even such supposedly basic constants as the velocity of light and acceleration of gravity. The factors affecting the atmosphere are many and complex, and the canopy theory has not yet been proved impossible and should not be dismissed.

A similar argument could be made about other difficulties that sometimes tempt us to adapt uniformitarian thinking in dealing with them. But the Bible exhorts us to let God say what He said, including the revealed fact that processes before the Flood — and especially before the completed creation — were not the same as they are now.

What is wrong with simply believing what God has revealed in His Word, even when we do not yet have a scientific explanation for a particular problem? As the apostle Paul would say: "What if some did not believe? Shall their unbelief make the faith of God without effect? God forbid: yea, let God be true, but every man a liar. . . ." (Rom. 3:3–4).

Appendix

The RATE Project

Don DeYoung

One essential component of evolution theory is an extremely long time scale for earth history. Biochemist George Wald, 1967 Nobel Prize winner, described the connection between evolution and time: "Given so much time, the 'impossible' becomes possible, the possible probable, and the probable virtually certain. One only has to wait: time itself performs the miracles."[1] On a cosmic scale, multi-billions of years are also required by versions of the big-bang theory. This incomprehensibly long chronology is sometimes called *deep time*. Geologists and astronomers seem to delight in describing vast time spans. However, it should be kept in mind that billions of years of history are not a certainty. In fact, there are many serious implications to deep time, both scientific and theological.[2]

RATE is an acronym for *Radioisotopes and the Age of the Earth*. This name was given to an in-depth research program conducted during 1997–2005. A team of creation scientists explored the evidence used to support evolutionary deep time. The team members, each holding an earned doctorate, included Steven

---

1. G. Wald, "The Origin of Life," *Scientific American* 191(August 1954): p. 44–53.

2. D. DeYoung, "Theological Implications of Deep Time," *Creation Research Society Quarterly* 39 (June 2002): p. 22–24.

Austin, John Baumgardner, Steven Boyd, Eugene Chaffin, Don DeYoung, Russell Humphreys, Andrew Snelling, and chairman Larry Vardiman. Each accepts the literal, biblical teaching of the supernatural creation of all things, occurring just thousands of years ago, not billions of years.

In support of the young-earth creation position, the RATE team conducted detailed experimental and theoretical research. In particular, the geologic discipline of radioisotope dating was evaluated. This dating technique was developed over the last century, and many thousands of derived ages have been reported for rocks, meteorites, fossils, and archaeological artifacts. The RATE team saw the need for a thorough technical evaluation of radioisotope dating. Over a nine-year period, more than one million dollars were invested in the research effort. The following sections summarize the major RATE results. Full details and documentation are provided elsewhere in technical[3] and popular-level[4] volumes.

Carbon-14 Dating
(Research by J. Baumgardner)

Of the several radioisotope dating methods, the carbon-14 technique is most familiar. There is a common misperception that radiocarbon supports an ancient history for the earth. The radioactive isotope carbon-14 has a half-life of 5,730 years. This is a relatively short lifetime compared with the other dating isotopes. Because of this, carbon-14 is typically used to date objects thought to be relatively young, a few half-lives or less. Plants and trees absorb carbon-14, which forms continually in the upper atmosphere. When the vegetation dies, its store of carbon-14 slowly diminishes, converting to stable nitrogen-14. The technique is used to date

---

3. L. Vardiman, A. Snelling, and E. Chaffin, eds., *Radioisotopes and the Age of the Earth: A Young Earth Creationist Research Initiative* (El Cajon, CA: Institute for Creation Research, 2000); L. Vardiman, A. Snelling, and E. Chaffin, eds., *Radioisotopes and the Age of the Earth: Results of a Young Earth Creationist Research Initiative* (El Cajon, CA: Institute for Creation Research, 2005).

4. D. DeYoung, *Thousands . . . Not Billions: Challenging an Icon of Evolution* (Green Forest, AR: Master Books, 2005).

wood, charcoal, and artifacts such as papyrus manuscripts. Truly ancient samples should no longer contain any carbon-14. Over one million years, for example, 189 carbon-14 half-lives would elapse. Any initial carbon-14 concentration in such a sample is reduced by the amount $(0.5)^{189}$. If you calculate this small fraction of remaining carbon-14, the result is clearly infinitesimal.

In the last decade, a major challenge has arisen in carbon-14 dating. There are reports of traces of carbon-14 still existing in samples thought to be much older than a few thousand years. These samples include fossils, petrified wood, buried shells, whale bone, coal, oil, and natural gas. The RATE team further explored this anomaly with new measurements of carbon-14 in coal. Ten distinct coals were obtained from the U.S. Department of Energy Coal Sample Bank. The samples represent the Paleozoic, Mesozoic, and Cenozoic eras of geologic strata, dating between 311 million and 34 million years ago. The actual carbon-14 measurements were contracted out to a leading geochronology laboratory using the latest technology called accelerator mass spectrometry (AMS). In each coal sample, measurable carbon-14 was indeed detected. The C-14 amounts translate into coal ages between 44,000 and 57,000 years. Note that these ages are thousands of times younger than assumed for the coals. Even so, the RATE team concluded that the coal samples are younger still. Much of the world's fossil fuels, including coal, result from vegetation which was buried during the global Genesis flood of Noah's day. Furthermore, there are indications that the pre-Flood atmosphere and biomass held much less carbon-14 than at present. Taking this pre-Flood carbon distribution into account, the carbon-14 ages for the coal samples are reduced to just several thousand years, in agreement with young-earth biblical chronology.

Following the coal study, the RATE team next sought a more extreme challenge to carbon-14 dating assumptions. Diamonds are thought to be some of the oldest materials available on earth, estimated at over one billion years old. They are thought to form deep in the earth's mantle under extreme pressure and temperature. The diamonds are carried to the surface by upward-moving magma. Still later, the magma cools into vertical underground structures called diamond pipes. In some cases the pipes later were exposed and eroded, scattering the diamonds across the landscape. For RATE analysis, 12 diamond samples were obtained from several African locations. As with the coal samples, careful handling, preparation, and carbon-14 analysis were completed by a commercial laboratory. Carbon-14 measurements in diamond had not been previously reported in the literature. Similar to the coal research, remnant carbon-14 again was found in every diamond tested. The apparent conclusion is that the diamonds are not nearly as old as assumed. Geologists and critics of RATE have struggled to explain the presence of carbon-14 in coal and diamonds. Perhaps modern carbon-14 "leaks into" ancient samples and contaminates them, or maybe the detected carbon-14 forms inside ancient samples by internal nuclear reactions. However, neither of these explanations survives theoretical and experimental analysis.

The RATE team concludes that carbon-14 in coal, diamonds, and a host of other earth materials provides strong evidence for their limited age, just several thousands of years. The measurements are in agreement with biblical creation; carbon-14 does not support an old earth.

Helium in Zircons
(Research by R. Humphreys)

Just as carbon-14 is found in unexpected places, there is a similar story for helium atoms found in granite. Igneous granite is a very pervasive rock variety occurring throughout the earth's solid crust. When granite forms from a melt it accumulates traces of radioactive elements, mainly uranium-238. This uranium decays through a series of intermediate radioactive isotopes, eventually becoming the stable element lead Pb-206. The U-238 half-life is 4.47 billion years. Along the path of uranium decay, eight alpha particles also are emitted. An alpha particle is identical to the nucleus of a helium atom. When the alpha particles slow down and capture electrons within the granite, helium atoms result.

Uranium atoms and their resulting helium atoms actually are concentrated inside tiny crystals which in turn are embedded within the granite mineral biotite. The crystals are called zircons and have the chemical formula $ZrSiO_4$ (Figure 1). These zircons are typically 50–75 microns in size, about the thickness of a page of this book. The zircons in granite have a distinct composition from the larger, *cubic zirconia* crystals which are synthetically made for jewelry.

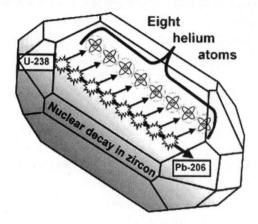

Figure 1. Illustration of a zircon crystal which frequently occurs as dust-size grains inside granite. Shown also are the zircon's internal uranium, intermediate atoms, helium, and lead. Eight helium atoms result from the complete decay of each radioactive uranium-238 atom, the end product being stable lead-206.[5]

Suppose one obtains a sample of granite that is considered to be millions of years old. Any helium atoms which formed within it from uranium decay over eons of time should have escaped from the rock and moved into the earth's atmosphere. This follows because helium atoms are chemically inert and do not combine with other atoms. They also are relatively small and can readily "leak" out of crystal structures. Several years ago, however, measurements indicated the surprising presence of helium atoms still existing in large numbers within "ancient" granite. It appears that the granite rock formations of the world may be much younger than thought. The RATE team explored this unexpected presence of helium atoms within the zircon crystals of granite. The effort began with

5. Vardiman, Snelling, and Chaffin, *Radioisotopes and the Age of the Earth*.

measurements of the diffusion, or movement, of helium atoms through zircon crystals and their surrounding biotite mineral. Some of this diffusion data had not previously been recorded. As expected, a relatively rapid loss of helium was observed. Next, granite samples were obtained from a deep drilling project in New Mexico. This drilling operation was conducted by Los Alamos National Laboratory in 1978. Rock samples were taken from depths reaching 1,490 meters, or nearly a mile downward. This granite was previously dated by radioisotope methods at about 1.5 billion years old. In the RATE work, many tiny zircon crystals were separated from the samples by an involved process of crushing and sorting. A commercial laboratory was contracted to measure the quantity of helium in the crystals and its escape from the zircons as temperature was varied. The results are shown in Figure 2.[6] The vertical axis is logarithmic and records diffusivity, which is a measure of the ease with which helium atoms migrate out of the zircon crystals. The black dots in the figure show the actual RATE measurements of helium diffusion with increasing temperature. The data points trend upward to the right because higher temperatures allow increased helium movement. The lower white squares show the calculated small diffusion values which are required if helium is actually retained in zircon crystals for a billion years or more. In contrast, the upper squares are the calculated diffusion values on a much shorter historical time scale of just 6,000 years. Clearly the young-age creation model gives by far a closer fit to the actual diffusion data. In fact the evolutionary age assumption is in conflict with the experimental diffusion data by a factor of at least 100,000.

In summary, the diffusion experiments show that helium can only be retained in zircon crystals for a few thousand years, not billions of years. Yet helium atoms are found in abundance inside granite zircons. As with carbon-14 in the previous section, helium is an indicator of a young earth. Granite, one of the most common rocks found worldwide, does not support an old earth.

---

6. Ibid.

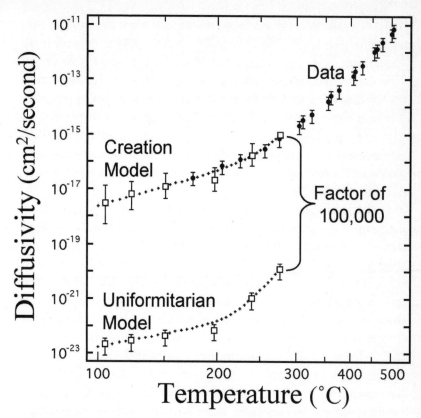

Figure 2. A summary of data for the escape of helium atoms from zircon crystals. Diffusion is plotted against temperature. The solid black dots show experimental diffusion data. Also shown are the calculated predictions for helium diffusion according to young-earth creation (upper squares) and conventional long-age (lower squares) models.[7]

Radiohalos

(Research by A. Snelling)

The previous section discussed uranium decay occurring within zircon crystals. For smaller-size granite zircons, those less than about 50 microns in size, many of the radiation alpha particles will exit the crystal. As they slow down they cause microscopic

---

7. Ibid.

defects while passing through the atomic structure of the surrounding mineral biotite. The alpha particles move outward in all directions from the zircon crystals which are called *radiocenters*. The crystal damage reveals itself as tiny spheres of discoloration called *radiohalos*, or *halos* for short. There results a shell appearance because most of the biotite crystal damage occurs at the end of the alpha particle path. Hundreds of millions of uranium decays are needed for a radiohalo to become visible. These microscopic halos or "burns" are useful since they provide a semi-permanent record of radioactive decay.

The RATE team conducted an extensive survey of radiohalos in granite rocks from around the world. These granites formed from magma which intruded sedimentary strata and then solidified. Collection sites included Finland, Australia, and six western U.S. states. The rock samples were first crushed to retrieve the component flakes of biotite, usually millimeters in size. You may have observed this biotite mineral which appears as black flecks in granite. The biotite occurs in multiple thin layers which can be peeled apart. RATE researchers mounted these biotite sheets on slides for microscope study. Any resident spherical radiohalos are revealed in cross section as dark rings. Each original decaying uranium atom releases eight alpha particles with varying energy (Figure 1), so the halos typically show multiple concentric rings centered on the zircon crystal.

The RATE radiohalo study included more than one hundred granite samples and the preparation of over 1,500 slides. About 40,000 radiohalos were counted altogether. The average number of radiohalos per slide was tabulated and then compared with the conventional geologic ages of the various granite samples. The result of this large-scale radiohalo survey is shown in Figure 3. We do not accept the conventional ages listed, but the radiohalos reveal an interesting trend. The oldest samples date from Precambrian times, 0.5–4.6 billion years ago, shown on the right side of Figure 3. Relatively few radiohalos were found in these samples. For the Paleozoic and Mesozoic eras, about 65–500 million years ago, the number of measured radiohalos greatly increases. Many creationists interpret the rock strata from this time span as Genesis flood deposits which accumulated in a single year. In this view the overall geologic column may be divided as shown in Table 1.

As Figure 3 shows, the Flood event appears to be accompanied by a great deal of radioactive decay with resulting formation of radiohalos. Further RATE research found a large number of fission tracks in the same strata. These results verify that radioactive decay was greatly accelerated during the Flood event, as discussed in the next section. And since radiohalos can form only in solid crystalline rock, not in liquid magma, their presence indicates that the strata of the earth and the many granite intrusions formed rapidly.

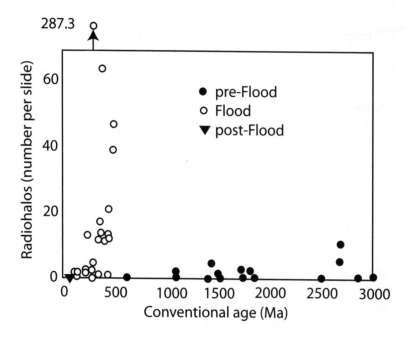

Figure 3. A summary of measured radiohalo counts versus conventional geologic time in millions of years (Ma). The vertical axis gives the number of radiohalos counted in many RATE granite samples. Notice that Flood deposits show by far the largest number of observed radiohalos.[8]

—————

8. Ibid.

Geologic Era	Conventional Time Span (millions of years)	Young-Earth Interpretation
Cenozoic	65–present	Late- and post-Flood deposits
Mesozoic	248–65	Mid- and late-Flood deposits
Paleozoic	543–248	Early-Flood deposits (about 4,500 years ago)
Precambrian	4,600–543	Creation week and pre-Flood deposits (about 6,000 years ago)

Table 1. Summary of the geologic eras, conventional time spans, and the possible creationist alternative view of history. The conventional ages vary somewhat and are taken from the Geological Society of America as of 1998.

Along with their distribution throughout the earth's rock layers, radiohalos also provide a second important area of creationist study. In Figure 1, three of the immediate steps between uranium-238 and lead-206 produce radioactive, short-lived isotopes of polonium. In past years it was noticed that polonium radiohalos often occur without the surrounding halo rings from uranium-238 and the other intermediate steps of decay. These have been called *parentless* polonium halos. One interpretation is that the short-lived polonium atoms were supernaturally placed inside solid granite during the creation week.[9] The RATE team firmly accepts the supernatural creation; however, the studies

---

9. R. Gentry, *Creation's Tiny Mystery* (Knoxville, TN: Earth Science Associates, 1986).

found evidence contradicting the idea of an instantaneous formation of polonium radiohalos and their host rock.

Among the many radiohalos counted by the RATE team were thousands of polonium halos. In many cases they are located in very close proximity to parent uranium halos, a millimeter or less distant. It is clear to the RATE scientists that the polonium atoms were transported away from their original locations. The polonium atoms then decayed and produced their unique secondary radiohalos at a short distance from the radiocenters where the parent uranium-238 source atoms were located. The transport mechanism within the granite rock involved hydrothermal fluids which include hot water solutions and gases. Often the polonium halos are found to occur along biotite cleavages, cracks, and crystal defects, all of which served as conduits for fluid movement. Geologists today realize that crustal fluids play a key role in many underground processes. These include the movement of magma, rock metamorphism, and the formation of polonium radiohalos. Radiohalos, found in rocks worldwide, do not support an old earth.

Accelerated Nuclear Decay
(Research by E. Chaffin)

We now come to one of the most significant and also the most controversial parts of the RATE project. The team concludes that there have been historical episodes during which radioactive decay was greatly accelerated. That is, nuclear half-lives were temporarily shortened on a global and even a cosmic scale. This radical conclusion is based on several points. First, there are a great number of nuclear decay products in earth rocks. These decay or daughter products were not created in place but clearly result from substantial nuclear decay. Based on the long nuclear half-lives as measured today, the rocks are indeed millions or billions of years old, hence giving rise to the old-age view of earth history. However, a realistic, literal view of the Book of Genesis allows for only thousands of years of history since creation. The obvious conclusion is that the daughter products must have accumulated quickly via rapid decay in the not-so-distant past.

As a second point, I earlier described the presence of helium atoms found in zircon crystals. This accumulated helium indicates a large amount of uranium decay, yet there has not been sufficient time for the helium to diffuse out of the zircon crystals. Accelerated decay in recent history is thus indicated. This is likewise the case for the many radiohalos found in granite. In addition, the existence of these radiohalos also shows that the rocks have never been heated above the halo *annealing temperature*. This is the temperature at which crystal defects are "repaired" by atomic movement and halos are erased. The radiohalo annealing temperature is about 200°C (392°F) for the mineral biotite. On a geologic time scale, the permanency of radiohalos is difficult to understand. After all, the earth is assumed to experience volcanism, tectonics, and magma movement throughout a multi-billion year history. The very presence of the halos in "ancient" granite indicates their rapid formation and a lack of subsequent heating since their formation. Several additional indicators of accelerated nuclear decay are explained in the comprehensive RATE books.[10]

It is readily admitted by the RATE team that a large-scale acceleration of nuclear decay is a radical proposal. But then so are other significant creationist predictions such as is the *ex nihilo* creation, the young age for the earth, the reprogramming of nature at the Curse, the global flood, and the rapid formation of the earth's fossils and sedimentary rock strata. The creation world view is not constrained by the uniformitarian limitations of secular science. Some critics argue that challenges to conventional science are a hindrance to progress. They say that belief in creation is a regression to outdated, naïve, medieval science. However, such critics are wrong. A reappraisal of earth history opens entirely new horizons for inquiry, research, data interpretation, and truth.

10. DeYoung, *Thousands . . . Not Billions*; Vardiman, Snelling, and Chaffin, *Radioisotopes and the Age of the Earth*.

When did the proposed accelerated decay of radioactive material take place? The RATE team proposes two distinct episodes. The first is during days 1–3 of the creation week. This follows because there was no plant or animal life on the earth at that time, and the speeded-up nuclear decay would release lethal amounts of radiation. Also, vast amounts of decay products are found in pre-Cambrian basement rock, much of it assumed to have formed at the creation. A second episode of accelerated decay then took place during the year-long Genesis flood. Figure 2 shows the pulse of radiohalo formation which occurred during this time. This heightened radioactivity would call for special protection for Noah's family and the animals on board the ark, not only from the storm, but also from intense radiation. A third possible episode of accelerated decay, at the time of the Curse of Genesis 3, is less likely because of the lack of accompanying tectonic activity.

Just how did the accelerated nuclear decay events occur? The mechanism remains uncertain. Nuclear lifetimes appear very constant as measured today. The nucleus of an atom is well-shielded from any outside influence. Under extreme conditions of pressure and temperature, nuclear half-lives typically can be altered by only a few percent or less. In contrast, the RATE team proposes temporary, dramatic million-fold increases in nuclear decay rates.

There are several theoretical ideas regarding the alteration of half-lives. Nuclear decay is very sensitive to parameters such as nuclear forces, the fine structure constant, the Fermi constant, and the energy of the emitted radiation particles. RATE computer calculations show that a 10 percent decrease in nuclear binding energy may result in a 100 million-fold decrease in an atom's nuclear half-life. More complex variables which control half-life involve quantum tunneling, string theory, and higher dimensions. The RATE team realizes that the actual mechanism of accelerated decay, and the theological and physical reasons behind it, may lie entirely in the Creator's realm. In this case, a full explanation of the adjustment of nuclear lifetimes is beyond the limits of scientific inquiry.

There is a separate serious challenge to consider. Nuclear decay produces a great deal of heat energy. This energy is harnessed in nuclear fission power reactors to generate electricity. If vast nuclear decay takes place rapidly on a global scale within rock strata, the resulting heat pulse potentially could vaporize the earth's entire crust. Some way is needed, either natural or supernatural, to safely channel this heat outward and away from the earth. Actually, this is a cosmic problem since accelerated decay is also indicated on the moon, planets, and the stars beyond. One tentative proposal is called *cosmological cooling*.[11] This involves a rapid expansion of the fabric of space, which would be an efficient heat absorption process. The idea somewhat parallels the rapid, inflationary stretching of space which is proposed by big-bang enthusiasts. However, big-bang space expansion is said to occur 13 billion years ago, while the RATE approach requires heat dissipation much more recently, occurring during the creation and Flood events. The RATE team sees the extreme heat generation during accelerated decay as a serious issue but not an insurmountable problem. The conclusion is that changing nuclear half-lives in the past bring a serious challenge to belief in an old earth.

Discordance of Radioisotope Dates
(Research by S. Austin and A. Snelling)

The RATE team invested major research effort in obtaining new dates for rock samples worldwide. This included two particular case studies on multiple rock samples from the Beartooth Mountains of Wyoming and the Bass Rapids sill in Arizona's Grand Canyon. The specimens were collected by RATE and dated by professional laboratories. Analysis was done on the whole rocks and also on the component minerals. The dating methods included potassium-argon, rubidium-strontium, samarium-neodymium, and lead-lead isotopes.

Isochron graphs were constructed from the resulting radioisotope data. These graphs are conventionally thought to give an

---

11. R. Humphreys, *Starlight and Time* (Green Forest, AR: Master Books, 1994).

optimum statistical age estimate while also accounting for the initial conditions of samples. However, the RATE results show several areas of major *discordance* or disagreement in dates. Four examples follow. First, potassium-argon ages, the most widely used isotope method, show wide variation. The results for different minerals taken from the same Beartooth rock sample ranged between 1.52 billion years and 2.62 billion years. Accelerated decay would falsify these numbers, but note that these age results differ by 72 percent. The conclusion is that potassium-argon dates in general should be looked at with suspicion. Second, amphibolite mineral ages from a rock formation in the Grand Canyon range between 0.840 billion years (rubidium-strontium) and 1.864 billion years (lead-lead), a 122-percent difference. Third, many of the samples produced well-behaved isochron plots with excellent statistics for particular isotopes, yet the derived ages varied greatly between the various dating isotopes. This raises a cautionary flag in accepting any isochron date. Fourth, hardened lava samples were collected from New Zealand's Mount Ngauruhoe which erupted just 50 years ago. The lead-lead dating method gave a false age of 3.908 billion years, a 7.8 billion percent discrepancy!

What are the reasons for these and many other discordant results? RATE analysis found evidence for frequent chemical mixing between moving underground magma and the adjacent rock layers. Additionally, there is evidence that magma can "inherit" chemical signatures, and false dates, from the earth's upper mantle. Either of theses occurrences would invalidate the measured radioisotope dates.

Three basic requirements are often recited as keys to the correct dating of rock samples. These include known initial chemical components of the rock, a closed, uncontaminated system during the rock's history, and a constant rate of nuclear decay. The RATE team finds that all three of these dating essentials fail at some level. Radioisotope techniques may indeed provide useful information on the *relative* ages of rocks and their interactions with surroundings. However, correct, absolute ages of rocks are not included in this information. The discordant dates documented for RATE rock samples challenge the old-earth view.

The RATE isotope data shows intriguing trends involving the two chief nuclear decay processes, alpha and beta decay. First, it appears that, as a general rule for a given sample, alpha decay gives an older date than beta decay. This implies that during accelerated decay episodes, the alpha decay process experienced a more extreme alteration than beta decay. Second, it is found that the heavier isotopes (samarium, uranium) experienced greater decay and give older dates than the lighter isotopes (potassium, rubidium). These unexpected trends may give important insight into the mechanism of accelerated decay.

Biblical Data
(Research by S. Boyd)

Biblical research also contributed to the RATE effort. In particular the creation passage Genesis 1:1–2:3 was considered. The Hebrew verb forms were analyzed to determine whether the passage was written as narrative history or as poetry. Results of this linguistic study are clear and compelling: The Genesis creation story is determined to be narrative history with a probability of virtually one. This means that Genesis 1:1–2:3 describes *ex nihilo* creation with literal 24-hour days. Other views including the day-age theory, gap theory, theistic evolution, poetry, or metaphor are not statistically defensible. Scripture does not support an old earth.

Conclusion

This chapter has touched only briefly on the multi-year RATE project and its findings. Further topics include fission tracks in zircons, insects in amber, isochron plot details, and nuclear theory. The RATE team suggests a credible alternative to the conventional ancient ages assigned to earth rocks. During two times in history, the creation and the Flood, nuclear decay processes appear to have been accelerated on a grand scale. One might say that the radioisotope clocks were temporarily sped up, and then adjusted back to the slower rates measured today. If true, then most radioisotope dates published over the last century are in gross error. The traditional old-earth evidence, radioisotope dating, has been recast in support of the young-earth. The RATE team finds that radioisotope data can be correlated with an earth which is about 6,000 years old. Carbon-14 atoms in samples found worldwide and helium in granite also place a similar limit on the earth's age. The RATE results provide significant support for the young-earth model of earth history.

Donald DeYoung, M.S., M.Div., Ph.D., is chairman of the physical science department, Grace College, Winona Lake, Indiana. Courses taught include physics, astronomy, and mathematics. He joined the Grace faculty in 1972 and has spent sabbatical leaves in California, Europe, and the South Pacific. Don is a graduate of Michigan Tech University (B.S., M.S., Physics), Iowa State University (Ph.D., Physics), and Grace Seminary (M. Div.). His writings have appeared in many periodicals. He has also written 15 books on Bible-science topics, including object lessons for children.

Dr. DeYoung is a member of the Indiana Academy of Science and the AuSable Environmental Institute. He is currently president of the Creation Research Society with 1,700 members worldwide. This group funds research, publishes a technical quarterly journal, and operates a laboratory in Arizona. Don speaks on creation topics and believes that the details of nature are a powerful testimony to the Creator's care for mankind.

Dr. DeYoung and his wife, Sally, have three married daughters. In their local church, Don is an elder, Sunday school teacher, and board member of Warsaw Christian School.

Eternal Ministries is a discipleship and
evangelistic ministry dedicated to
teaching and proclaiming the Word of God.
For more information regarding the Bible
and the Christian life, or to contact
Dr. Ron J. Bigalke Jr., please
do so through our website:
www.eternalministries.org

Soli Deo Gloria!